Caught in Play

Caught in Play

How Entertainment Works on You

Peter G. Stromberg

Stanford University Press
Stanford, California

For Nelly

Stanford University Press
Stanford, California

© 2009 by the Board of Trustees of the Leland Stanford Junior University. All rights reserved.

Printed in the United States of America on acid-free, archival-quality paper

Library of Congress Cataloging-in-Publication Data

Stromberg, Peter G.
Caught in play: how entertainment works on you / Peter G. Stromberg.
p. cm.
Includes bibliographical references and index.
ISBN 978-0-8047-6110-9 (cloth: alk. paper)—ISBN 978-0-8047-6111-6 (pbk.: alk. paper)
1. Amusements—Social aspects. 2. Play—Social aspects. 3. Recreation—Social aspects. I. Title.
GV1201.38.S78 2009
306.4'81—dc22
2008041877

Designed by Bruce Lundquist
Typeset at Stanford University Press in 10/14 Adobe Garamond

Contents

Foreword

WE ALL KNOW what it means to be completely in the grip of an activity—playing a game, watching a film, pursuing a hobby, reading a book. So absorbed are we that we somehow lose track of time and place and are carried away into an alternate, imagined universe. Peter Stromberg calls this experience "being caught up." His book is a high-flying set of reflections on what lies behind our capacity to get caught up in this way. In this landmark study, Stromberg carves out a new terrain for anthropological analysis: the world of entertainment. It's almost shocking to think that it took so long for anthropology to stake its claim.

What makes "entertainment" an apt subject for an anthropologist rather than a sociologist, psychologist, or historian? Obviously, entertainment is a cultural domain of great significance in modern life. But in Stromberg's synoptic vision, the modern notion of entertainment straddles general human capacities and specific historic and cultural circumstances. It's perfect grist for the holism of the anthropologist's mill. To understand the relation of this general capacity for being caught up to the historical evolution of modern forms of entertainment requires the kind of bridge between human nature in general and human culture in particular that can best be provided by a psychological anthropologist.

On the human nature side of the equation is Homo sapiens' evolved capacity for "simulation" of experience and what Stromberg calls "meta-action." People, it turns out, don't occupy only the world of immediate physical reality. They have the ability to place themselves in imagined worlds and take on alternative roles in those worlds that may be very different from any role they play in "real life." Stromberg explores this kind of role taking through captivating analyses of kids playing role-playing games and the impact on readers of romantic fiction.

He argues convincingly that these capacities to create and occupy imagined roles in imagined worlds, to mentally put ourselves in others' shoes, are crucial cognitive skills that are basic to human socialization and social learning. Whereas mental simulations cannot always be observed from the outside, Stromberg's data—role-playing games caught on film—shows in a powerful way the kind of virtuosic role switching between physical and imagined realities that is an essential aspect of being human.

Particularly important are Stromberg's insights that, although play occupies a "liminal zone" between fantasy and reality, it is not normally confused with reality. So getting caught up in imagined worlds does not entail confusing that world with ordinary life. In this context, Stromberg's discussion of the research on the complex effects that romantic fiction has on readers is especially illuminating. What all this implies is that these forms of play serve very special and nonobvious functions in relation to those ordinary realities that they at once simulate and oppose.

However potent these general insights about simulation and meta-action, taken by themselves they don't make complete sense of the contemporary entertainment scene. Entertainment may be a variation on the general theme of human play, but there is something distinctly modern about the world of entertainment Stromberg describes, and he knows it. Stromberg wisely avoids reducing entertainment to its universal cognitive features.

The world of contemporary entertainment has a history, and Chapter Three takes us on an eye-popping tour of what Stromberg considers key historical moments in the evolution of the modern culture of entertainment. It may be self-evident that modern entertainment has been significantly shaped by recent developments in technologies of representation. But Stromberg goes well beyond the obvious, tracing the roots of the culture of entertainment to the emergence in the 18th century of an ideal of a kind of rapt engagement in aesthetic representations such as novels and paintings. This idea of psychological engrossment in art forms grew out of an older ideal of aesthetic contemplation as a path to religious devotion, an idea brilliantly explored by the art historian Michael Baxandall in his book *Painting and Experience in 15th Century Italy.*

With the development of modern consumer capitalism in the 18th and 19th centuries, the ideal of cultivating religious devotion became secularized. Religious devotion became aesthetic sensibility and eventually evolved into an ideal of the cultivation of desire as an end in itself. So modern entertainment develops in tandem with modern marketing, and the result is a harnessing of some universal cognitive capacities for some very new and special ends.

What we have here is nothing less than retooling of the human psyche to lay the cognitive foundations of modern consumer culture. After all, capitalism proposes a world of action governed and justified by private desire. So it is no surprise that cultivating the inner experience of desire eventually becomes an end in itself, and a pivotal goal of modern entertainment.

Stromberg's brilliant synthesis of this historical material covers a lot of ground in short order. But it is ultimately provocative and convincing. His excursion into the history of modern desire gives us a new way to think about some of the less-obvious forces shaping the world of contemporary entertainment.

Although Stromberg explores the many faces of entertainment, he avoids the trap of passing easy judgment on modern entertainment as good or bad. It is telling, however, that many of his case studies describe pathologies of engagement. In contemporary American youth culture, there seems to be a thin line between getting caught up and becoming addicted; this book does not skirt the issue.

I was especially intrigued by the role that boredom plays in the culture of smoking and drinking among college students. Stromberg stresses that boredom is a universal human experience that is culturally malleable. The modern fear of boredom that Stromberg's research with college students uncovers is a powerful example of how boredom is culturally conditioned. This particular species of boredom is characteristic of late modernity. It cannot be fully understood without exploring the deliberate cultivation in consumers of ever-intensifying "stimulus hunger," an appetite that is surely a hallmark of late capitalism.

What is especially notable here is that even though modern play may appear to privilege a rich inner life, college students seem to most fear being alone and understimulated. Stromberg's analysis embraces the many contradictions illuminated by the study of entertainment. It turns out that the surfaces of play mask some surprising hidden dynamics of modern life.

But we don't want to give too much away. Enough of coming attractions! I only hope I have convinced you to stay tuned for the main event. It's a thriller, I assure you, so hold onto your seats and turn the page.

Bradd Shore
Atlanta, Georgia
July 1, 2008

Acknowledgments

I HAVE BEEN WRITING this book for fifteen years, and in that amount of time one can get a lot of help. I continue to be astonished and humbled by the willingness of others—including scholars who are very busy—to devote hours of their time to reading and offering suggestions on my work. Of course, the long-term result of this is that much of what is good in this book is the accumulated insight of others. I have undoubtedly lost track of some of the people I should acknowledge, and to them I apologize. But I do remember these people who have read parts of this book in manuscript or who otherwise have offered their help: Jessica Kuper, William Arens, Greg Urban, Vincent Crapanzano, Don Brenneis, Keith McNeal, Steve Duck, Lamont Lindstrom, Michael Nunley, Michael Mosher, Jennifer Helé, and Maija Stromberg. I am also grateful for financial support from the Robert Wood Johnson Foundation and the University of Tulsa Faculty Research Grant Program.

I owe special thanks to the men and women who taught me what I know about being a social scientist, some of them now gone: Michelle Rosaldo, Ann Swidler, Robert Paul, Mel Spiro, Roy D'Andrade, Guy (Ed) Swanson, and Jane Hill. Each of these people is, or was, more than a teacher or senior colleague to me; these people have given me a career that I have found meaningful.

I would also like to thank my colleagues in a number of disciplines (history, sociology, cognitive science, developmental psychology, to name a few) who have done so much of the careful research on which the argument in this book is based. I have had to read broadly to write this book, although any expert will immediately spot important books and articles that have not been consulted here. Nevertheless

I have learned an enormous amount from several books that are cited again and again throughout this work. Careful readers will know which authors I am talking about, and I want to thank these scholars and encourage those who have an interest in this topic to begin by reading some of these books. There is a tremendous volume of high-quality work bearing in one way or another on the culture of entertainment.

Finally, I especially want to thank a few people who have made special contributions to the process of writing and finishing this book, while stressing that none of these people can be associated with any of my errors. Alex Hinton organized the publisher's review of this book. He figured out very quickly what I wanted to do in this book and then efficiently set about helping me do it. Ron Jepperson has been a valued intellectual interlocutor and friend for decades and has intervened repeatedly with excellent advice. Bradd Shore encountered the book in a late version, but his extraordinarily detailed comments and hours of conversation have decisively shaped the final form of the argument. The most substantial study reported on in this book was planned and carried out with Mark Nichter and Mimi Nichter, and surely some of the sentences in Chapter Eight began their lives as collaborations with these two. But more broadly, I started talking to Mark Nichter about this topic years before I started writing about it, and my numerous conversations with him are so much a part of this book that I could never say for sure where his influence stops.

Year in and year out, writing this book was made possible by my wife, Nelly Vanzetti. Authors sometimes—appropriately—thank their spouses for picking up more than their share of life's tasks. I am lucky enough to have a spouse who can not only do the laundry and take the dog to the vet but is a gifted writer and researcher in her own right, and she has been editing, commenting, and playing devil's advocate with chapter drafts for all of those 15 years. It is to her I dedicate this book.

Caught in Play

1

Caught Up in the Game

SKIP CRACKS HIS KNUCKLES as he prepares to roll the dice. With his bulky body, his unkempt, cascading hair, and his pharaoh-style beard, he looks like an imposing warrior from a bygone age. Indeed, Skip is currently engaged in battle, hand-to-hand combat with an upstart who has issued a challenge to fight. Raising the left side of his body out of his seat, he grimaces and bellows "wham" as he kicks out with his left leg, contacting his enemy in the stomach.

Some of Skip's friends are focused on the fight; one shouts "Stay down!" as the kick is completed. Others seem oblivious to this altercation, which has been going on now for six or seven minutes. The latter chat with one another and help themselves to repeated servings from an enormous receptacle containing malted milk balls. Skip himself looks proud of his kick, for an instant, and then slightly anxious as he returns to the task of his next dice roll. The game continues with further powerful strikes by Skip and loud grunts of pain, also issued by Skip as he acts the part of his imaginary opponent.

Skip is participating in a role-playing game, a form of entertainment in which players pretend to be characters in imaginary worlds[1]. Players might, for example, imagine themselves to be the crew of a spaceship or a group of adventurers seeking a treasure. Although the kick described here seems a natural part of playing the game and might pass unnoticed, something about it strikes me as peculiar. My question is this: If Skip is really just imagining the character he is representing in the game, why does he kick with such obvious emotional intensity? An even more basic question: Why does he kick at all?

1

Some might answer by saying something like, "Well, he's playing a game and when he pretends to kick the guy he's fighting, he's just really getting into it." But "getting into it" is a matter that deserves some thought. This kick is really sort of odd: as he strikes out with his leg Skip is not only imagining himself to be his character but going a step beyond that—he is doing what his character would do.

Anecdotes circulating among Skip's peers make frequent reference to over-the-edge role players who lose track of the line between fantasy and reality, who *become* the characters they portray (see Fine 1983: 211ff). "Role players are scary," says Chris, who off and on has immersed himself deeply in these fantasy games. He goes on to say that he has discovered there are two sorts of players: "There's the people that are self-aware, and understand. And then there are the people who *literally* aren't aware of what reality is."

Skip doesn't seem to belong to the latter group. He is well aware that he is sitting in a shabby room with a group of male friends, the acrid odors of fast food—today's and last week's—permeating the atmosphere. Skip would smile at the suggestion that he or any of his friends ever lose track of the fact that the high-tech outer space setting of the game is imaginary.

But, then, there's the kick. I have been able to study it carefully because I made a film of the game in which this occurred. Anyone who sees the kick would probably agree that it is a spontaneous gesture, unrehearsed, and certainly not presented to the group as "this is the sort of thing my character would do." Everything points to the conclusion that Skip does not make a conscious decision to kick. Put it this way: Skip is playing a game, and he knows it is a game, but sometimes his body seems to forget that it's a game, and at those moments what Skip is imagining is made incarnate; it assumes the status of a reality in the world.

Getting Caught Up in Entertainment

One way of labeling Skip's kick is to see it as evidence he is very caught up in the game he's playing. Of course, this is only one example of becoming caught up. There are dozens of other in-character gestures and speech on that tape, and they are all testimony to the players' deep immersion in the game.[2] Johan Huizinga (1955: 14), the author of what is arguably our most influential study of play in Western culture, captures this sort of immersion in his description of a child engaged in pretending: "The child is quite literally 'beside himself' with delight, transported beyond himself to such an extent that he almost believes he actually is such and such a thing, without, however, wholly losing consciousness of 'ordinary reality'."[3]

It is not only children and role players who become caught up in play.[4] Presumably, most of us have at some point become immersed in a book or game or movie such that—on the cognitive and emotional levels—the activity temporarily assumes a profound significance and the importance of the outside world begins to fade. Other authors have used their own terms to designate this experience; Mihalyi Csikszentmihalyi (1990) talks of "flow," for example, while Diane Ackerman (1999: 12) has described "the ecstatic form of play" as deep play.[5] Although I have learned much from these authors, I have not adopted their terminology, because even though their formulations overlap with my own, they are not the same. Most significantly, both Csikszentmihalyi and Ackerman place a moral value on this sort of play, stressing that this is a form of activity human beings everywhere should cultivate for reasons of personal growth. They may be right, but I prefer to remain agnostic on moral questions of this type. In this book, I look instead at the *social* role of this sort of play. My question is not whether we should seek to engage in this sort of play, but rather what happens when we do so.[6]

This brings me to another difference between my approach to the subject and those of previous authors. Both Ackerman and Csikszentmihalyi extend their terms to cover ecstatic experiences that occur in such domains as skilled work or religious experience. Although I would not deny that one can become deeply absorbed in many activities, for my purposes it is not useful to lump them all together, and in this book for the most part I confine myself to the possibility of becoming caught up in play.

For me, becoming caught up in play is worth our notice because this phenomenon can be the basis for an approach to understanding "entertainment," a broad term that in my usage includes parts of consumption and advertising as well. Entertainment is by now so thoroughly woven into the fabric of our existence that we rarely stop to think about our relentless quest to be entertained, and if we try to do so the appropriate language and concepts seem elusive. This difficulty is one hint that entertainment is at the hub of our culture. Of course, its importance extends well beyond the Americas and Europe. For its effect on contemporary human life and especially for its sheer exotic weirdness, the culture of entertainment is arguably the most influential ideological system on the planet. Yet precisely because it is so pervasive and close to us, entertainment is difficult to understand, and even to talk about.[7]

Some readers might find this last statement odd, because there is a nearly incomprehensible volume of written material, in both scholarly and popular discourses, about entertainment. Simply reviewing the literature on entertainment in all social science and humanities disciplines would itself entail a multivolume work. But much of the laudable work that has been carried out in sociology, communications, cultural studies, and related fields has focused primarily on questions of aesthetics, politics, technique, and so on, while for the most part avoiding the kinds of general cultural analysis that anthropologists have pulled off in distant lands. How does entertainment *fit* with other parts of our culture? That is, how is it part of a pattern integrated with our world view, our ethics, and our concept of person? For all that has been written on individual pop icons and sitcoms and the liberating (or oppressive) power of popular culture, such basic questions remain for the most part unanswered.

Think of it this way: What do we know about the overall effect of living in a society in which entertainment is so central? What do we know about how entertainment affects society and the people who participate in it? Consider a contrast to religion: although there remains much to be learned, social scientists have a solid and reasonably consensual understanding of such matters as how religious rituals support values and social norms, how religion can be called on to facilitate social change, how it helps believers face life's difficulties. Scholars interested in specific issues such as sacrifice or religious language can build on a solid foundation of broadly accepted work and attempt to offer refinements or extensions of our knowledge.

There is, sad to say, no parallel foundation in the study of entertainment. One could unearth authors from the Frankfurt school who sought to demonstrate the importance of the "culture industry" in maintaining the domination of the capitalist class in industrial and postindustrial democracies. One can cite somewhat inflated claims, most famously associated with the French sociologist Baudrillard (1981), that we now live in a cultural climate of hyperreality, in which the boundaries between reality and image are blurred or even indistinguishable. Or one could turn to more recent work, mostly in cultural studies, that sees entertainment as a site for creative and heroic resistance to dominant discourses. One will search in vain for any consensus, among the social science disciplines or anthropology in particular.

There are any number of reasons this might be so in anthropology. Among the more important: first, in spite of much effort, cultural anthropology has yet to completely exorcise its increasingly covert agenda of focusing on the "exotic." Hence a study of television in Nigeria seems somehow less prestigious than one of a religious tradition that has survived in a rural region. But either one carries more panache than a study of how people respond to sitcoms in Bakersfield. Faye Ginsburg (2005: 17), admitting that until recently the study of mass media was "almost a taboo topic for anthropology," sees the end of such attitudes in recent work. I am less optimistic. As she goes on to note, entertainment has become less off-putting for anthropologists now because it has increasingly penetrated non-Western settings. However, it would seem to me that a strong theoretical framework for interpreting the cultural effects of entertainment would require first of all an understanding of its place and significance in the societies that have led the way in the development of entertainment.

Second, in recent decades much of cultural anthropology has been gripped by a neoromantic fervor in which coherent explanations and generalizations are regarded as oppressive imposition of a rationality that is simply one culturally determined form of understanding the world. From this perspective, a gradual accumulation of consensual knowledge about a topic such as entertainment is not a goal to be pursued.

Such views (which are often associated with the label postmodernism) are understandable as an attempt to come to terms with anthropology's history of rendering the lives of others as mere grist for the mill of social scientific theorizing. However, I cannot accept that the solution to such problems of exploitation is to abandon the attempt to generalize about human action. Those who have the privilege of being paid to study social and cultural life incur an obligation to the society that supports them. The obligation is to articulate in the clearest possible way useful statements about the societies they observe. These useful statements may bring injustices to light or point to more effective ways to deliver health care or increase our general fund of knowledge about human social life; there are many possibilities. Entertainment is a dominant force in contemporary life, and the more we understand about it the better off we will be.

Careful analysis of entertainment should take us a certain distance down the road toward understanding our own odd relationship to entertainment: why we find entertainment so compelling while claiming to regard it lightly, why entertainment often seems to clash with dominant moral values in the society, why so many of us come to focus on fame and celebrity as the most available models of our purpose. Entertainment, in ways that are difficult to articulate and therefore troubling, is closer to defining the meanings in our lives than we would like to admit. Any progress toward the goal of sorting out how entertainment influences us and our social life would be a contribution to our self-understanding and ultimately to our civic life.

Entertainment, Pleasure, and Play

I have said that entertainment is important and—despite its utter familiarity—somewhat mysterious. I have suggested too that getting caught up in the playful activities of entertainment might offer a useful foothold in the challenging task of beginning to grasp the most general effects of entertainment in our society. But I have not yet defined what I mean by entertainment, and before I proceed it is probably advisable to do so.

When I refer to entertainment I am talking at once about a kind of activity and a social context in which the activity occurs. If this seems abstract, consider a simple example, that of playing a game. When I play a game such as tennis, I engage in certain activities, such as swinging a racket. But swinging a racket does not count as playing tennis if I am idly doing so in my living room. Rather, I need to swing my racket in a particular context that includes things like a tennis court, an opponent, and a commitment to follow the rules of the game of tennis.

Focusing for a moment just on the activity, how can we characterize it? At the core of the idea of entertainment is that it is activity that provides pleasure, especially a particular kind of pleasure my dictionary (the *Oxford English Dictionary*) identifies as amusement. Not all pleasure-seeking behavior is entertainment, of course. One might find pleasure in the appreciation of beauty in poetry or music, in the love of one's family, in sex. Happily, the possibilities are endless. So what is it about certain pleasurable activities that defines them as a component of entertainment?

The word *amusement* is helpful here, which is undoubtedly why the dictionary writers chose it. The word connotes diversion, a certain lightness; to return to my dictionary: "pleasurable occupation of the attention without seriousness." I agree that we usually do not think of entertainment as serious activity, but we should also keep in mind that seriousness may enter into entertaining pursuits. It seems to me the heart of the matter is that when one is engaged in entertainment, one's *end* is pleasurable amusement, and not some practical goal. I can play tennis for entertainment and diversion. I can also play tennis to practice my strokes or engage in a competition. To the extent I have the goal of winning a tennis competition, it does not seem correct to say that I am playing for purposes of entertainment; this becomes especially clear if it is a professional competition.

The word *diversion* is worth noticing as well. In years of discussion of the matter with hundreds of college students, I have learned it is not possible for something to be entertaining unless at least to some small extent it diverts us from our day-to-day reality. It is not just that we can become caught up in entertainment, it is that unless we become at least slightly caught up in something, we do not consider it to be entertainment. An activity must pull one in to be entertaining; if one observes or acts without this ever happening, one says something like "Well, some people find that entertaining, but I don't."

In sum, then, one part of entertainment is pleasure-seeking activity that diverts one's attention from the day-to-day world. But perhaps this is enough to define entertainment. Go back to me and my tennis racket: if I am just swinging my tennis racket in my living room, isn't it possible to say that I am entertaining myself? Is it really necessary to have the game of tennis to constitute what we call entertainment? Well, how long am I likely to keep up this racket swinging? If I were to do so for the length of a tennis match, and it was clear that I wasn't practicing my strokes or imagining myself in an actual game, then an observer would have good reason to think me insane. In other words, a little bit of random racket swinging might be entertaining, but we know that the "little bit" is crucial. This may seem like a trivial consideration, but it is in fact important. Even though it may be possible for a person to engage in an entertaining activity with little or no larger context framing the activity—no show, or game, or fantasy—we acknowledge that this is an unusual situation. When we think of entertainment, we think in the first instance of a person acting in concert with something stimulating the action or imagination so that the person is engaged, responding to something that has independent form.

This larger context of entertainment, the entertaining framework, can take many forms. The most efficient way to specify the institutional level of entertainment is to say it is always some form of play. Defining my concerns in this way is not as restrictive as it might initially seem, for I adopt a broad definition of play.[8] I follow French sociologist Roger Caillois (1961) in adopting a four-part classification of play and games. Caillois divided play and games into *agon* (contests such as chess and basketball), *alea* (games of pure chance), *mimicry* (pretending), and *ilinx* (activities that induce vertigo). The advantages of this classification arise primarily from its breadth and flexibility. It allows one to see the element of play in a broad range of activities that might not initially be categorized in this way. For example, mimicry includes situations in which one imagines oneself as another, something that is likely to occur in any sort of spectating. Furthermore, Caillois points out that activities may consist in combinations of his categories. A professional sporting event is agon for a few of the participants and mimicry for the rest.

All of entertainment fits into this classification of play. This does not mean that all play is entertainment. To return to the previous paragraph, professional football players *play* the game of football on Sunday afternoons in large stadiums, but they are not doing so for purposes of their own entertainment. People play for all sorts of reasons, not just for entertainment. To summarize, then, entertainment is playful activity undertaken for its own sake, in pursuit of pleasure that diverts the player from the day-to-day. But when I use the term *entertainment* in this book, I also intend to designate something that is to a large extent unique to contemporary consumer capitalist societies such as those of the Americas and Europe. This needs to be explained.

Entertainment in Contemporary Society

Have all people in all ages sought entertainment? It is difficult to imagine what evidence would enable one to answer that question. Certainly we can quickly call to mind activities from other times and places—gladiatorial contests, puppet shows, story telling, carnivals, and so on—that were staged to entertain their audiences. But the purposes such activities serve vary over time and space, and it would be a gross error to assume that anything conceivably entertaining is precisely the same sort of activity that we label entertainment. I take it for granted there are some distinctive elements of entertainment in contemporary consumer society—that is, societies such as the United States, the European countries, and Japan, in which a basically capitalist economy is combined with democratic political institutions and a wealth of available consumer goods. In the first place, these societies provide a material standard of living to most of their members that is, by historical standards, extraordinary. Thus, people who live in these places have, in relative terms, more time and resources to pursue entertainment than has usually been the case in human history.

Second, there is obviously a lot of entertainment available. In addition to the proliferating institutions of entertainment, such as movies, television, portable music players, game consoles, theme parks, and on and on, there is also the fact that many of the activities of day-to-day life[9] have come to conform to the standards of entertainment: one hopes for a car that is a pleasure to drive, one expects one's food (and one's friends) to be diverting and interesting, teachers seek entertaining ways to engage their students, political campaigns seek to present their messages amusingly, and so on.

There are more opportunities for entertainment now than there have been in other times and places, and people have more resources to engage these opportunities. In such a situation, what could be called a logic of entertainment begins to dominate: in many realms of life the values of entertainment begin to pervade institutions that originally had a different goal. As Darwin argued for the survival of the fittest, we now have survival of the most entertaining: those forms that are not entertaining lose out to those that are.[10] The entertaining politician gets elected, the entertaining class gets the enrollment, the entertaining car is the one that sells, and over time a competition emerges to enhance entertainment value wherever possible. Thus it is not just that there is more entertainment going on in our society; it is that entertainment begins to dominate over other standards of value in the society. As many authors have commented and demonstrated, we live in a culture of entertainment.[11] Again, this probably distinguishes the nature of entertainment in contemporary life.

Finally—and this is less widely acknowledged but equally important—in contemporary society entertainment is in part a process of finding the meanings that ground us in the world, and such may not be the case in other cultures.[12] We engage entertainment for diversion, for fun, but it does not follow from this that entertainment is trivial in its effect on our lives. In the contemporary world, entertainment and the pleasures it generates are fundamental to our vision of the good life. Furthermore—and this is one of the main themes of this book—in our society entertainment works to create and sustain many of our culture's fundamental ideas, practices, and values. One reason this is not widely appreciated is that although these values and ideas are fundamental, they are often denied as such. In entertainment we learn to value our own pleasure and stimulation, embrace disruptive passions such as romance, and develop insatiable appetites. These desires, shaped and fed by entertainment, are necessary to our way of life; but unlike patriotism, self-sacrifice, and integrity, they are not the values we most often choose to acknowledge in our official discourse.

The stories we tell ourselves about ourselves, and what we actually do, often do not mesh very well. This situation can perhaps be linked to what was famously labeled "doublethink" by George Orwell. The term referred, in the novel *1984*, to the ability to simultaneously accept and discount a proposition. In Orwell's original formulation, doublethink was the capacity to ignore the contradictions generated in a totalitarian worldview, and this is (arguably) a different matter from the conflicts between sets of values that I am describing here. However, there is enough similarity here to be intriguing, for the fact of the matter is that many in contemporary society find themselves in the odd position of simultaneously accepting and rejecting certain beliefs and practices. I will have a good deal to say about this before I am through.

In keeping with my sense of the wide-ranging significance of entertainment, in this book I use the word *entertainment* itself broadly. Rather than limiting the term to the sorts of things that are the most obvious examples of entertainment (TV dramas, for example), I include phenomena that some might see in other terms. In this book, a television advertisement for a political candidate that consists of a series of soft-focus images from an imagined past (the friendly milkman waving at a child along his morning route, a child laughing gleefully while playing on a swing set with her suspender-wearing grandfather) may be politics, but it is certainly also a part of entertainment. As I have hinted, I consider some of our consumption to be entertaining. Cultural critic Neal Gabler has summarized this point eloquently. Speaking of turn-of-the-(21st)-century American culture, he writes (1999: 205):

> One could see how entertainment and consumption were often two sides of the same ideological coin. Entertainment was about release, freedom, transport, escape. Aside from the purchase of necessities . . . so too was consumption. Entertainment was about the power of sensation. So too was consumption, in this case, the sensations generated externally by how one looked and internally by how one felt. Entertainment relied heavily on instant gratification. So too did consumption.

To descend to a concrete level, in my definition a number of activities are likely to be examples of entertainment[13]: watching narrative fictions on television or in movies; reading narrative fictions (or some forms of nonfiction); spectating at events such as sporting contests, concerts, and theatrical performances; shopping (although not all shopping); playing games of all sorts; listening to music; visiting theme parks, resorts, museums, and so on; consuming food and other substances for purposes of enjoyment; and fantasizing stimulated by cultural objects such as advertisements. Examples of activities that are typically not entertaining: waiting in an airport, undergoing dental surgery, anything we call work (career, yard cleanup, child care, cooking dinner), sleep, and any activity with a specific practical goal.

Yet another point about why we should not consider the sort of entertainment we enjoy today as simply a universal aspect of human experience: I follow sociologist Colin Campbell in assuming that we members of contemporary society possess some distinctive psychological skills that give us a special ability to immerse ourselves in the fantasies of entertainment. In an innovative and compelling book entitled *The Romantic Ethic and the Spirit of Consumerism* (1987), Campbell suggests it is the development of modern hedonism that laid the foundation for the consumer society of the 20th century. By *modern hedonism* Campbell means to refer to the imaginative faculty of creating illusions known to be false but believed to be true. Campbell locates this faculty above all in the everyday practice of daydreaming, which he holds to be pervasive in contemporary society.

According to Campbell, the secret of modern consumption is that in fact consumers do not seek fulfillment from products. Rather, they derive pleasure from longing for products and for what they represent, those symbolically perfect worlds of the fantasy. Thus Campbell sees modern hedonism as a direct parallel to romance in sexual matters; the pleasure is in the *longing*, the fantasy of fulfillment. Once the product (or the romantic partner) is actually obtained, its value begins to deteriorate. It is no longer the object of fantasy; now it is an object of reality, and like all real objects it can never measure up to its correlate in the fantasy world. Campbell would therefore contend—and I agree—that our "materialism" is not materialistic at all. It is not *things* we long for; it is the *idea* of those things. This capacity to find pleasure in our longings (a product of several centuries of a particular sort of cultural history) is again not something that we can assume to be present in all lands and among all peoples.

Is Entertainment Activity a Form of Ritual?

The arguments I am outlining here take shape around a vision of the social landscape that is somewhat different from the one adopted in the emerging literature on this topic in anthropology.[14] Frequently those who work on the topic depend heavily on the concept of ritual in their attempt to understand the place of entertainment activities in society (see, for example, Hughes-Freeland and Crain 1998). Rothenbuhler and Coman (2005: 3), in their recent edited volume entitled *Media Anthropology*, write: "The concept that has received the most numerous applications and the most interesting developments in media anthropology has been *ritual.*"

These authors are correct in commenting that in this literature the term *ritual* is ubiquitous, and it is easy to understand why this is so. In the first place, conceptualizing entertainment activities, or some of them, as ritual has the great virtue of provoking us to think carefully about the social and moral significance of entertainment (broadly construed) in our culture. For example, many have noticed that the various forms of entertainment convey deep and unquestionable meanings, much as rituals often do (Esslin 1982b, Miller 1998, Hughes-Freeland and Crain 1998). Or take a more specific example: the similarities between something like a fan's devotion to a celebrity and the kinds of devotion that occur in religious ritual may indeed be striking. The fan may create a shrine to the celebrity idol, and regard the celebrity as having superhuman status and a connection to a world beyond this one, and be convinced that supplication of the celebrity will yield the solution to intractable problems, and so on.[15] If one assumes that ritual is typically associated with religion, there are further reasons to consider the possibility that entertainment activities are ritual forms. For example, as I show in Chapter Three, many forms of entertainment have their historical roots in religious activities.

Nevertheless, in this book entertainment activities are primarily interpreted not as ritual but rather as play. Because I deviate from the dominant approach, I need to carefully explain my choice. I consider entertainment activities to be play first of all because, generally speaking, this is how the men and women engaged in these activities understand them. Ritual is activity undertaken, as Caroline Humphrey and James Laidlaw (1994: 68) say, "in earnest;" play is not in earnest.[16] In this sense the very idea of entertainment—that it is fun, a diversion from serious endeavors—goes directly counter to the character of ritual. Second, in spite of this obvious observation, entertainment activities have not often been interpreted as types of play, and therefore such an approach may offer fresh insights.

Third, the term *ritual* has been promiscuously overused in the social sciences, and as a result it has acquired a slatternly looseness. Play is also a broad term, but it continues to convey at least some specificity of meaning. As many have commented, "ritual" is used so often and in so many ways that it is hard to know just what an author means when she claims something is a ritual. Sometimes authors attempt to turn such ambiguity to their advantage; they evidently think that simply claiming an activity is a ritual constitutes analysis of it. However, rather than asserting that some entertainment activity is like a ritual and declaring that one has done a good day's work, one needs to go on from there to show how this perspective enables us to understand the activity in a new and deeper way. At times it seems as if ritual is invoked to suggest the gravity of some entertainment activity without engaging in the heavy lifting of showing how and why the activity is important.

In fact, ritual is a rhetorical figure in many discussions of entertainment. It alerts the reader to some sort of claim of continuity between religious and secular action without pursuing the continuity very far. If one does pursue it, in some ways the insight starts to break down. For example, at the end of the day, or of the analysis, it turns out most entertainment activities do not seem like religious behavior. If entertainment is like religion, then show me the men and women who find answers to life's greatest questions in entertainment. Show me those who are willing to lay down their lives for entertainment. Show me the parent who finds solace in entertainment after the death of a child.

At the same time, it would be a grave error to simply throw out the concept of ritual as we attempt to grasp the nature of our engagement with entertainment. The considerations I offered at the beginning of this section alert us to the fact that although a facile assertion of entertainment as ritual will not do, it also will not do to dismiss the connections between entertainment and ritual. All of this would be much easier if social scientists worked out a clear understanding of the distinctions among play, ritual, and art. But such understanding is not even on the horizon. None of these concepts is clearly understood, much less the relationships among them. On the conceptual level, play and ritual are cousins, or siblings. Maybe they are fraternal twins. Nobody knows, so it will not work to be overly dogmatic about precisely where entertainment fits.

I offer some thoughts about the place of entertainment in a later chapter. For now, two points are important to understand. First, I have adopted a pragmatic approach to my use of grand concepts such as ritual, art, and play. In applying all of these concepts at different times, I walk around the great mystery of entertainment and look at it from different angles.

Second, in this book I explain how entertainment in contemporary society often serves some of the same social purposes as ritual, play, and art do in other societies. In our society, entertainment works to valorize[17] some of our most important (though often denied) ideas, groups, and activities. Every society needs ways to create and enforce its dominant values and commitments. The great French sociologist Emile Durkheim set an important part of the agenda of modern social science with his argument that a society's most significant symbols and solidarities are forged in collective rituals. Since his time, social scientists have demonstrated repeatedly that when human beings live together in relatively stable small communities, the intense social interaction of ritual is a dominant means of building commitment to social ideals.

I suggest that oftentimes entertainment activities do something similar in contemporary society. That is, we live in a social order in which entertainment has assumed some of the significance that interactive ritual has in other sorts of societies. In our society ideals, commitments, and communities that have considerable cultural significance are often formulated in and expressed through entertainment activities,[18] which as I have noted at times seem similar to ritual but in other ways are more appropriately conceived as a type of play.

In short, play and ritual may both be adapted to strengthen our ties to people and ideas. In a later chapter I offer a reason for this: I argue that play and ritual are best understood as two related forms of a broader category I call *meta-action*. But whereas ritual tends to be associated with the ideas and symbols we acknowledge to be important, play is often associated with the ideas and symbols that we understand to be powerful but less worthy of admiration. This distinction perhaps takes on special importance in a society such as ours, a society in which people must sustain two rather contradictory streams of motives. There are the motives of the daylight, those of work, production, and responsibility. And there are the motives of the night, those of leisure, consumption, and enjoyment. We might be inclined to call the former stream of motives values and the latter stream desires. In our society, these desires of consumption are often created and reinforced through play, the play of entertainment.

Losing Yourself in Entertainment and Losing Yourself in a Crowd

Entertainment is an important though elusive component of contemporary life. Those who have suggested that entertainment activities are forms of ritual are on to an important insight: entertainment is not just idle fun, but a social and cultural process through which values and commitments are generated. However, this insight is not enough. We need to look closely at the peculiarities of how people engage entertainment, for these activities generate commitments in ways that go beyond the mechanisms that have been discovered by students of ritual. Above all, in entertainment we become committed to something—an idea, an image, a person, a product—by becoming caught up.

When a player becomes caught up in an entertainment activity, she temporarily allows herself to lose track of her day-to-day world in order to immerse herself more fully into the world of play. Like the role player Skip, she may begin to react—cognitively, emotionally, physically—to the world she is imagining. As she does this, she feels the reality of the imagined world.[19] She is not momentarily insane, for she knows the world of play is imaginary. Although I will have reason later on to offer a refinement of Campbell's phrase (1987), for now it is sufficient to agree with him: she knows the world of the fantasy to be false but she feels it to be true.

As the player becomes more caught up in the entertainment, her own physiology gets into the act and leads her downs paths of engagement she does not really choose. The player may be taken over by the play. We embark on this path for the most part because we think it is fun, but becoming caught up in play is by no means a trivial embellishment on more serious forms of human behavior. On the contrary, our capacity to function as serious people is dependent, throughout the life course, on our capacity to play effectively.[20] (Of course, this is not the only example of a vital human activity being enthusiastically carried out because it is pleasurable.) What we experience as fun is a fundamental cultural process through which we discover and renew our commitments to the values and symbols that make us human. Social scientists have shown over and over how this can happen through religious rituals, but they have not paid enough attention to how it can happen through play.

To most fully understand becoming caught up, it is necessary to understand that it is one manifestation of something that reaches deep into human experience. Specifically, I argue throughout this book that becoming caught up in play activities is very similar to becoming deeply immersed in compelling social interaction (such as a successful party or a lively conversation). The parallel is no coincidence; rather it is based on the fact that similar cognitive and emotional processes underlie important aspects of our sociality and our ability to immerse ourselves in imaginative situations.

What I have said so far makes clear that becoming caught up is a complex process in which social, cultural, and biological components of human behavior work together to create experiences in which cultural symbols (including images, narratives, beliefs, physical objects, and substances) take on a particularly affecting salience. It is the salience that comes from one's physical experience of being transfixed by a symbolism that has the power to redirect thought, feeling, and action. Thus in strong experiences of becoming caught up, we may feel that our environment and even our selves have been utterly transformed.

These experiences have considerable sociological importance, on the cultural and psychological levels. The first of these, as I have noted, is primarily cultural: as persons become caught up in the play of entertainment, they come to feel, on a level that far surpasses the merely intellectual, the significance of images, symbols, and ideas. Whether it is a matter of becoming caught up in a highly produced advertisement for a consumer product, a fiction about people like himself, a celebrity image, or some other game, the components of the game assume profound salience for the player. These components—images of products or persons, ideas, consumer products—thereby develop a potency that seems to transcend the day-to-day world. In short, the play of entertainment is the context in which some of our most important cultural symbols are valorized, infused with the charge of emotion that lifts them to the status of ideals.[21]

Here again I restate Durkheim's argument (1995), albeit in a different context. He held that the human capacity to conceive ideals, abstract versions of our perceptions, is based in the transformative experiences of ritual. Durkheim insisted that because people experience a transcendent state in collective rituals, they are able to conceive a level of perfection that transcends experience. This conception is the foundation of the capacity to conceive ideal forms. As I will discuss at length, one does not need to look very far in our society to find images of perfection that transcend our experience. Sit in front of your television for a few minutes and you will see, in both the programming and the advertising, a world populated by beings and objects that are familiar but on the whole newer, more attractive, and generally more appealing than anything in your day-to-day world. These images are some of our most powerful ideals.

The situations I discuss in this book entail becoming caught up in ideal images, images that are utopian[22] in the sense that they offer satisfactions transcending what is available in the everyday world. This is one more reason I repeatedly emphasize the importance of play. Play inevitably offers improvements on our reality; we are drawn to play because it is more suspenseful or exciting or rewarding—on the whole it is just more fun—than life in the day-to-day world. As I have just pointed out, if our play in entertainment really engages us, our faith in these better-than-reality images is confirmed and strengthened. The process of getting caught up in play both builds on and reinforces our capacity to conceive utopian versions of our experience in the everyday world.

No doubt few of us give much thought to our capacity to conceive utopian images, but this is a vital aspect of how we sustain our interest in the world. It is in no small part our ability to conceive something better than what we have here and now that keeps us plodding through daily life. This brings me to the level of psychology. Another argument I make in this book is that the very success of this process in our society conditions the nature of our experience. One example is that the vitality and excitement of our entertainment experiences seem to render us prone to dissatisfaction and boredom with our existence when there is nothing entertaining available. Another example is that the appeal of various substances and activities can be constructed so successfully that we begin to consider ourselves as powerless to resist them, and highly prone to what we call addictive behavior. Finally, I want to attend to the fact that one of our most powerful ideals is a perfected version of ourselves. Thus many of us are prone to wander through our lives in search of experiences that will transform us into the beings we sense we could and should be.

Taken together, these themes allow me to argue that becoming caught up in entertainment activities can explain much not only about what people do when they seek entertainment but also about the role of entertainment in the contemporary social order. Ultimately, it is my hope that such an argument might provide part of the groundwork for a reflective discussion about the role of entertainment in contemporary society, a discussion that goes beyond debate over the merits of this or that entertainment activity.

Where the Book Is Headed

In the following chapters, I discuss becoming caught up in three realms: entertainment activities proper, certain kinds of consumption, and certain kinds of interaction. Neither consumption nor interaction is typically conceived as play, but I argue that a number of playful activities are included within these broad categories. I cannot necessarily claim that in composing my argument I have selected the most telling or appropriate examples. Rather, the activities I examine are dictated by the constraints of the material available to me: I write about activities that I have some familiarity with through my own research, or that others have effectively researched for me. A more comprehensive book on the culture of entertainment, with less idiosyncratic examples, will have to remain a project for the future.

In keeping with the analytic language I have introduced, I sometimes refer to the phenomena I discuss as games. By this I mean merely that they are forms of play. One of the most important games I talk about is what I call *romantic realism*. Our cultural environment is suffused with images, physical places, and collections of verbal symbols that are constructed in such a way that they improve on our day-to-day reality. The product in an advertisement gleams and performs to perfection, often accompanied by persons of unblemished beauty and grace. We visit a theme park in which the complexities of, say, a historical period are reduced to a few meaningful and compelling features. Though we recognize romantic realism as a fiction, we play with it. We go along with these utopian images because doing so can be fun and enjoyable. But as we become caught up in romantic realism, our activity in the day-to-day world may be affected in ways I have already mentioned.

One can also interpret some activities in the everyday world as play. There are, for example, playful interactions with other persons. Such interactions may or may not be classified as entertainment, but it is undeniable that a *person* can be entertaining.[23] I argue that certain kinds of relationships, in particular romantic relationships, are either entertainment or something much like it (the same could be said of some kinds of sexual relationship).

The other major category of real-world playful behavior in our society is consumption. Such behavior may occur for a number of reasons: economic necessity, as a part of establishing or maintaining relationships, but also for purposes of entertainment. No small portion of our economy is based on goods and services provided for entertainment, or to make potentially mundane experiences (such as driving) entertaining.

One way to grasp the nature and significance of entertainment activities is to understand their history, which helps us better appreciate their place in our politics, economy, and way of life. In Chapter Three, I offer a rough sketch of the birth of entertainment culture, with particular attention to the question of how getting caught up has been implicated in entertainment. I am no historian, and this account offers nothing new or startling to those who have studied the history of entertainment.[24] But originality is not my goal here. Rather, I want to help place entertainment in a particular cultural context. First, I show how certain of the interpretive practices that help us enjoy and make sense of entertainment may well be modified forms of religious behavior. Second, I demonstrate the close relationship among entertainment, these interpretive practices, and the growth of a high-consumption economy. In all of this, I emphasize the point that understanding the contemporary high-production, high-consumption society as a manifestation of the march of technological progress is a seriously impoverished misconception.

Chapter Four examines role-playing games and is the first of several empirical studies that illustrate some of the mechanisms and significance of becoming caught up. Role-playing games are significant because they afford a rare opportunity to observe and document in detail what happens when people become caught up. I use two videotapes of role-playing games to deepen our understanding both of how people become caught up and what the implications of this activity seem to be. In Chapter Five, I analyze facets of becoming caught up by breaking them down into component processes such as rhythmic entrainment, affective mimicry, and absorption. These processes are rooted in the human capacity to adopt a physical and social position that is different from the one a person occupies in the day-to-day world. Aided by a good deal of recent work on what is called "simulation theory," I show why this shift of position is done with such ease and skill that for the most part it goes unnoticed. But adopting a vantage point in our imagination is only the beginning of the story, for we can also—even from a very early age—think, feel, and act as if we were in that position. Ultimately, it is these mental and physical processes that can, individually and in interaction, create the sensation of being immersed, caught up, in an alternative world.

In Chapter Six, I address the questions, What sort of process is becoming caught up? In what category does it belong? What else is it like? I introduce the concept of meta-action and grapple in earnest with the relationship between play and ritual. Reviewing Durkheim's well-known theory of the efficacy of ritual, I point out that he traced this efficacy to many of the same cognitive and emotional processes that can be observed in becoming caught up. Furthermore, I call on a recent study by sociologist Randall Collins (2004, his book *Interaction Ritual Chains*) to support the position that these processes can also be observed in many forms of intense social interaction. Overall, I raise the question, If it is widely accepted that the valorization of a society's central symbols may be established and strengthened through their appearance in conjunction with intense interaction, is it not possible that play can have similar effects?

I consider this question in Chapter Seven, in the context of a particular set of potent symbols in our society, those associated with our ideas about romantic love. Romantic love is in some contexts dismissed as a fantasy, but at the same time it may manifest in our lives as a force more powerful than the individual will, stronger than our closest and most enduring family relationships. However it is that symbols are valorized, clearly the process is effective in the case of our ideas about romance. I trace the role of becoming caught up in valorizing the concept of romance. The task is rendered more interesting by the fact that romance is both a form of fiction and a form of interaction.

Chapter Eight is another empirical study; here I look at the early phases of using the legal drugs tobacco and alcohol. Initially it may seem that such activity is distant from the games and fictions I consider earlier in the book. However, there is a fundamental continuity here. The routines through which the young men and women I have studied (college students) introduce themselves to these substances are often playful. This may not be particularly surprising when one recalls that both legal and illegal nonmedical drug use is often labeled "recreational." It is indisputable that in our society much drug use is pursued for pleasure and escape, undertaken in pursuit of the same sorts of experience that entertainment provides.

Drug use is also indisputably a form of consumption, and in that way this brief study offers a bridge to a complex domain I only begin to discuss in this book. Much consumption in contemporary society is undertaken for purposes of entertainment, and the role of play and becoming caught up in activities of this sort has to be developed in other work. However, drug use can function as a revealing case study, especially in light of its very strong relationship to the issues of addiction that I have mentioned. Drug dependency is a striking case in which the human capacity to choose activities seems compromised. If a person develops dependency on a drug, she typically appears (to herself and others) to be unable to choose to stop using the drug. As I discuss in Chapter Eight, the common sense that interprets this situation as solely a result of the chemical properties of the drugs is oversimplified. Although the interaction between mind-altering chemicals and the body is undeniably an important part of dependence, various cultural factors are also important. I show that experiences of being caught up in play, especially in the early phases of drug use, help to create the idea that drugs have the power to overwhelm the user's capacity to choose. In arguing that the concept of being caught up can assist us in our thinking about dependency, I am also suggesting that this idea might be useful in understanding the character of human agency in other contexts, particularly in entertainment and consumption activities more broadly.

Chapter Nine addresses what might be considered the antonym of becoming caught up: boredom. Throughout the book, I emphasize how becoming caught up enhances the tangibility and desirability of fictional worlds. But as we strive for a higher level of satisfaction we often experience a nagging dissatisfaction with things as they are right now. This manifests itself, most obviously, in a pervasive sense of boredom. Here I analyze more of the material from the tobacco study mentioned earlier as well as two interviews with young men who struggle with boredom and find some relief in their activities as fans of the television series "Star Trek." But both men are also stymied by what they see as an inability to choose the world of the day-to-day over the more potent stimulants of entertainment.

In the tenth chapter of the book, I summarize my answer to the basic question of just what it is that is valorized through the mechanisms I describe in the earlier chapters. There are any number of specific examples, but at the most general level the idea that is consistently recreated and made plausible through experiences of becoming caught up is of a particular idea of the self. Repeated and powerful experiences of self-transformation as one becomes caught up in entertainment activities cannot help but create and sustain the conviction that the self is essentially flexible, that transformation is commonplace. Thus a particular form of social character (Riesman, Glazer, and Denney 1961) takes shape, what might be called a flexible self.

The flexible self is well adapted to life in a context of entertainment. Because we understand ourselves to be easily capable of transformation, we are unsure of our place and therefore receptive to suggestions about what we should be or do. In this we are ideal consumers. Also because the self is flexible, it is capable of fully exploiting the possibilities of entertainment by immersing itself in surrounding experiences. Above all, this self is convinced that transformation is possible, that a diet or a product or a makeover or a relationship can be its salvation.

To the extent that we see ourselves as in essence flexible, we are vulnerable to the notion that we cannot resist the powerful symbols creating our experiences of transformation. The flexible self, in other words, is easily overwhelmed. Throughout the book, I return to the theme of addiction, which in its full-blown form is a source of enormous destruction and suffering. But there are also milder forms of compulsion that people compare to addiction, for example an uncomfortably strong relationship to a form of entertainment.

I conclude the book by touching briefly on some of the implications of this study and the further questions this material suggests. Our society has developed a powerful cultural technology for generating compelling symbolic forms; we call these forms entertainment. People find enormous pleasure in their play with these forms; as noted, there are also costs to individuals and to society as a whole. Taken together, the various terms and ideas I introduce here (or borrow from colleagues)— caught up, entertainment as play, valorization, simulation and extended imitation, the flexible self—suggest a particular sort of discussion about the place of entertainment in contemporary society.[25] As I have said, entertainment is so central in our culture that it eludes us. If this book contributes to a new approach to talking and thinking about entertainment, I will consider it a success.

2

Romantic Realism

WHY IS IT that everywhere we turn in contemporary society we encounter elaborate images that are fictional but that closely mimic the features of the day-to-day world? These fictions are all around us, in movies and television programs, in magazines and mail-order catalogues, in theme parks, in advertising. In all of these realms, we observe scenes that are quite like the reality we live in, but they are always a little bit better, a little bit more attractive, a little bit more entertaining than our mundane lives.[1]

Such images are characterized by what I will call *romantic realism*. The word *realism* is often used to label, in the words of art historian Michael Fried (1990: 3), fictions that are "accurate transcriptions of a world outside themselves." Although this attempt to reproduce some aspect of the world is indeed an important characteristic of realism, this characteristic is not (as Fried would be the first to tell you) the whole story. Fiction by Jorge Luis Borges aside, no map is a landscape, no photographic portrait a person, no novel an experience. Fictions, as human creations, necessarily depart from what they depict, and for all practical purposes this means fictions are constructed in such a way as to accentuate what their creators take to be significant.

This is especially true of romantic realism, realism that is in some sense utopian. Romantic realist fictions are discernibly an improvement on the day-to-day world[2] in some way. They are symbolic worlds in which there is more adventure or romance or pleasure, and less tedium and pain and disorientation than we typically find in the day-to-day world. As Campbell (1987: 84) has observed, "In romantic novels and films, heroes and heroines rarely have hiccups, headaches, or indigestion unless this proves essential to the plot."

In sum, romantic realist fictions are at once like and unlike the day-to-day world. In the first place, these fictions are familiar. Like utopias, they are always just over the horizon, beyond the next hill, slated for the very near future.[3] But at the same time, romantic realism always somehow perfects the realities it depicts.[4]

To descend into concrete details for a moment, when referring to romantic realism I am talking about such phenomena as the image of a celebrity, an advertisement for a consumer product, or a blockbuster movie. I am talking about the alluring images and cozy, reassuring copy in mail-order catalogues; the appealing world of close but slightly antagonistic characters in the television sitcom; or, to return to where I began this book, the less polished imaginary world of the fantasy role player. All formulaic fiction, such as the mystery novel or the romantic movie, can be classed as romantic realism.

These minifictions may be as simple as a photograph: a handsome couple, and two adorable children laughing as they enjoy their meal from Kentucky Fried Chicken. Our interaction with them may last only an instant. Nevertheless, our engagement with these images is a form of play. This play, like games in general, may create suspense and offer players a chance to participate in its resolution. But it may also consist in sheer pretending. Like daydreaming or simple pretend play, these fictions may afford pleasure simply by stimulating enjoyable fantasies.

If you want to observe romantic realism in its most acute form, go to a Disney theme park, where in the words of one Disney employee "what we create is a 'Disney Realism,' sort of utopian in nature, where we carefully program out all the negative, unwanted elements and program in the positive elements" (Rymer 1996: 77).[5] What you will experience at a Disney attraction, or in any of these examples, is a world that is familiar but also somehow more appealing than the world in which you live from day to day, and this world will entice you to the pleasures of participation, in spite of your knowledge that advertisements are trying to manipulate you, that movies are not real, that the Polynesian village is not much like any part of Polynesia. But we have grown comfortable with at least this form of doublethink, and the contradiction is not likely to cause you to lose any sleep.

Much of what we call entertainment comprises romantic realist fictions.[6] These fictions add up more completely than real life does, and for this reason they offer us gratifying worlds to inhabit. As I discuss here, romantic realism is a prominent feature of much advertising, which is another reason I classify much advertising as entertainment. In this chapter I argue that our interaction with romantic realism is in principle much the same as more conventionally recognized games; both of these activities are based on interpretive practices that also allow us to enjoy fictional narratives. Even though our engagement with a romantic realist image may be brief, we may become caught up in it; throughout this book I show that becoming caught up is often ephemeral, interspersed with ongoing activities.

There are a number of questions one might want to ask about romantic realism. First, What are some examples of the phenomenon, and where does it occur? Second, Why is it so widespread in our society, and is it present in other societies as well? Third, Do people become caught up in the play of romantic realism? Fourth, and probably most important, What is the significance of romantic realism? Suppose people do become caught up in these images; does it matter in any significant way? I answer each of these questions. But let's begin with a series of examples.

The Formulaic

In introducing romantic realism, it is a little hard to know what to choose, for in fact there are so many examples of this phenomenon swirling around us that it is difficult to know where to fix one's gaze.[7] But considering a few examples at a superficial level helps pin down the nature and significance of romantic realism.

My first example is formulaic literature, and here I am relying heavily on John Cawelti's elegant book on this topic called *Adventure, Mystery, Romance* (1976). Much of the narrative fiction that constitutes entertainment—and under narrative I include not only print works but also television and movies—is highly formulaic. The situation comedy, the soap opera, the romance, the detective story, and so on: all of these genres (and many more) incorporate stock characters and plot lines. Although a great action adventure movie might present a new twist or two on the formula, for the most part it will stick to a familiar plot about a protagonist encountering and overcoming challenges that seem overwhelming.

Like all of romantic realism, formulaic fiction is both familiar and fantastic; it is like our world yet with the volume turned up, the contrast sharpened, and the plodding boredom of the everyday edited out. We enjoy formulaic fiction because it pulls us into a world in which passions are strong, answers are clear, and in the end right triumphs over wrong. In Cawelti's formulation of the point: "The mimetic [by this he means "realistic"] element in literature confronts us with the world as we know it, while the formulaic element reflects the construction of an ideal world without the disorder, the ambiguity, the uncertainty, and the limitations of the world of our experience" (1976: 13). The fact that we in effect know what is going to happen in a mystery or a romance does not detract from our pleasure; if anything, it enhances it. We find comfort and meaning in engaging a new version of a familiar story, another repetition of a reassuring encounter with suspense that ultimately ends in the triumph of all that is right and good.

According to Cawelti (1976: 19), formulaic literature is "analogous to certain kinds of games or play." From my broad perspective on play, I rather simply say that formulaic art *is* a form of play. It is a rule-bound activity willingly entered into for the purpose of amusement and stimulation. As with the other forms of play we have looked at, the rules of the formula are grasped by the player as the stipulations that establish a separate world, subject to many but not all of the rules of operation that characterize the day-to-day world. Paul Harris (2000: 66) clearly explains this characteristic in talking about how we appraise developments both in pretend play and in interpreting fiction. The events of the fictional world, he hypothesizes, "are appraised from the particular vantage-point that has been adopted within it. More specifically, we do not appraise the inputs from a perspective outside of that imagined framework, although in principle such a stance is available to us." The formula, then, is a world of its own that we may enter and pretend to dwell within. We agree to accept the formulaic fiction as a tentative reality and to follow along wherever it might take us.

This capacity both allows and is abetted by identification[8] with the characters in the fiction. In role-playing games, the player adopts the perspective of an improvised character. In formulaic art, players adopt the perspective of a protagonist, with whom they identify. In fact, this is what happens in all of the play I examine in this book. One enters into an alternative world and takes the perspective of a being dwelling in that world. This is fundamentally a form of imitation, what I call (following Alvin Goldman 2005: 91) extended imitation. Once one dwells in this alternative symbolic universe and adopts a "vantage point" within it, the stage is set for the other emotional and cognitive processes whereby one becomes increasingly caught up in that world.

As Cawelti points out, there is a point to all of this that goes beyond amusement. To put it another way, what we disguise or dismiss as amusement has important social implications. Through formulaic art, members of a society come to share fantasies embodying significant commitments and values (1976: 34). Inevitably these stories present a threat to treasured cultural convictions: it is possible to find meaning through enduring love, justice will prevail, problems can be worked out. In the end, the threat is resolved. As a result, Cawelti (1976: 35) says, "Literary formulas help to maintain a culture's ongoing consensus about the nature of reality and morality."

Advice

Now consider a second example, something that is so much a part of our everyday lives that it is likely to pass unnoticed. This is advice. I have before me as I write this an insert from my Sunday newspaper.[9] On the cover of this insert, I am informed that it reaches 41.7 million readers each week. The cover story is a compendium of advice, pointers from (among others) natural healing expert Andrew Weil, a fitness coach, a therapist and relationship expert, and a ubiquitous lifestyle consultant cum felon.

Most of what I read is unexceptionable, sensible, hard to argue with. The natural healer advises me to take time for myself: "One afternoon or evening a week, resolve to do something just for you: Take a drive in the country, listen to music you love, get a massage." That sounds good; I'd love to do that, although I'm not sure my employer will be completely supportive of my taking an afternoon off for a drive in the country. The fitness coach suggests a minimum of three or four days a week of strength training with weights, "combined with 30 minutes of cardiovascular exercise."

The relationship expert insists that I take at least 20 minutes every other day to give my partner my undivided attention, as well as stressing the importance of a monthly "romantic overnight getaway." Let's see, so far we're running (with showers after the exercise) around 11 hours a week out of my normal schedule, plus a couple of full days a month gazing into my partner's eyes at a bed and breakfast. Then there's the advice about things to accomplish. The lifestyle consultant suggests that I restock my pantry with "pastas, cooking wines, wasabi, [and] dried spices," that I create my own cookbook "by organizing [my] . . . recipes in a loose-leaf binder," and that I experiment with table decorations.

I could go on, but the point is probably clear. There is little possibility that any of the 41.7 million readers could actually follow all this advice, or even a small part of it. The situation becomes especially clear in light of one of the natural healer's stress-beating recommendations: downsize your life. "This is a good time of year," he counsels, "to think about what you can get rid of." OK, I can do that, and probably the best place to start is the 20 or 30 things I've just been advised to add to my life.

So if there is no possibility, and no serious expectation, that anybody is actually going to do all this, why is this the lead article in this very popular magazine? The reason, of course, is that it's enjoyable to read about doing these things. The "advice" is in fact a form of entertainment that presents images of an improved existence—a realistic fiction. Yes, I believe I'll take a deep breath and spend the morning reorganizing my pantry, and then take the afternoon off just for myself. It's not going to happen, but it's pleasurable just to think about it.

In general, advice is not to be followed; its purpose is to present fictions about what life could be like. Notice that, precisely because the advice is quite reasonable, those fictions are not outrageous; they are quite conceivable and therefore more believable and enjoyable. Taking an afternoon off: that could really happen, couldn't it? Thus the fictions of the advice are but a step away from my life, a familiar but slightly improved version of my experience. As such, they are a particularly effective means to stimulate my imagination: they are believable enough to give me emotional stimulation, yet sufficiently separated from my day-to-day reality that I do not rationally regard them as actual plans for life. (We would regard the person who actually sets out to do all the things recommended by Martha Stewart as a comic figure, or perhaps as insane).

Thus, note the extent to which advice operates as play. Specifically, it is a form of pretend play, like pretending to be a cowboy. As I engage in this play, I remain aware that I am fantasizing about the pleasures of stocking up on wasabi, impressing my guests by having it on hand, and so on, as opposed to actually doing these things. As with daydreaming about being a rock star or acting like a cowboy, however, it is more fun if I can at least partially forget my awareness that this is all pretending. That is, the emotional stimulation I get from the play will be greater if I can become somewhat caught up in the activity. As I mentioned in the previous section, players have the capacity for extended imitation, for placing themselves in a particular imaginary position and working from there. Further, doing so can produce behaviors, thoughts, and feelings that are rooted in the world of the fiction.

For these manifestations of becoming caught up to occur, players must become engaged in a feedback loop that uses their own cognitive, emotional, and imitative faculties. For example, as one becomes more absorbed in a fantasy about taking time off just for oneself, one begins to relax just imagining it. As one becomes more relaxed, one may well seek to play with this feeling, to enhance it by becoming more deeply absorbed in the fantasy.

Such activity may sound trivial, like meaningless reverie, but I doubt that such a judgment is correct. In playing the game of advice, I may very well formulate some actual plans ("It's true! I would feel better if I were getting more exercise, but I don't need a gym membership. I could just get one of those fitness balls"). More broadly, deriving emotional pleasure from advice play helps to sustain our faith in an idea that underwrites both our economy and our culture: we can transform ourselves in ways that will bring happiness. Were this to begin to seem like an implausible idea, think of how economic activity would slow down, as people stopped buying products and services they believe may improve—even transform!—their lives. Sales of fitness balls would plummet. Thus playing with advice is one way, among many, in which one of our key cultural values is sustained.

Celebrities

Another pervasive example of romantic realism is the celebrity. The celebrity is the ideal in human form, a concept that should be familiar in a predominantly Christian culture. The celebrity of film or radio was, in the early 20th century, a relatively new phenomenon. Although certain men and women were celebrated prior to the late

19th century, it is only after this time that the celebrity system took the form in which it is familiar today.[10] Stage actors, for example, could attain a wide following in the 19th century. However, they were not the focus of public interest in the way that, for example, film stars are today. In the 19th century, there seems not to have been any overwhelming public interest in the private lives of stage actors (Schickel 1973: 6).

But in the 20th century, there arose a type of personality, usually an entertainer of some sort, who was at once widely known and felt by the public to be an intimate. The public's reaction to this figure was an astonishing level of curiosity about the celebrity, above all perhaps a desire for some kind of contact with the celebrity, as if he or she could do something for the fan. In part, the appearance of the celebrity is dependent on technological factors; new media such as film and radio made it possible for individuals to enjoy a level of public exposure that had been rare in earlier centuries.[11]

However, celebrities as we know them are not created only by wide exposure; the other necessary component of celebrity is intimacy (Barnouw 1966; Schickel 1985). Early radio announcers used a speaking style modeled on public oratory; in this phase of development they (like the earliest silent film actors) were not identified by their names. Gradually, announcers began to adopt a more intimate voice, as if they were having a conversation with the individual listener. As announcers' voices became ever more familiar, audiences became increasingly curious about the people doing the announcing (Barnouw 1966: 163). The result was an avalanche of mail directed to the mysterious radio personalities by listeners who often seemed to regard the announcers as their closest friends.

The phenomenon of celebrity is born out of precisely these two somewhat opposed tendencies, wide exposure and intimacy.[12] The celebrity is simultaneously realistic and romantic, at once very close to us and decisively different from the environment with which we are familiar.[13] The celebrity is a romantically realistic human being, one who is an intimate—very close to us—and yet a slightly improved version of a mortal human. This increment of superiority possessed by the celebrity arises out of the perfect meaningfulness of the realm of the celebrity: the celebrity is precisely the person whose every act is meaningful.

If a person has entered into the public eye, the most commonplace features of his or her character and experience acquire significance. The celebrity is a person who has been removed from the context of everyday life and made into an object of contemplation, not entirely unlike an object of art.[14] Consider what critic Martin Esslin (1982a: 8) has written about a famous work of modern art:

> When in 1917 the French avant-garde painter Marcel Duchamp submitted a urinal
> to be displayed in an art exhibition in New York, he drew attention to a phenom-
> enon of basic importance: once an object, man-made or natural, is taken out of its

ordinary context and put onto a pedestal or into a frame, it is made to say, "Look at me, I am here to be observed!" and immediately that object acquires some characteristics of a work of art.

The celebrity is the human equivalent of Duchamp's urinal: what was mundane, a person like any other, becomes an object of wonder. To be famous is to be a framed human being, a work of art, a romantic realist version of a person.

The rest of us live in a world in which we are regularly confronted with suffering, boredom, and minor discomforts, a world that often fills us with doubt: Is there any purpose to all this? Although in reality the person who is celebrated is no more likely to escape this situation than anyone else, from the outside her life seems to be something quite different. Hers is a life in which everything has significance. Her going to a restaurant may be newsworthy, or at the very least occasion for comment from other diners. Her divorce may precipitate a small avalanche of media coverage. We are used to thinking that the celebrity does extraordinary things, but it is more to the point that whatever the celebrity does must be extraordinary.

The devoutly religious person can sustain, at least some of the time, a conviction that he knows the overall story and how his life fits into it. I would guess, however, that most of us can only dream about such a level of faith. This is why we envy the celebrity. For us, the celebrity lives a perfectly meaningful life, not because she does not suffer but rather because she appears to live in a world where every detail *means* something. Above all, she has a purpose, her purpose is to be her, something that galvanizes the whole society. It is this promise of perfect meaningfulness that the celebrity offers us through her life, and in one way or another most of us indulge in the pleasures of dreaming of that realm where the celebrity dwells.

Like advice, the celebrity masquerades as an element of our reality, but even though the celebrity is known to be a real person, he or she is not really of this world. We must keep in mind here that although the celebrity exists as a human being, this human being is not the celebrity. Even in a brief encounter, you will notice that he (the actual physical person) turns out to have pimples or is far shorter than you imagined. Especially if you were get to know the celebrity, he would fairly quickly become a person, talented perhaps but not different in principle from other people. The celebrity can exist only in the realm of the imagination.

To think about a celebrity is to play a game in which a particular human being counts as a romantic version of a human being, a human being with an otherworldly allure. One plays this game, in the end, for the same sort of reason that one plays other games: it's stimulating, it's fun. Of course, many people come to be highly caught up in this game, and as a result at times they begin to focus more on the game than on the everyday world. Their awareness that they are playing a game, that the celebrity is a person like anyone else, begins to fade. As a result, they find themselves fascinated by the celebrity in a way that may seem excessive, even to them; the whole business seems to be not entirely under the fan's conscious control.

In general, then, the image of the celebrity can be seen to serve a number of basic functions in contemporary social organization. First, the celebrity vitalizes the conception of the free individual in a society that at once reveres individuality and (in less immediately obvious ways) feeds on conformity. The celebrity is the person who shows us that individuality is not only possible but spectacularly profitable, in financial and cultural terms.

Second the celebrity vitalizes our faith in a world beyond the day-to-day. Celebrities prove that the romantic realism in which we are awash represents actual possibilities for us, for celebrities are mortal men and women who have come to dwell in a realm that overlaps with the everyday but that (unlike our day-to-day world) is alive with significance, clarity, and meaning. Note, then, that celebrities are emotionally charged images in which people may become caught up, and in so doing experience the palpable reality of the central ideological myths of late modernism. We too should organize our priorities to pursue self-realization and fame; no one can deny that the celebrity has transcended the mundane and monotonous level in which most of us wearily dwell. The celebrity proves to us that the ideal may enter into the real, and thus strengthens our conviction that such a transformation is possible for us as well.

Advertising

A final realm I would like to point to as one in which we may clearly see the principles of romantic realism at work is advertising. In the words of Pat Connolly, catalog manager for Williams-Sonoma, "We are certain that if the [catalog] picture is just right, you will say, 'My life would be great if I just had that desk, or that couch, or if I could just sit at that table and take a bite of that lifestyle.' "[15]

"Utopian visions are the very essence of advertising," observes Margaret Duffy (1994: 5–6). This is the point I want to develop, although one probably needs to be a little more careful about generalizations at this level. After all, not all advertisements present romantic realist fictions. Even if one restricts one's attention to television advertising, there are many kinds of advertisements.[16] Many commercials on TV, especially those locally produced, are "retail advertisements," ads designed for the most part to inform consumers that this or that store or car lot has desirable products at a low price. For the most part, these advertisements make little attempt to establish a meaning or image for the product; they consist, for example, of an announcer shouting about the prices at the Ford dealership while one sees pictures of representative cars and trucks.

Nationally distributed advertising is much more likely to undertake the task of cultivating the symbolic meaning (often called a brand) for the product. A certain proportion of these ads are to some extent informational; advertisements for automobiles, for example, may quote independent reports rating their car, or talk about standard equipment, and so on. However, even advertising that presents information of this sort in a straightforward manner is likely to also attempt to appeal to consumers by glamorizing the product. The automobile may be shown gleaming as it rotates on a pedestal, or is driven through a scenic landscape, or is driven by attractive people.

Furthermore, much national advertising depends little, if at all, on presentation of information about products. To some extent this is dictated by the nature of the product being sold; how much information is there to convey about a soft drink? However, it is also true that furnishing product information is often not the most effective form of promotion.

Instead, the most effective way to promote a product is largely to associate the product with realistic fictions. My understanding of the role of romantic realism in advertising was enhanced when I read Michael Arlen's book *Thirty Seconds* (1980), an entire book about the making of one 30-second AT&T commercial. (From this point forward, I am talking about the sort of noninformational advertising I have been describing, rather than advertising in general.) This ad is a "vignette" commercial, a type that became popular in the 1980s. Such commercials consist, on the visual level, in a large number of somewhat interconnected short scenes. What astonished me was the amount of complexity entailed in making a 30-second commercial. To take the AT&T commercial as an example: it was carefully conceived on the basis of much research and an overall corporate strategy (What image do we want? Who are we trying to reach? and so forth). The people who do this work, who are described and quoted in the book, are thoughtful and convincing; incidentally, I assume, they are paid a great deal of money.

AT&T then contracts its basic idea for the commercial out to a production company with numerous employees who audition perhaps hundreds of actors and actresses, scout locations, come up with props and costumes, and attend to the various aspects of actual filming. They spend weeks setting up and filming the various vignettes, perhaps working for an entire day to get a few seconds of usable tape. Meanwhile, other groups of professionals are composing and recording the music for the ad. Finally, miles of film are edited and combined with the music, with enormous attention being paid to such questions as the amount of echo in the sound of a dancer's foot on the stage, the precise timing of music with film cuts and action, and the balance of color in each scene.

Arlen himself is astonished at how much of the care and detail that has gone into making the commercial is too fast or blurred to be noticed in the final product. Aspects of scenes that took hours to film are not even noticeable unless one knows what one is looking for. What is going on? The answer to this question is clear if one has been paying attention to the dialogue in the book. In every stage of the process, the makers of this commercial have been asking versions of the question, "How do we communicate what we have in mind?" The wicker chair isn't quite right for the condominium; it doesn't say condominium. The phone doesn't "read" in this scene. The bulls at the rodeo must have horns. Hundreds of such judgments are made as the commercial is planned, filmed, and edited. What emerges is a set of images that look like reality but conform to our expectations in a way that reality never does.

The images used in the commercial have been perfected through thousands of hours of work by perhaps hundreds of people. In the day-to-day world, a bull might lack horns; a condominium might be furnished eclectically. But not in a carefully contrived commercial. The enormously complex iconography of American culture is being harnessed to construct a potent image that is *similar to but decisively different from* the everyday world. The commercial presents familiar beings in familiar settings doing familiar things, but in the commercial everything is the way it should be. Even when a commercial depicts disorder, as might be done in an ad for a cleaning product, the disorder has a form of perfection, a circumscribed spill on an otherwise immaculate tiled floor.[17]

The power of the commercial stems from the subtlety of its depiction. The fact that the images in the commercial are so much like the day-to-day world means that viewers (who are, of course, not prone to reflect consciously on the commercial) are likely to accept them as directly relevant to the everyday world in which they dwell. Fictions are seamlessly interwoven with actual events and situations, with the result that the viewer is comforted, reassured, inspired by images at once like and more fulfilling than everyday reality.

Why bother? What does it matter if people observe scenes in which all the signs line up, in which the bulls at the rodeo always have horns? It matters because the romantically realist imagery offers an extraordinarily powerful means to valorize symbols. The viewer who becomes caught up in the play of attending to a romantically realist image experiences the same sort of feelings that we observed in the role-player Skip. Viewers experience real feelings and perspectives generated by an imaginary situation. In so doing, they will undergo a palpable transformation of themselves. What has wrought this transformation? Why, of course, it is the elements of the romantic realist form that sparked this transformation, and prominent among those elements was a particular product or service.

Note that the mechanism here is the same as in the other examples I have discussed. People engage these images according to an unarticulated agreement: for the moment, these images will be accepted as depicting a world understood to be different from the familiar world of the everyday. But like advice (take the afternoon off!) or the celebrity (he was born in the city where I grew up!) the advertisement also seems exceedingly close to our reality. Like a formulaic fiction, we understand that the advertisement is not reality, but we are willing to play the game of pretending that it is reality. It entices us to pleasant imaginative flights in which the cares of the everyday world begin to fade as we become increasingly caught up. Of course, the product may then appear as an element of this world that might bring us closer to this better place.[18]

Is Romantic Realism Unique to our Society?

How did romantic realism come to be such a commonplace? Has it always been so pervasive? Human beings have certainly dreamed of finding perfect worlds since they began to dream. Among the most prominent and historically important dreams of perfection are those formulated in religious terms. Some scholars (see, for example, Cohn 1961) have suggested that the pursuit of utopia through religious social movements has its roots in the Judaic tradition, but it seems more likely that utopian movements have arisen in other times and places as well.[19]

In the Christian tradition, pursuit of a perfect world is most often called *millenarianism.* "The millennium" is an image of paradise, so named because of the New Testament prophecy that Christ will return and reign over the faithful for a thousand years (the word *millennium* itself stems from the Latin for "one thousand"). By now this terminology has been generalized and is used indiscriminately for non-Christian as well as Christian movements. Millennial utopias are the perfect worlds that appear in the visions of the prophet and are generally characterized by three features. First, the transformation to the new and perfect world will have its origin in forces that are beyond the knowledge of most people; these forces may be supernatural, beings from outer space, and so on. Second, the transformation to the new world will be sudden and probably catastrophic; believers in the forces will live to see the new world, but nonbelievers will perish. Third, this transformation is imminent: it will happen soon, and therefore the world of perfection is close at hand.

The vision of the millennium, together with its forebear the legend of Eden, is among the most powerful and widespread ideas in Western thought, always dwelling just below the surface of the mind, waiting to be awakened. It has been roused to life again and again in Western history—in the origins of Christianity and Islam, in the Crusades, in the movements of the Reformation, in the great awakenings in American society, perhaps also in the totalitarian movements of the twentieth century—in sum, in social movements that promise an imminent paradise.

Whether one would want to see the secular utopias of romantic realism as manifestations of the millenarian dream is largely a matter of how one wants to define one's terms. Seeing this sort of continuity helps to understand some of the deep cultural similarities that unite human beings who dwell in different places and historical periods. However, it is also important to understand how the suffusion of romantic realism throughout our culture creates a situation that is historically unique.

In the next chapter I turn to the continuity and differences between our culture's romantic realism and the dreams of perfect worlds that occurred in earlier phases of our cultural history. I suggest that the solution to this problem lies in the period of European history we have come to call Romanticism. In a sense, the Romantic period represents a cultural and historical sea change through which artistic genres and eventually economic behavior assimilated the millenarian themes and imagery of the Reformation and earlier phases of the Western religious tradition.

This interpretation of the fusion of millenarian expectations and artistic genres is the central theme of M. H. Abrams's classic treatment of Romanticism, *Natural Supernaturalism* (1971). Here Abrams discusses the general project of Romantic writers as an attempt to reshape basic Christian beliefs in a post-Enlightenment intellectual climate:

> A conspicuous Romantic tendency, after the rationalism and decorum of the Enlightenment, was a reversion to the stark drama and suprarational mysteries of the Christian story and doctrines and to the violent conflicts and abrupt reversals of the Christian inner life, turning on the extremes of destruction and creation, hell and heaven, exile and reunion, death and rebirth, dejection and joy, paradise lost and paradise regained. . . . But since they lived, inescapably, after the Enlightenment, Romantic writers revived these ancient matters with a difference: they undertook to save the overview of human history and destiny, the experiential paradigms, and the cardinal values of their religious heritage, but reconstituting them in a way that would make them intellectually acceptable, as well as emotionally pertinent, for the time being [1971: 66].

Putting the matter in somewhat cruder terms than Abrams does, we could say that Romantic literature and philosophy were attempts to reconfigure traditional Christian concerns in the domain of art. To quote Abrams again: "Characteristic concepts and patterns of Romantic philosophy and literature are a displaced and reconstituted theology" (1971: 65). Now of course, this transformation was not the age's only attempt to reshape Christian doctrine and promises in a secularized format. The French revolution, to take a single and overwhelming example, can be interpreted in part as an attempt to bring about the millennium through political revolution (Abrams 1971: 65). But, still speaking very broadly, disillusionment with the ultimate failure of that attempt was one of the reasons the Romantics were encouraged to pursue the same end in another domain, that of the imagination.

It is above all the concern with the millennium that Abrams considers the key to understanding Romantic literature. In the broadest interpretation, the Romantics sought "to reconstitute the grounds of hope and to announce the certainty, or at least the possibility, of a rebirth in which a renewed mankind will inhabit a renovated earth where he will find himself thoroughly at home" (1971: 12). Abrams's interpretation of the Romantic achievement points to the conclusion that Romanticism was not only heavily influenced by Christian thought; much of Romantic literature can be considered as a form of secularized millenarianism. Abrams is concerned to show that this understanding can help us grasp certain themes and continuities in Romantic literature, for example the recurring stress on the redemptive function of the poet, and of art more generally. In the present context, the point is not so much to understand Romantic literature in itself but rather to grasp the general process whereby the traditional images and expectations of millenarianism entered into the realm of art and literature.

I turn to this task in the next chapter. To fully understand just what romantic realism is and how it has come to dominate so many realms of our culture, it will be helpful to take a brief detour through some of the historical writing on this issue. Although there is no account of the history of romantic realism as such, a number of authors have studied related issues in looking at art and literary history, the rise of consumer capitalism, and the nature of Romanticism. Together these works offer compelling evidence that romantic realism is a cultural pattern that took shape as a part of the broader movement we call Romanticism, and that it developed alongside—and as an important part of—the work and leisure practices so prominent in late-modern consumer capitalism.

3

Romanticism and the Birth of Consumer Culture

A **FRENCH CRITIC** of the 18th century, the Abbé de La Porte, commented on a painting by his contemporary Jean-Baptiste Greuze as follows:

> A father is reading the Bible to his children. Moved by what he has just read, he is himself imbued with the moral he is importing to them; his eyes are almost moist with tears. His wife . . . is listening to him with that air of tranquility enjoyed by an honest woman surrounded by a large family that constitutes her sole occupation, her pleasures, and her glory. Next to her, her daughter is astounded and grieved by what she hears. The older brother's facial expression is as singular as it is true [cited in Fried 1980: 9–10].

Michael Fried, from whose book I have taken this passage, summarizes La Porte's evaluation of the painting: "What he himself found most compelling about the Pere de famille was what he saw as its persuasive representation of a particular state or condition . . . i.e., the state or condition of rapt attention, of being completely occupied or engrossed or (as I prefer to say) absorbed in what he or she is doing, hearing, thinking, feeling" (1980: 10).

The capacity for absorption or engrossment is undoubtedly universal. However, engrossment as a suitable topic for a painting is not universal. Fried notes, in the work from which I have been quoting, the extraordinary level of concern with what he

---

Parts of this chapter appeared previously in an article published in the journal *Ethos* (Stromberg 2000).

calls absorption among French painters in the latter half of the 18th century. What is responsible for the emergence of this theme? More directly related to my concerns in this book, does the concern with depicting engrossment in paintings have anything to do with the development of getting caught up in other symbolic realms?

There is considerable evidence that getting caught up is a mode of engagement with symbolic resources such as art, literary fiction, and (eventually) entertainment that developed alongside of and as a necessary correlate of the modern worldview. Others, most recently and notably Jonathon Crary (1990, 1999), have studied the development of distinctive forms of attentiveness in 19th-century European society, and my argument is intended to be compatible with this approach.[1] Crary points out that contemporary observers identified a form of "passive attention" during this time, a category embracing states such as reverie and daydreaming. However, for the most part he is interested in another (more active) sort of attention, the forms of concentration and focus that support contemporary productivity in economic life.

In a sense, I want to look at the other side of attention, the forms that support activities of consumption and leisure. The growing literature on this topic points clearly to the late 18th century (the period most associated with early Romanticism and with rapid development in the consumer economy) as the time at which contemporary practices of becoming caught up took shape.[2] Developments in religion and art closely paralleled this economic transformation and helped adjust patterns of social behavior in ways that encouraged certain sorts of action in the marketplace. It turns out that the development of concern with absorption in painting is a good place to start in the attempt to describe this relationship, so I begin with a fuller exposition of the facts set out by Fried in his classic book *Absorption and Theatricality*.

Absorption and Becoming Caught Up

Although Fried is concerned with the tradition of depicting absorption that developed in mid-18th century France, he notes that this tradition was a revival of themes that first emerged in European painting in the 17th century. These earlier depictions of absorption tended to focus on religious themes, although Fried notes that already in the 17th century a process of secularization—whereby absorptive states occurring in nonreligious contexts became a possible topic for the artist—was under way. This secularizing tendency was more or less complete in a French painter such as Chardin, who (says Fried) displays no difference in attitude whatsoever "between the pictures of games and amusements on the one hand and ostensibly more serious or morally exemplary scenes on the other" (1980: 47). Fried finds here:

> a new, unmoralized vision of distraction as a vehicle of absorption; or perhaps one
> should say of that vision that it distills, from the most ordinary states and activi-

ties, an unofficial morality according to which absorption emerges as good in and of itself, without regard to its occasion [1980: 51].

As Fried traces the development of concern with absorption through the 18th century, he observes that the attempt to portray absorption necessarily implies certain things about the relationship between a painting and its beholder. Early in the period, representation of absorption entailed picturing subjects utterly engrossed with something, and thus necessarily not oriented to the observer of the painting. However, as the conventions of the depiction developed, this was no longer adequate: "By the first half of the 1760s, however, the presence of the beholder could no longer be dealt with in this way; it demanded to be counteracted and if possible obliviated in or by the painting itself" (1980: 67). Obliviating the beholder came down to the practice of portraying extremes of absorption, thereby rendering the viewer utterly irrelevant to the subjects of the painting.

The emotional extremes of the paintings of this decade have made them seem sentimental and cloying to critics of later ages, but Fried points out that what we interpret as an attempt to pull in a wide audience through sentimentality was in fact an attempt to *exclude* the viewer (1980: 68–69).[3] It was precisely this, he argues, that was the basis for the enormous impact of these paintings (1980: 69; see also Schama 1989: 152). Although Fried refers to this situation as a paradox, its resolution is facilitated if one assumes that the beholder's reaction to these paintings was an early form of getting caught up; the viewer is able to be emotionally moved by the painting *precisely because* she is separated from it. Indeed, this was the explicit attitude toward painting during this period. Summarizing the attitude of contemporary critics such as Diderot, Fried writes: "A painting, it was claimed, had first to attract (*attirer, appeler*) and then to arrest (*arrêter*) and finally to enthrall (*attacher*) the beholder, that is, a painting had to call to someone, bring him to a halt in front of itself, and hold him there as if spellbound and unable to move" (1980: 92).[4] This is no different from the mechanism of getting caught up, emotional and cognitive immersion in a fiction that is enabled by a rational separation from the form, a recognition that it is a fiction and engagement with it can be considered play.

In fact, one can go so far as to say that the very reason for selecting absorption as a topic in this period was to produce absorption in the beholder. The attitude of the time is summarized in this way by Fried: "Only by establishing the fiction of his [the beholder's] absence or nonexistence could his actual placement before and enthrallment by the painting be secured" (1980: 103). Why so? Although I depart from Fried's analysis in explaining it this way, I would say that getting caught up becomes possible when artistic conventions are oriented around the goal of creating an alternative symbolic universe in which the subject may momentarily dwell.[5] Depictions of extreme absorption constitute the fiction of a person or group utterly fixated on something other than the viewer, and in so doing they establish a symbolic world set apart from the one in which the viewer stands.

Such an image shares an important characteristic with the sort of configuration I have referred to as romantic realism: the artifact must be both close to the familiar day-to-day world and decisively different from it. Again, it is precisely because one is so firmly aware of its contingent, created nature that one can allow oneself to become immersed in the work.

The Novel

Thus one can look at certain 18th-century painters as setting out to induce what I have called getting caught up. Furthermore, the techniques of doing this entailed some of the basic conventions of romantic realism (although, of course, what art historians call Realism is a later phenomenon).[6] It is not only in painting that these themes can be observed in this period. It is suggestive, for example, that the second half of the 18th century is also often cited among students of English literature as the period giving rise to the genre we now call the novel.[7]

Here I wish to stress three points about the novel that parallel Fried's discussion of absorptive painting. First, the novel has often been interpreted as a result of the secularization of narrative conventions that originally took shape in explicitly religious contexts. Second, it is common to name realism as a significant characteristic of the genre (perhaps the defining one). Third, the novel is a form amenable to appreciation through practices of absorption. I discuss each of these points in turn.

Robert Darnton, whose discussion of reading practices in the late 18th century will be mentioned later, argues explicitly that reading practices in France during this period were a secularized version of earlier forms of reading carried out in ritual contexts: "[The approach to reading advocated by Rousseau] revive[d] a way of reading that seems to have prevailed in the sixteenth and seventeenth centuries: reading in order to absorb the unmediated Word of God" (1985: 232). A number of well-known studies have made similar arguments about fiction during this period. One of the classic works on the origins of the novel, Ian Watt's *The Rise of the Novel* (1957), stresses throughout close connections between the novel and an earlier generation of inspirational literature. Daniel Defoe, author of the book (*Robinson Crusoe*) that Watt (1957: 74) characterizes as "certainly the first novel,"[8] was "born and bred a Puritan" (75). Watt carefully considers the relationship between Calvinism and the novel and concludes that in a number of ways it is indisputable that Calvinism prepared the way for the novel.

Of particular interest in this context is the relationship between the novel and the genres of spiritual literature that immediately preceded it, books such as Bunyan's *Pilgrim's Progress*. In such works, Watt (1957: 80) points out, "The significance of the characters and their actions largely depends upon a transcendental scheme of things." In the novel, of course, conventions of realism focus the significance of the story on the individual characters and their lives; this is where we readers look for meaning.

Note, then, that at the most basic level the genre of the novel reflects a shift in how subjects pursue meaning. The meaning of the novel is not in an external cosmic order to which the work of fiction testifies; rather its meaning is to be sought within the structure that is established by the work itself. This is the same idea we observed above in the context of painting: the work of art becomes a world separated from this one, yet related to it.[9] It is within the unity created by the work— this separate world—that meaning is to be sought. In this the novel can be assigned in principle to the category of romantic realism, for the very idea of the genre is to present a recognizable world in which meaning is somewhat more coherent than in the day-to-day world.

This judgment is as close to being uncontroversial as one can get in the realm of literary studies. Watt cites "formal realism" as the distinguishing characteristic of the genre of the novel. By this he means the novel is a form relying not on traditional formats in the areas of plot and ethical stance but instead mimicking the sort of epistemological realism—an attempt to record things "as they are"—that had begun to prove so successful in the sciences. Later critics have questioned Watt's understanding of realism; in particular it now seems clear that Watt underestimated the element of romanticism in the realistic conventions of the novel (see, for example, McKeon 1987). But this merely strengthens the association of novelistic form and the form of realism I am focusing on in this book.

Finally, to my third point: it is well known that the rise of the novel was accompanied by reading practices that entailed deep absorption in fiction for purposes of emotional stimulation. After all, Austen's *Sense and Sensibility* (1811), certainly among the best known of all Romantic novels, not only presents extensive evidence of such practices; they are at one level the topic of the book. To cite a single, if prominent, example: early on in the novel we learn much about the three main characters—Elinor, Edward, and Marianne—through Marianne's expression of disappointment that Edward was insufficiently moved in reading Cowper's poetry: "To hear those beautiful lines which have frequently almost driven me wild, pronounced with such impenetrable calmness, such dreadful indifference" (Austen 1995: 14). As I discuss below, one of the key features of the romantic worldview is the conviction that one is morally bound to find emotional stimulation in art; it is the excesses of this position that Austen is satirizing here.[10]

Darnton (1985: 251) maintains that in France "the quality of reading changed in a broad but immeasureable public toward the end of the old regime." He attributes this change largely to Rousseau and to the reception of his extraordinarily popular work, *La Nouvelle Héloïse*. In a preface, Rousseau maintained the love letters that constitute the novel to be authentic, and evidently no small proportion of his readers took him at his word (Darnton 1985: 233). Furthermore, and equally relevant from the perspective I am advocating here, Rousseau implored his audience to put themselves in the position of the protagonists ("at the foot of the Alps"). Again, his words seem to have made a deep impression on his readers, who identified passionately with the characters in the book. As Darnton (1985: 248) puts it, "His 'fans' read him in the way that he asked to be read and threw themselves into the role called for in the prefaces."

This level of emotional involvement with a fiction, made possible by the imaginative immersion in the familiar world of the depiction, is what I have called getting caught up. As I have stressed, this immersion consists of accepting a vantage point within the fiction. Of course, I do not mean to say here that the reading practices outlined by Darnton reflect those of our own period; in fact, Darnton carefully warns against this conclusion. Nevertheless, there is at least one basic continuity between the interpretive conventions of that time and of today, that being the practice of becoming caught up as a way of enjoying the novel.

The Birth of the Fashion Pattern

I have briefly surveyed two realms of cultural activity, painting and literary fiction, and have found evidence in both of these areas of the emergence of the conventions of becoming caught up in realistic fictions during the second half of the 18th century. Furthermore, I have suggested that these interpretative practices were in both cases revivals of earlier traditions established in specifically religious contexts. I now want to broaden this inquiry somewhat by looking at another social transformation of this period, the birth of the modern fashion pattern. I argue that the same themes—secularization, becoming caught up, and romantic realism—can be located in patterns of consumption that begin to appear during this time.

I am fortunate to be able to call on a historiography of consumer behavior that has appeared over the last two decades, after this important topic went largely ignored for many years. Although there is slight disagreement over matters such as dates, authorities such as McKendrick, Brewer, and Plumb (1982); Campbell (1987); and McCracken (1988) are in general agreement that the mid-to-late 18th century was a decisive period in the emergence of the modern fashion pattern.[11] Although some attention to fashion is probably universal, the European fashion pattern that emerged at this time is distinguished by the rapid rate of change in style of consumer goods.

Novelty became a significant marker of the symbolic value of goods during this period; McCracken (1988) points out that this idea contrasts sharply with a mode of consumption established in earlier centuries, what he calls the patina system.[12] Attention to patina, the various characteristics acquired by objects as they age, yields a relationship to consumer goods that ensures some level of stability to status claims: new silver illustrates your recent achievement of the means to afford silver and thus is distinctly less valued than silver that has obviously been in the family for generations.

To become established as the dominant mode of decoding the symbolism of goods, fashion had to overcome a deeply entrenched way of thinking about this matter. Crudely but accurately phrased, the symbolic value of newness had to migrate from bad to good. Furthermore, establishment of the fashion pattern requires overcoming some rather basic attitudes about the utility of goods; to participate in the fashion pattern I must want the new style of shoes even though my old shoes are still usable. Campbell (1987) is especially attentive to this problem, which persists in contemporary consumer behavior and which he labels "the puzzle of modern consumerism":

> A mystery surrounds consumer behavior. . . . [It] concerns the very essence of modern consumption itself—its character as an activity which involves an apparently endless pursuit of wants; . . . the modern consumer . . . is characterized by an insatiability which arises out of a basic inexhaustibility of wants themselves, which forever arise, phoenix-like, from the ashes of their predecessors [37].

Campbell's Account of the Ethic of Consumerism

Campbell's attempt to solve this mystery takes shape as an inquiry into the development of a consumerist ethic, the idea that there is moral value in consumption. Campbell's argument is modeled on, and intended to supplement, Weber's celebrated account (1958) of the Protestant work ethic. Campbell claims that Weber, in showing how Calvinist theology was transformed in practice to an ethic promoting rational labor in an earthly calling, missed half the story. Weber, as is well known, isolated the Calvinist position on predestination as decisive in creating the psychological climate in which early capitalism flourished. Calvin held that a perfect God must have foreknowledge of all of history, and therefore would be aware of the state of grace of all believers. To say that a believer could do anything to alter this state would be to suggest that God would have been uncertain about something, a claim detracting from his perfection and majesty. This is the foundation for the belief in predestination: God's perfect knowledge becomes the believer's fate.

Weber (1958) argues that Calvin's followers were unable to bear the tension created by this doctrine, for in its purest state it demanded that believers accept there was nothing in the course of their lives that would indicate or influence whether they were bound for heavenly bliss or eternal damnation. The result of this situation was the development, over generations, of often covert doctrines and practices that offered signs to the believer as to whether he or she was among the elect. Believers sought ways to demonstrate to themselves and others that they were destined for heaven. Diligent and rational labor in a calling, issuing in prosperity, came to be seen—in spite of the doctrine—as a good indication of salvation. Consequently, Weber suggests, religious energies were eventually diverted into economic activity in a way that encouraged and valorized the latter.

Although Weber concentrated on the importance of rational economic activity as a sign of salvation, Campbell (1987) points out that there were a number of other indicators of grace that took shape in the centuries after Calvin. Campbell is particularly concerned with the development of an emotionalist ethic, ideas that certain feelings such as charity and compassion were signs of the "divine which is within" (1987: 118). In many Protestant communities, emotion came to play a central role as a sign of the presence of God.

Campbell attends in particular to the Cambridge Platonists, a group of 17th century theologians who softened Calvin's views on predestination by stressing the importance of feelings of benevolence, charity, and pity in the life of the Christian.[13] Such emotions were evidence of the spirit of God working within the individual believer, hence functioning as a sign of the believer's state of grace (see Campbell 1987: 107ff). This "other Protestant Ethic" was an important source of Sentimentalism and Romanticism, secularized ethical systems within which tender and sensitive feelings came to be seen as signs of moral rectitude.

This transformation came about in part through development, in the early 18th century, of a middle-class aesthetic, a philosophy of beauty. Such a philosophy was of crucial significance in a time when the middle classes were competing with the aristocracy for political, social, and cultural hegemony (1987: 149). In particular, one must understand that battles for social dominance were likely to revolve around charges that members of the middle class were vulgar and lacked taste (1987: 149). In this context, a strong defense of middle-class aesthetics was of utmost importance.

Campbell contends that it was the Earl of Shaftesbury who offered such a defense by marrying neoclassical aesthetics with the ideas of the Cambridge Platonists. Shaftesbury suggested that humans "possessed an intuitive moral sense" of good and beauty (1987: 150) and that one's feelings are the expression of this sense. It is therefore through one's emotional reactions to life and art that one's virtue—one's harmony with the good—is demonstrated. As Campbell comments, "Responsiveness to beauty thus became a crucial moral quality, such that any deficiency in this respect became a moral lapse" (1987: 152).

In this way, appreciation of art and beauty became a form of morality. Here Campbell has deepened our understanding of the transformations between the ritual practices of the 17th century and the aesthetic practices of the late 18th century. Paintings or novels came to have moral value in the latter period because emotions had come to have spiritual value in the earlier one. Because there was an emergent culture industry turning out forms of art (poetry, fiction, painting, and so on), an arena in which one could demonstrate one's taste, and hence one's worth, was taking shape. How one responded to, say, a poem became (particularly in the Romantic period) an index of one's taste, and by extension one's worth. This, of course, is the basis of Marianne's dismissal of Edward in *Sense and Sensibility* (Austen 1995).

Thus in this period there occurred a shift in earlier understandings of the value of feeling, such that feelings of pleasure in art became the true indicator of moral worth: "Pleasure indeed becomes the crucial means of recognizing that ideal truth and beauty which imagination reveals—it is the 'grand elementary principle' of life—and thus becomes the means by which enlightenment and moral renewal can be achieved through art" (Campbell 1987: 205). This elevation of pleasure in imaginary experience was not only a commitment of airy intellectuals but can be seen in the attitudes of the novel-reading public, as well as in social commentary and satires of this public. Campbell argues persuasively that Romantic ideas and practices of fiction reading helped "to bring about a critical change in attitude towards the world" (1987: 176). The new attitude was that the pleasures of imagination, fostered through immersion in fictions, might be preferable to the mundane pleasures of everyday life.

Note, then, just as Weber argues that through Protestantism religious energies were eventually channeled into the secular realm of labor, that Campbell maintains such energies were also channeled into the secular realm of leisure activities. In this realm it was above all one's emotional reactions that were cultivated as a sign of moral value. Gradually, the groundwork was thereby laid for "emotional hedonism," the idea that it is good to indulge and enjoy one's emotional reactions to the world.

Emotional hedonism is significant for the development of modern patterns of consumption because it sanctions, and indeed encourages, cultivation of the ability to derive enjoyment from one's emotions. In its most developed forms, emotional hedonism becomes autonomous; the matter of what is *really* happening to the subject is irrelevant if the subject has mastered the psychological skills of fostering emotions through his or her imagination. In fact, this autonomous form of emotional hedonism is likely to offer greater possibilities for satisfaction than practices linking enjoyment to actual experiences, because actual experiences are limited in availability and duration.

The experiences of emotional stimulation that were so important during the romantic period occurred first of all in response to art. However, Campbell's argument confronts us with the possibility that the growing taste for a wide variety of consumer goods occurring at this time also reflects the effects of autonomous hedonism. He suggests that the necessary link here is found in the practice of daydreaming about the effects of products. Fantasizing about the possible effects that products might play in our lives generates our longing for them.

The possibility of turning the wish into a reality entails the daydream being not merely a fantasy. To be a daydream a fantasy must not be too outlandish. It must contain an element of realism: "Daydreaming can perhaps best be envisaged as an activity which mixes the pleasures of fantasy with those of reality" (Campbell 1987: 85). Putting the matter in the terms I have advocated, the daydream is a romantic realist fantasy.

Now, if a subject is able to experience intense emotional pleasure on the basis of imaginary experiences, he or she comes to place enormous value on novelty. It is an occasion for imaginative speculation on what might be, as opposed to the familiar, the limitations of which are known (Campbell 1987: 85–86). The basic point here is that it is always possible for the modern autonomous hedonist to imagine pleasures more intense than those of actual experience, so that actual experiences are always at a disadvantage relative to anticipated ones.[14] Hence the fashion pattern: the consumer gets excited about the new product and imagines how it will give pleasure. The product is perhaps obtained, and if it is, it disappoints. At this point the consumer is ready to entertain suggestions about a newer product. And so on.

Thus, according to Campbell, the basis of the consumption practices underlying the fashion pattern is that in fact consumers do not seek fulfillment from products. Rather, they derive pleasure from longing for products and for what they represent, those realistic worlds of fantasy. Thus Campbell sees modern hedonism as a direct parallel to romance in sexual matters; the pleasure is in the *longing*, the fantasy of fulfillment.[15] Once the product (or the romantic partner) is actually obtained, its value begins to deteriorate. It is no longer the object of fantasy; now it is an object of reality, and like all real objects it can never measure up to its correlate in the realm of the ideal. This is the explanation for the observation with which I began, the insatiability of the consumer enmeshed in the fashion pattern.

Consumption practices that were taking shape around the turn of the 19th century, then, share certain themes that I have identified in other cultural arenas. First, Campbell presents a strong case for the view that these practices of consumerism were a secularized version of Protestant attitudes about emotion in the 16th and 17th centuries. Second, the consumer's engagement with products was likely to be mediated through fantasies about the pleasures the product could provide. These fantasies entail becoming caught up for the purposes of emotional stimulation,[16] in this case through fantasies associated with the product. Finally, these fantasies are a form of romantic realism, unified and meaningful fictions that both reflect and perfect the everyday world.

The Birth of the Culture of Entertainment

I have suggested that late-18th-century Europe saw the growth of opportunities for becoming caught up in the domains of art, literary fiction, and consumption. Together, the trends in these three areas suggest a broader social process, the early stages of the development of a socioeconomic order hinged upon high production and high consumption. That is, cultural practices through which people are encouraged to derive pleasure through their imaginative interaction with art and goods are a firm foundation for consumption of leisure and goods.

However, it is important to note that these cultural changes predated the high-consumption economy in which these values were to become so important. Although the industrial revolution of the 18th century significantly enlarged productive capacities in the European economies, it took another century before an economy based in delivering consumer products to a broad range of social classes began to emerge. During the 19th and early 20th centuries, social, technological, and cultural changes paved the way for the coherent system of entertainment and consumption that characterizes life today. It was during this period that monopoly capitalism emerged and techniques of mass production in manufacturing began to dominate the economy. Formation of a broad middle class with a national culture, increasing use of electronic media for communication and entertainment, the growth of advertising and the consumer economy, and integration of communities of immigrants into the American mainstream are a few of the other noteworthy changes that occurred during this period. In the words of William Leach (1993: 111), these changes "greatly extended the frontiers of consumer society and . . . carved into the older American culture a newer culture, a culture that seemed to offer everyone access to an unlimited supply of goods and that promised a lifetime of security, well-being, and happiness."

Many scholars have devoted their careers to studying parts of this emerging new culture, and I can only touch on a few of the themes that are most relevant here. In particular, this period (roughly 1875–1925) saw development of increasingly sophisticated methods for displaying various kinds of social perfection. Social and cultural resources began to be devoted to ever more tangible forms of romantic realism, actual physical depictions of the utopian world existing beyond the day-to-day. Here I briefly sketch this process of development, which culminated in contemporary technologies for realistic display of perfected images, such as advertising and motion pictures.

The Transformation of Advertising

A number of the institutions examined in this chapter have taken shape as secularized versions of earlier religious practices. Advertising in the broad sense has existed for centuries, and it certainly does not fit into this pattern. However, the sort of advertising I mentioned in the previous chapter is a much more recent phenomenon, and here the argument can be made that religious models were important. In its earliest form, romantic realist advertising was oriented around simple messages of renewal: your problem is based in lack of our product and your salvation shall be its acquisition. In a sense, this brings us back again to millenarianism; advertising can offer a message of salvation that is similar to that offered by the prophet. In fact, historians such as William Leach and T. J. Jackson Lears have extensively documented the links between the rise of national advertising and the American millenarian tradition.[17] Lears (1994), for example, points to a direct connection between millenarian revivalism and advertising in American society.[18] Because of the popularity of Evangelistic preaching and the stress on self-transformation through conversion, people accepted the idea that one's life could be permanently changed in a moment. Advertisers successfully exploited this idea by creating persuasive claims that self-transformation could occur in the realm of consumption. Here I want to look a little more closely at how this approach to advertising emerged.

Certainly, the way was paved prior to the late 19th century. As I have noted, the fashion pattern was well established in urban areas early in the century, and already by 1856 *Harper's* magazine had referred to "the shopping mania" as "a species of absorbing insanity."[19] However, in the years around the turn of the 20th century the American economy underwent changes that entailed tremendous increases in productivity. Although one may speak of mass production earlier than this time, it is really in the 20th century that factories began to be organized in assembly lines to turn out large numbers of commodities such as automobiles. These new techniques of mass production would have been useless without corresponding expansion of markets; it is profitable to make a lot of something only if one can subsequently sell such quantities.[20]

The literature on this period often refers to a shift from a "production oriented to a consumption oriented" economy, shorthand that encodes a very complex transformation in a probably overly convenient phrase. This development is at base changes in social character, changes in the sorts of people living in the society. The economy did not, of course, change from production to consumption; there must be continued production if there is to be anything to consume. The point is rather that people began to identify more with their role as consumers than their role as producers, a change that entailed new sorts of economic behavior.

Some historians have claimed that it was primarily advertising that *caused* the change in social character[21]. A developing strategy of advertising, consciously devised by social scientists and advertisers, resulted in an explosion in the effectiveness of and resources devoted to advertising during the early decades of the 20th century. Earlier advertising had tried to sell products on the basis of the utilitarian value of the product being sold; the developing techniques of modern advertising focused increasingly on the problem of how the product would help the consumer improve or maintain his or her social standing.

The point is that the product is sold not by information about it but by creating an emotional situation in which the product becomes necessary if one is to be the right sort of person. This is an effective way to sell products, but there is something even more significant going on here: this is an effective way to create consumers, because if all ads work this way, and if people are surrounded with advertising so that it is hard for them to pass a waking hour without encountering an ad, the general message will start to take hold. The general message is that one can transform oneself through consumption.[22]

Though this argument (which I have summarized from Stewart Ewen 1976) is thought-provoking, the broader historical picture suggests that innovations in advertising in the early 20th century were more a response to than a cause of changes in social character. After all, many of the signs of such changes were present in the late 19th century, before the time when advertising began to be a dominant force in the American economy. What seems most likely is that broad social currents around the turn of the century left many people in a position to be receptive to appeals that told them how to attain well-being, fulfillment, and improved social standing. Advertisers quickly perceived and addressed these needs.[23]

Lears (1983: 29ff) points to the career of Bruce Barton as exemplary of the sorts of changes happening in American society at this time. Barton was the son of an influential Protestant minister, a writer of inspirational literature, and one of the founders of modern advertising. Born in 1886, Barton began working in advertising shortly after graduating from Amherst College. It is particularly the overlap between Barton's religious and advertising interests that make him significant for my argument here. Barton pioneered in producing a sort of advertising copy that promoted individual products by associating them with the promise of an improved life. Barton gives overwhelming evidence of having been sincere in this belief: through salesmanship modern business would bring about a better world.

It is here that an affinity arose between his faith in business and his faith in God. The purpose of both religion and advertising was to improve the world by promoting entrepreneurship, industry, consumption for pleasure, and positive thinking. Barton often commented that the Bible was a great advertising text, and his most famous work, a biography of Jesus called *The Man Nobody Knows,* explained why. In Barton's interpretation (his book was a best seller for years in the 1920s), Jesus was "the most successful advertising man in history" (Lears 1983: 33). He was an enthusiastic consumer ("the most popular dinner guest in Jerusalem!" Lears 1983: 33) and "the founder of modern business'"(Lears 1983: 31). According to Barton, to paraphrase Calvin Coolidge, "the business of God is business."

Authors such as Lears and Phillip Rieff (1966) have interpreted the changes in advertising strategies as one sign of an emerging "therapeutic ethos" around the turn of the century. There was a convergence of thinking in several social realms, most prominently, religion, medicine, and product marketing, that tended to reinforce the same set of ideas, ideas about the possibility and value of gratification, fulfillment, and exuberant well-being in this world. That is, advertising recognized the possibility of responding to the same sort of meaning problems to which religious systems have traditionally tried to offer answers. What advertisers began to recognize was that it was very effective to sell products by presenting them as contributing to eventual states of profound well-being. Symbolic representations of such states are romantic realism. The end result of this was the situation we have today, in which advertising has become a dominant component of our cultural environment. A basic message echoing throughout the millions of advertisements produced each year is that via consumption one may attain paradise; the product will usher the consumer into a romantically realist version of everyday life.

The Exhibitionary Complex

As is well known, the economic changes of the late 19th century were accompanied by a shift from farm to city. The new urban environment, both necessitated and made possible by advancing technology, was capable of offering symbolic spaces to everyman that had previously been accessible only to elites. These spaces displayed the treasures and wonders of the Euro-American powers and allowed the populace access for purposes of education, advertisement, and nation building. Displays of the plundered treasures of the orient or the latest massive electric powered machines naturally provoked ruminations on the greatness of the society that had one way or another gained access to these marvels.

Tony Bennett (1994: 123) labels these symbolic spaces the "exhibitionary complex"; its constituents were art, science, and history museums, "dioramas and panoramas, national and, later, international exhibitions, arcades, and department stores." Part of Bennett's point is that these institutions channeled political power by presenting a particular view of the world as advancing scientific knowledge. But he also emphasizes that this power is not exercised through any form of constraint; rather it is based on citizens' pursuit of knowledge and amusement.

The result is that the exhibitionary complex helps to "organize a voluntarily self-regulating citizenry" (1994: 124).

In several ways, then, the exhibitionary complex represents the emergence of a new form of entertainment, occurring in public spaces and directed at the entire populace.[24] Several authors have made this argument directly, pointing to the mass exhibitions of the mid-to-late 19th century as precursors of contemporary entertainment. For example, Rosalind Williams (1982) studied the expositions of the late 19th century and concluded that the purpose of the expositions gradually shifted during this period from education to entertainment (1982: 199).[25] This shift entailed an increasing emphasis on "the sensual pleasures of consumption . . . over the abstract intellectual enjoyment of contemplating the progress of knowledge" (1982: 199).[26]

What is it to emphasize the sensual pleasures of consumption? To explain this, Williams calls on the words of a contemporary observer, Maurice Talmeyr. Talmeyr was troubled by the absurdity of exhibits that concentrated on the exotic or titillating details of some object of interest while ignoring its other features. An exhibit might depict India, for example, as a land full of strange animals and rich fabrics, with no reference to famine or Hinduism. Williams summarizes the new approach evident in the expositions, and her opinion of that approach, as follows:

> Fantasy which openly presents itself as such keeps its integrity and may claim to point to truth beyond everyday experience, what the poet Keats called the "truth of the imagination." At the Trocadero [a sector of the 1900 Paris exposition], on the contrary, reveries were passed off as reality, thereby losing their independent status to become the alluring handmaidens of commerce. . . . What is involved here is not a casual level of fantasy, a kind of mild and transient wishful thinking, but a far more thoroughgoing substitution of subjective images for external reality [1982: 65].

Throughout this book you will note that I am not very sympathetic to the claim that audiences are likely to mistake fantasies for realities. Rather, I cite this observer to show that the great expositions of the late 19th century, entities that were ambiguously educational, entertainment, and advertisements, were already well developed in their capacity to present romantic realist fictions of the sort we associate with, say, theme parks today.

Vanessa Schwartz (1998) has identified Paris as a site where growing availability of and interest in amusements transformed the very nature of culture and experience by the late 19th century. "Life in Paris," she writes, "became so powerfully identified with spectacle that reality seemed to be experienced as a show" (1998: 10). By this, Schwartz means that new social technologies processed aspects of experience and presented them back to the public as spectacles, spectacles that were also understood as aspects of the real. One of her most striking examples of this phenomenon is the Paris Morgue, "where bodies were laid out behind a large display window for consideration by anyone who stopped by" (1998: 11). Although this particular avenue for romantic realism did not lead into the future and hence seems odd to us today, again the underlying principle is the same as what we are used to: we are fascinated by what is at once close to our reality and beyond it. A number of institutions emerged in their contemporary form around this time, all based in techniques of displaying valued objects in idealized scenes suggesting the meanings of those objects. In addition to exhibitions and the department store, one could point to museums and to developing forms of visual entertainment such as the wax museum and the stereoscope (Schwartz 1998).

These same techniques were at the very heart of the organization of new retail outlets such as the department store. In this realm (much like the others I have been discussing), there was a more or less conscious strategy to integrate strategies of the theatre into realms such as education and consumption.[27] The goal was to create spectacular environments that would give onlookers a taste of hitherto un-imagined possibilities, realizable through citizenship and consumption. When a new Marshall Field's arrived in Chicago in 1902, notes William Leach (1993: 31), no expense was spared in creating an unprecedented scene at the opening: "Containing more than one million square feet of selling space," the store was adorned with fresh flowers on every counter and shelf and featured six string orchestras entertaining on different floors.

Unprecedented displays were not limited to special occasions. They were a part of the everyday in the flagship stores in large urban centers. In the department store, as Neil Harris (1990: 184) has pointed out, there was increasing appreciation of the possibilities of presenting goods in contexts that emphasized their potential role in some idealized scene in the consumer's life, so that customers purchased "their ideals of fantasy as well as the specific commodity."

These new strategies of display and marketing raised the fashion pattern to a new level of importance. Leach (1993: 91) writes of the turn of the 20th century: "Fashion merchandising was a theatrical strategy *par excellence*. . . . Its intent was to make women (and to a lesser degree men) feel special, to give them opportunities for playacting, and to lift them into a world of luxury or pseudo-luxury, beyond work, drudgery, bills, and humdrum everyday." The effect of such a strategy was to strengthen the already existing hunger for novelty, first in clothing but eventually in a range of consumer products. Originally the fashion pattern was fundamentally a social phenomenon; the goal was to demonstrate that one had the resources (financial and otherwise) to stay abreast of trends. What changed in the late 19th century was that in addition fashion became a realm of fantasy and meaning. It began to be accepted that one could make consumer choices not to show or argue for a particular social standing but rather as a form of play.

I might choose a product because it fits in with a fantasy about who I would like to be or what I would like my life to be like; I might buy to convey a particular impression or just for fun. Fashion becomes a link, a step along the way between my mundane world and the world I have seen in the fashion show or the shop window, the world I aspire to. Fashion is in this sense like celebrity. The fashionable product is the celebrity in the world of things; it dwells at once in this world and the world beyond.

Motion Pictures

As advertising developed ever more effective techniques for promoting products, technological developments were occurring that would make it possible to present advertising messages in an extraordinarily potent new form.[28] These techniques, of course, are those that make it possible to present highly realistic images of human beings and those things that interest them. The most relevant history here is that of the motion picture, which Williams argues was the successor to the expositions (1982: 212).

Once again, it is tempting to understand the appearance of cinema as based primarily in technological advances. However, as Jonathon Crary (1990) has pointed out, many of the significant innovations that eventually enabled production of "realistic" images were social and ideological. Modern optical devices, for example, could be devised only after certain ideas and understandings of vision had taken hold. Crary writes (1990: 14), "What occurs [in the early 19th century] is a new valuation of visual experience: it is given an unprecedented mobility and exchangeability, abstracted from any founding site or referent." That is, what we call realism is based in theories of vision that separate the activity from the real world (1990: 14). Here, then, is the theoretical basis for one very important form of what I have called romantic realism: the conceptualization of vision as a process that can be separated from ongoing reality.

The earliest optical devices able to produce moving images for viewers date from the mid-18th century; however it was late in the century when the technology of projection that paved the way for contemporary cinema took shape. (See Sklar 1994 for an account.) In the closing decades of the 19th century, urban areas were beginning to feature phonograph parlors where, for a fee, one could listen to popular songs, political speeches, and the like. By the middle of the 1890s, similar venues began to offer Edison's new kinetoscope, an early machine for displaying moving pictures.[29] Projection technologies also date from this period. Schwartz

(1998: 178) points out that moving images were being projected at a leading wax museum, the Musee Grevin, by the early 1890s.

Although a series of technological improvements generated continuous improvements in the quality of the moving pictures, they remained basically a curiosity through the early years of the 20th century.[30] Moving pictures were simply one form of diversion, typically mixed together with other forms. David Nasaw (1993: 152) writes of this period: "The audience for moving pictures was composed not of dedicated 'spectators' but of individuals, whose attention had, for the moment, been directed to one set of moving images and would, a moment later, be diverted to other 'attractions.'" The real growth of cinema as a public attraction occurred in the next two decades, when new editing techniques enhanced the story-telling possibilities of the medium and made it possible for the first time for "viewers to immerse themselves in the illusional world represented on the screen" (Nasaw 1993: 153).

It is this capacity to create a powerful experience of becoming caught up[31] that makes motion pictures such a decisive institution for development of the contemporary culture of entertainment. The point was simply stated more than half a century ago by my fellow anthropologist Hortense Powdermaker (1950: 14): "Movies have a surface realism which tends to disguise fantasy and makes it seem true." Or, in my terms, motion pictures are a beautifully adapted technology for production of romantic realist fictions, which combine the authority and the familiarity of reality with the compelling significance of the fantasy. By the second decade of the 19th century, then, with the increasing sophistication of cinematic technology and technique, the foundation was in place for a culture of entertainment. We have been building on that foundation ever since.

In the conclusion of this book, I return to more recent developments in the culture of entertainment and their implications for concepts of person and community in contemporary society. In the next chapter, however, I consider in detail some instances of becoming caught up in the play of entertainment. This allows me to begin to develop a more detailed understanding of just what "becoming caught up" is, and to propose some initial guesses about the social significance of this phenomenon. Eventually, this more in-depth view will form the foundation for a preliminary account of the place of getting caught up in entertainment in contemporary society.

4

Role Playing

IN "HOMO LUDENS," his classic discussion of play in human culture, Johan Huizinga (1955: 28) defines the word:

> Play is a voluntary activity or occupation executed within certain fixed limits of time and place, according to rules freely accepted but absolutely binding, having its aim in itself and accompanied by a feeling of tension, joy and the consciousness that it is "different" from "ordinary life."

The first thing to notice here is an echo of Coleridge's "willing suspension of disbelief": Huizinga specifies that play proceeds "according to rules freely accepted but absolutely binding." That is, the player willingly enters into the conventions of the play and in a sense gives herself over to the play. She proceeds within the boundaries and rules set by the play and immerses herself therein; the player gives herself up to the trajectory of the play. Koepping (1997: 20) observes that this possibility is ever-present in play: "The dialectic between awareness and unconsciousness, between playing as active form of enactment and the process of being taken over by the text (the word, the movement) also entails the risk of loosing [sic] the self in the game." Play is a world within the world (different, as Huizinga says, from everyday life), and in giving herself up to it the player may find herself transformed in ways she does not foresee.

Parts of this chapter appeared previously in an article published in the journal *Ethos* (Stromberg 2000).

In this chapter I closely examine one example of play, role-playing games, in order to study this transformation more closely. My case study demonstrates that the game influences the players' speech, behavior, and feelings in ways that they almost certainly do not plan or intend. Such findings are good evidence of the sort of change entailed in becoming caught up. The examples discussed here also show that a player may be immersed in and partially transformed by the game while maintaining an almost flawless footing in the world of the everyday. This social position, essentially being in two places at once and taking one's cues for behavior from the everyday world and the world of the fantasy, is important because it makes it clear that becoming caught up can occur right under our noses without producing disruptive aberrations in a person's behavior.

Role-playing games are a good place to begin in investigating entertainment activities because they are undertaken by groups, and therefore the evidence of becoming caught up in the game is more obvious than it is in individual activities. In a later chapter I use the example of readers of romance novels, and I assert that these readers become caught up in these novels. One can ask readers to verify this, but it is difficult to actually observe it. The role player, on the other hand, sets out to be entertained in, and together with, a social group, which means that immersion in the game may be richly documented because it is a public activity.

What Is Role Playing?

In role-playing games, each player creates a character, and the characters then embark on some sort of adventure set up by the rules of the game and a player-referee. Unlike more familiar board games such as Monopoly, the format and outcomes of role-playing games are quite flexible and reflect the imaginative contributions of players and the referee. One of the earliest, and still most well-known, of these games is called Dungeons and Dragons. This particular game enables players to enter a vaguely medieval environment and embark on fantasy quests featuring treasures, heroism, mayhem, and the like. More recently, the dominant domain for role playing has been the Internet. At the time I write this, a game called Worlds of Warcraft is all the rage, though by the time a reader encounters these words the torch will surely have been passed to something else.[1]

Some readers may question the assertion that these games, played by a small and often slightly offbeat demographic, are an appropriate representation of mainstream entertainment activities such as, say, viewing TV. The connection between these two phenomena certainly is not obvious, but it is significant. At the most fundamental level, a role-playing game is a set of special conventions through which a recognizably fictional suspense is created and eventually resolved. The same is of course true of a TV show. Sociologist Erving Goffman (1986: 555) observes that any form of dramatic performance (which includes much of what we call entertainment) is "gamelike activity." By this he means that the drama consists in a fictional encounter through which a problem is set up and resolved:

> In the game [that] the playwright provides us . . . the scripted characters do not engage one another in the narrow capacity of game partners and opponents who then deal with one another at still further remove through the figures available in a deck of cards or a box of chess pieces. The world onstage is more perverse than that. For in the gamelike activity the dramatist presents, the cards and pieces are themselves personlike figures.

Role-playing games, in fact, can be considered a hybrid, a combination of game and drama in that they too are carried out through the use of "personlike figures" (the player's character). Thus these games can with equal plausibility be considered an adaptation of either pretend play or improvisational acting (that is, role-playing games could be considered either as play or as theatre). In any of these activities, a person pretends to be a particular sort of character drawing upon memories and imagination.

This is also fundamentally similar to what happens when we read a fictional narrative. Kendall Walton (1990), in his book *Mimesis as Make-Believe,* hypothesizes that a reader's involvement in a fiction is parallel to what we experience in play.[2] He draws a parallel between the stipulations that establish a particular narrative trajectory in a fiction and the imaginings that constitute an episode of pretend play. He uses the term *fictional* to refer to any such proposition (1990: 35). If John is pretending to be a cowboy, then "John goes on a cattle drive" is fictional. In suggesting this parallel, Walton is defending the assertion that games of make-believe are an excellent model for our interaction with art and fantasies in general; just as a child may make believe she is a doctor, an adult may make believe that the images of a painting or a story are real. So it is fictional that there is a sailor named Ishmael who knows much about Ahab's obsession with a white whale, and it is fictional that Lucy and Ricky are a wacky but happy married couple. A painting or a story, like a game of make-believe, establishes fictional worlds in which participants may become immersed.

All of these fictional worlds contain certain props. Props are elements of the world that impart directionality to our imaginings and thereby enrich them. A particular painting establishes one world and not another; it prompts imagining in a certain way, just as a stipulation "I'm a doctor" leads to one sort of game and "I'm a cowboy" to another. The painting and the stipulations here are props. A game might be established in the woods, to take an example Walton returns to repeatedly, by the stipulation that tree stumps are bears. The stipulation is a prop, as are the stumps. Actual stumps are props that establish the distribution of bears in a fictional world, the world of the game.

Notice, then, that our understanding of fictional worlds requires continuous blending of the stipulations of a fiction into our commonsense knowledge of the day-to-day world. Once pretend play of any sort—including interpretation of fiction—gets under way, the basic principles of causality and the features of the situation function for all practical purposes just as they do in mundane experience. Harris (2000: 11) writes, in discussing cooperative pretend play, "Once set in motion, a make-believe stipulation has various implications and restrictions for both partners."

Thus all forms of engagement with fictions depend on an imaginative shift to another position, and then consistent application of interpretations generated by the question, "What would it be like to be there?" Whether it is a child engaged in pretend play, a role player, or even a reader following a fictional narrative, the player must have the ability to take up a vantage point within the simulated world and reason from here. I call this taking up of the vantage point just described—using a term suggested by Harris—the *deictic shift*. Harris, a leading expert on children's play, regards this capacity to adopt a perspective different from that of the everyday self as the foundation of pretend play. (In fact, I go well beyond this in the next chapter, following those who claim that this ability to shift to an alternative perspective is basic to all human cognition). Harris (2000: 10) writes: "A pretend episode includes causal chains with an unfolding structure much like a narrative." No matter what sort of fictional world is in question, the capacity to participate depends on the ability to improvise or follow along those causal chains, and not constantly check back in with the day-to-day world.

This cognitive capacity is present, says Harris, by the age of two. Its essence is the ability to adopt a perspective from within the fiction. Figuratively speaking, one must be able to appropriate the "there" of the story and make it one's "here." This is a mysterious business, though it is not a mystery most of us think about. Even to understand a story on a basic level, we must follow it. We must be able to grasp where it is going, what is important and what isn't, and so on. W. B. Gallie (1968: 22) directs our attention to how following a story is a form of *submission*:

> Following a story is, at one level, a matter of understanding words, sentences, paragraphs, set out in order. But at a much more important level it means to understand the successive actions and thoughts and feelings of certain described characters with peculiar directions, and to be pulled forward by this development almost against our will: we commonly appreciate, without needing to articulate to ourselves, many of the reasons and motives and interest upon which the story's development up towards its climax depends.

Note Gallie's point that the story pulls us forward "almost against our will." The phrase is a powerful hint of the nature of agency in play. To follow a story is to give yourself up, momentarily and voluntarily, to the trajectory of the play. Doing so requires some degree of suppression of normal mental function, or what we usually take to be normal function, in which an autonomous intentional subject presumably sets the trajectory of one's behavior. It is significant that Gallie lumps his discussion of following a story together with the problem of following a game. To play a game, or to appreciate it as a spectator, also necessarily entails submitting to the trajectory of the game. Only by doing so can one make the right moves or appreciate others doing so.

Thus playing and understanding a game entails some level of what might be called taking the perspective of the game. A game, like a story, is only minimally conveyed in its formal conventions. Playing a game or following a story demands that one enter into this world and feel one's way around in it, according to one's largely inarticulate knowledge, based in experience, of how the social and physical worlds work. This is not only a cognitive process. There is an emotional component to the basic skill of pretending or following a narrative. It is the capacity to identify with a protagonist or other fictional character and thereby invest the developments the character undergoes with emotional significance.[3]

To summarize: role playing games, while they may be a somewhat limited and quirky phenomenon, are excellent examples of something that is not limited and quirky at all, that being our capacity to adopt a position within a fictional world. That capacity is essential to the ability to play games and to engage fictional narratives, and it helps us to better grasp the kinship between these phenomena.[4] Ultimately I argue that adopting a position in a fictional world is an extension of our capacity to imitate. This suggests that these skills of playing in fictional worlds are linked to basic neurological functions; in the next chapter I discuss the role of these functions in mediating social interaction. All of this eventually leads to a considerably more detailed understanding of what it is to become caught up in play and serves as the basis for appreciating the social and cultural importance of this phenomenon.

The Games

Rather than try to describe role-playing games in general, I will focus on a small number of such games. My examples are taken mostly from several episodes of two games: one an advanced Dungeons and Dragons game that took place in the spring of 2000, and the other a Mekton game of late 1996 (Mekton is a futuristic science fantasy game in which players imagine themselves to be piloting gigantic robots; Fields and Sappenfield 1997). With the help of a professional camera operator,[5] I filmed several hours of both games.

Some basic awareness of what one might call the plot of these two games is helpful in interpreting my examples. The player referee (or "DM"[6]) is, in the games I have observed, the person responsible for setting up the basic framework within which the players pursue their adventure. Generally, the player referee spends some time at the beginning of each session explaining or reminding players of this framework; this is the case in both of the games I am focusing on here. In the Mekton game, the scenario is that the players have four hours before they are placed in "sleep chambers" for a long interplanetary journey. It is uncertain when, or even if, they will emerge from this state of suspended animation. Thus the play consists primarily in the various characters getting their affairs in order before they begin their journey.

In the Dungeons and Dragons game, I prompted the DM to summarize the game situation for the purposes of the film I was making. Here is what he said:

> One of the party members had a magical sword which was evil and for about a year kept on trying to corrupt him, and eventually it kind of wore through, it did corrupt him and he traveled to the abyss, which is kind of a hell. And once there made a deal with a uh demoness, and became like her second hand man and he went to a interplanetary like city that's kind of a hub of a multiverse. And was planning on taking it over until they [points to other players] came looking for him and sort of foiled it and he escaped from them, back onto the abyss, and they're now, they followed him through the portal and they're trying to find him on the abyss and . . . ["kill him," says one of the other players].

Although the two games differ noticeably in some of their conventions (discussed below), the players in both games are for the most part jocular and casual. Moments of intense focus on the game occur, but they are the exception rather than the rule. Some people who have seen parts of the films have commented that the players do not seem caught up in the game at all. Rather, for the most part the game seems to be a rather flimsy excuse for a bunch of men to sit around a table and socialize, which they do through small talk, telling stories about themselves and others, and cracking jokes. As they talk, the men frequently "poach" from other realms of popular culture (see Jenkins 1992). That is, they regularly refer to arcane details in the areas of their shared interests: Star Trek, science fiction, Japanese animation. At times, it can be difficult to find the game being played among all the cross-talk, digressions, and munching.

This is what engagement with entertainment looks like. I suppose that in some cases interacting with entertainment may manifest itself as a glassy-eyed, trance-like immersion in an activity such as video game playing. But for the most part, people engage entertainment in settings such as, say, a living room where members of a family are watching television. People wander off to get a snack, carry on a conversation, split their attention between the television and a book, and so on. In this sense—again—the role-playing games I have observed are fairly representative of broader patterns of how people engage entertainment. Thus the evidence given here, which shows that moments of becoming thoroughly caught up in the game are interspersed with a great deal of ancillary activity, demonstrates that becoming caught up often occurs momentarily. Becoming caught up in a fiction can manifest itself as a moment of involvement in the midst of disengagement[7] and therefore may not be noticed by observers, or even by the player himself.

Confusion of Game and Reality?

Role-playing games allow us to look in detail at what happens when a person becomes caught up in a fiction, as happens when Skip kicks. But what are we looking for? In the first place, some transparent evidence of just what happens when someone becomes caught up would be helpful. What sort of observable change accompanies becoming caught up? I also hope to go beyond this question and to offer at least the beginning of an answer to another one.

This second question is, What is the status of the fiction for the player who is caught up? As I noted in the first chapter, those who participate in role-playing games agree with a number of cultural critics and academics that role players (and users of entertainment more generally) actually confuse reality and the fictions they engage for purposes of entertainment. They cannot tell the difference between these two levels. This confusion was a theme that was central to the influential Frankfurt School theorists, who wrote in the first half of the 20th century.[8] They traced this situation to a technology that had made possible what they called mechanical reproduction of images, and they considered cinema to be the context in which entertainment finally merged with reality:

> The more densely and completely its techniques duplicate empirical objects, the more easily it creates the illusion that the world outside is a seamless extension of the one which has been revealed in the cinema. . . . According to this tendency, life is to be made indistinguishable from the sound film [Horkheimer and Adorno 2002: 99].

The claim that users of entertainment cannot distinguish fantasy from reality is overstated.[9] Although I have no doubt this may occur among certain individuals from time to time, I am extremely skeptical that this is an adequate description of what happens when most entertainment users play. The fact that most role players, and most people who engage other sorts of entertainment, can flawlessly negotiate the real world while they are playing suggests that the "confusion" position is both wrong and oversimplified. Even in cases where temporary confusion occurs

(I discuss one later), they are easily corrected, and the primacy of the everyday world is never threatened.

A far more accurate formulation of the situation is Colin Campbell's reformulation of the notion of doublethink: not only role players but most of us in contemporary society are prone to fall into fantasies "known to be false, but felt to be true" (1987: 78). This captures the dissociative component of the player's situation, the fact that the player can choose to experience the thrills of the fantasy at a physical level while retaining clear awareness of the fictional status of the game. However, as Campbell himself recognizes when he writes about consumption behavior, what we know is ultimately based in what we feel, and thus what we know cannot be completely separated from what we feel. Another way of summarizing this is to say that participation in entertainment activities is not just a matter of temporary stimulation. We may walk away from entertainment experiences changed in some way.

Ultimately, the matter of whether entertainment users sometimes confuse fantasy and reality is not really the important question. The important question has to do with the normal and expected consequences, on the social, economic, and cultural levels, of our immersion in the fictions of entertainment. Throughout this book, I try to show that the temporary self-transformations occurring when a player becomes caught up in a game may have some important long-term repercussions. These stem from the fact that in such experiences of self-transformation we feel the potency of certain ideas and symbols and physical objects in ways that are not typical of our lives in the day-to-day world. We may as a result form convictions about the capacity of these ideas and symbols and physical objects to change us noticeably. This knowledge is carried into the day-to-day world.

So let us turn now to a detailed examination of the process of becoming caught up in role-playing games, looking at the sorts of changes that occur as players become caught up. In general, I want to emphasize how the player dwells in the fictional position he adopts in the game, experiencing the world from that pretended perspective. First, a discussion of the mechanics of adopting this perspective.

Deictics

Deictics are aspects of language that are interpreted in terms of the situation in which speech occurs. If I say "this," or "now," you will know what I mean only if you have knowledge of the physical surroundings in which I utter the word. Deictics are important in the present context because they are evidence of where (in space and time) and who the speaker claims he is. That is, if the deictic landmarks in a player's speech point not to his actual situation but to the fictional situation of the game, he is carefully using language to sustain the collective illusion that the players are actually in the situation they imagine. Because deictics occur frequently in speech, it is not possible for the player to plan ahead each time one of these terms appears in his speech. Rather, he must imaginatively put himself in the place of the character and speak from this place.[10] This is based on what I have termed (following Harris) the deictic shift.

Deictics can separated into three types: personal, spatial, and temporal (Crystal 1987: 106). Personal deictics are pronouns, such as *I* and *you,* that point to the participants in a speech situation (these are discussed later). Spatial deictics depend on the place where speech takes place, and temporal deictics depend on the time.

Spatial deictics that refer to the world of the fantasy are ubiquitous in the games. A player says, for example, "I'm not actually here," meaning his character is not present in the scene where the current action is taking place. Much of the referee's discourse necessarily relies on forms that refer to the spatial framework of the fantasy ("They're coming towards you" and so on). Anytime a player announces an action, he is likely to make some reference to activity in the place of the fantasy ("I can't two-hand sword these people"). Thus participants in the role-playing game must thoroughly master a large and subtle set of conventions that both depend on and constantly recreate the world of the fiction.

Temporal deictics follow much the same pattern, often being used in players' speech to refer to the fictional situation. However, I have observed more confusion in temporal deictics, perhaps because time, being invisible, is less clearly separated into imaginary and here-and-now realms. A good example of such confusion occurs in the Mekton game. The game itself takes up time—a great deal of time as it turns out (the game I videotaped went on into the early morning hours). But the characters are also concerned with time, for you will remember that they have only four hours before they enter suspended animation. Now and then, an observer can see signs of players mixing up these two time frames.

As Ben works in the mech (mechanical and electrical) bay, trying to make modifications to the ship's engines, he knows he has a deadline to meet. Ben and the referee have this exchange:

Ben: So, quick check on the time, just [to] see how I'm going

Referee: You've got about five minutes left

Ben: Five minutes left?

Referee: And remembering the disposition of your chief petty officer you probably
    don't want to be late

This seems like an unremarkable exchange, but if one looks closely at the videotape one notices that Ben glances at his watch as he says the words "quick check on the time." But it is clearly game time he wants to know about here. So why does he look at his wristwatch?

Of course, I can't answer that question with complete certainty. But it seems as if Ben momentarily forgets that he can't find out how much game time he has by looking at his watch. That is, for an instant Ben loses track of the fact that game time and real time are separate systems. This indicates a rather deep level of involvement in the fantasy in which he is involved, that of modifying the engines in the mech bay of a space ship.[11]

A few minutes later, Skip does precisely the same thing. In preparing to fight the opponent he will eventually kick, he asks the referee, "How much time have we got left?" and as he does so, he rotates his left arm and glances down at it. Again, it is not the case that Skip's question refers to real time; the context makes clear that his concern is whether he can fight and then finish up the activity he has already begun in the game.[12]

The general point here is the same as one that I made in the previous section. Skip and Ben are not confused about what time frame they are in. They are attending to the time frame of real life, in which they are participating in a role-playing game. But—as is shown in a number of the examples I discuss here—these instances of checking the time illustrate the fact, that on some level of Skip's and Ben's minds, they are deeply absorbed in the fantasy of the game while remaining effectively oriented to their real-life environment.

The third type of deixis comprises personal pronouns, and again pronouns that refer to the fantasy pervade the games. This emerges immediately in the Mekton game, even before it really begins; as they are getting ready to start the game, players produce exaggerated imitations of characters in different situations ("I'm taking direct hits! Boom!" or "You can't shoot me, I'm the star!").

Notice how they are using the first person pronoun. As these utterances make clear, when a player says *I* during these games, he is usually referring not to himself but to his character. In fact, this convention is so taken for granted by players that it can be difficult to reestablish *I* as referring to the speaker. Even presumably obvious real-world statements such as "I'm getting bored with this" and "I'm going to go get something to eat" may be interpreted by other players as "character comments." In some cases, exaggerated gestural work may be done to establish the referent of the first person pronoun. Here is a transcript of a brief episode from the Mekton game, illustrating both the conventional practice of using pronouns to refer to characters and the effort that must be expended to suspend the convention. The situation here is that player 2's character is in a fight; the excerpt turns on the fact that the character is a woman.

Player 1: Hold it, who would I be rooting for?
Player 2: [laugh]

[Referee?]: The female (I'd say) *[in falsetto]* kick his ass kick his ass.

Player 2: Oh well but yeah he's part zentran.

(5) *Player 1:* Yeah

Player 2: So he might be [laugh] rooting for his own

Referee: But you were naturally, you were naturally born human, you were raised as a human

(10) *Player 1:* That's true

Player 3: Let's put it this way—who do you like better, your squad leader

Player 2: Or this bozo

Player 3: Or some strange bozo

(15) *Player 2:* [laugh]

Player 3: Who are you betting on

Player 1: Yeah [in falsetto] kick his ass

Referee: The babe or the guy

Player 1: [falsetto, voice breaks] kick his ass

(20) *Player 4:* By no stretch of the imagination would Skip's character be a babe. I'm sorry[13]

Player 2: What do you mean?

Referee: Why would they clone someone ugly?

Player 2: That's sorry

(25) *Player 3(?):* That's right

Player 2: All militran [?] are babes I gotta attract just me as it's hard to envision me being who I am that way

Throughout this episode, *I* (as well as other pronouns, such as *you*) is used to refer to characters in the game. Player 1 mentions he might have split loyalties as he observes the fight between player 2, his squad leader, and a "zentran," a member of a group that is part of player 1's heritage. The players discuss this situation, and in doing so the referee calls player 2 a "babe," a characterization to which player 4 objects. This leads directly to the point I want to illustrate: player 2 then states that in spite of his (the speaker's) rather unfeminine appearance, his character is an attractive female. To do this, the speaker must recapture his first person pronouns. So at lines 26–27, player 2 attempts to reestablish the referent of the first person pronoun as the speaker. He begins this attempt with an emphatic *me* and then explicitly mentions the imaginative effort in which the players are participating. In doing the latter, player 2 steps outside the frame of the game; he says, in effect, "I know that we have a situation here in which it is difficult to sustain the imaginative effort in which we are all engaged."

He then makes a joking reference to his (the speaker's) characteristics being difficult to reconcile with the image of an attractive female. Thus player 2 steps out of the game here in part by using an emphatic *me* and in part through the content of his speech; in referring to imaginative effort, he takes a position on the "other side" of the frame the players have established. However, perhaps the most important part of the work that player 2 does here is not conveyed in the transcript: lines 26 and 27 are accompanied by an elaborate self-touching gesture in which the player uses both hands to emphatically point to the center of his body. In combination with the verbal performance, this gesture serves to reestablish the referent of the first person pronoun as the physical being producing the speech. In summary, we can say, at least for this group, the convention is that *I* refers to character, and contravening such a convention takes a good deal of work

Gesture and Physical Movement

Much of the material presented in the previous section is evidence not only of a shift to an imaginary perspective but also of the motor implications thereof. As a player begins to talk or experience or interpret from the alternative perspective, he may begin to produce movements appropriate to the fictional position. Looking at one's watch and shouting encouragement to an imaginary character in an imaginary fight are both examples of acting from the imaginary perspective. As I discuss later, research from several disciplines seems to be converging on a fuller understanding of how and why we human beings find it quite natural to imagine experience from a perspective other than that of the day-to-day self. However, in this section I simply want to present further examples of the physical manifestations that may occur as one occupies a fictional position.

People move when they speak. They gesture constantly, they pantomime actions they are describing, and so on. Thus it is no surprise that players in these games move. It is initially a bit surprising, however, how much of players' movement is oriented not to their physical situation but to the situation of the fiction.[14]

I began the book with one such example, Skip's kick in the Mekton game. There are numerous such instances in these two games; in general, for example, players tend to mimic characters' movements and utterances when they are engaging in imaginary fights. However, almost any kind of activity in the game tends to be accompanied by physical correlates. In the Dungeons and Dragons game, for example, one player says "We're standing in some of the goo" and he and his interlocutor both glance down at their feet. Another character gets a mysterious substance on her arm, and the player holds up his forearm and sticks out his tongue, licking off the substance.

It is worth noting that most of this sort of behavior occurs among the more involved and more expert players. This is particularly obvious in the Mekton game, where the skill level of the players varies considerably. The most expert and (along with the player-referee) most respected players in this game are Skip and Ben. Their expertise lies primarily in the fact that they play their characters thoughtfully and consistently. Novice players lack the skills necessary to put themselves in their characters' place; too many of their actions and responses are clearly linked not to the fiction but to their own concerns. Although Skip and Ben retain their own concerns, of course, they are able to integrate them into the game in a way that sustains and extends the fiction.

So, when it comes Ben's turn to reveal how he will spend his time before being placed in suspended animation, he announces he will use part of the time available to him to write letters to his family. He begins to compose the letter and then wonders aloud how he can phrase a certain point so that it will "get past the censors." The player-referee has not stipulated that there are censors; rather, Ben reasons that a person in such a position would have this concern. Thus he extends and deepens the fiction for all the players, and it is not hard to see why something like this makes playing with Ben enjoyable for all the participants.

Ben then moves to the mech bay to check out the mechanical and electric aspects of the ship in which he will be traveling. He begins to make some modifications in the ship's engines, a task that requires reprogramming the ship's computers. Using his right hand, Ben shakes the dice as he prepares to roll to determine whether he will be successful in this endeavor. With his left hand, meanwhile, he types on an imaginary computer keyboard. So, while Ben's right hand does something that is a necessary and clearly understandable part of the game he is playing, his left hand does something that is neither necessary nor easy to understand. Ben knows he is not sitting at a computer keyboard; that is, if you asked him you would find he was not confused about this. He is not portraying "a person typing on a keyboard," because he has no audience. Neither Ben nor anybody else shows any sign of noticing the movements of his left hand. (I was there too, and I certainly didn't notice this until I saw it on film.)

So what is up? There is only one possible interpretation here: this activity is simply another example of the sort of thing that Skip's kick represents: an unconsciously generated physical movement that testifies to Ben's deep immersion in the world of the game. The fact that he does this while playing the game with his other hand is a good indicator of what sort of thing being caught up is. It is dissociated activity that may occur while the person is attending to something else, while the person conceives himself as doing something else.

On the other hand (if I may), the fact that a player is becoming deeply caught up may be noticed by players, and in the one instance I have of this on videotape it seems to be clearly embarrassing to the group. At one point in the Dungeons and Dragons game, a player elects to flee a dangerous situation by flying down an unknown passage in a subterranean environment. He informs the DM that he is doing this:

> *Player 1:* I think it's time to fly down the other tunnel
>
> *Player 2:* [laughter] you will be required to maneuver straight through
>   [indistinguishable]
>
> [general laughter]
>
> *Referee:* Is that what you're doing this round?
>
> *Player 1:* Yeah
>
> (5)   *Referee:* You're gonna forgo your casting?
>
> *Player 1:* Hell yeah
>
> [general laughter]
>
> *Referee:* Go
>
> *Player 3:* I love Llewelyn [Player 1's character's name]
>
> *Referee:* Are you ready?
>
> (10)   *Player 4:* He's flying
>
> *Player 3:* He's flying zhuuu [flying sound]—
>
> *Referee:* Yeah I've got you flying
>
> *Player 4:* He's flying as—
>
> *Referee:* Go—
>
> (15)   *Player 4:* Fast as he can through the air
>
> *Player 1:* Go what? [sarcastic]
>
> *Referee:* I mean you make it
>
> *Player 2:* [laughter]
>
> *Referee:* Is what I'm saying
>
> (20)   *Player 2:* Go! [laughter]
>
> *Player 3:* Yeah
>
> *Player 2:* Go. Act it out!
>
> [general laughter, accompanied by elaborate gestures of flying by several
>   players]

Here it is the referee who is revealed to be so deeply immersed in extended imitation that it is embarrassing to his comrades. This episode centers around line 14, where the referee says "Go" to player 1, meaning "Go fly down the tunnel we have been talking about." This is immediately interpreted by player 1 as entailing an overly deep identification with the game, and then this theme is picked up by the other players, who use it to tease the referee. A careful look at the transcription will substantiate this interpretation.

At line 1, player 1 announces that the character he animates chooses to fly down the tunnel. At line 3, the referee clarifies that this will be the character's action for the present round, and at line 7 he says "Go," that is, "Fly down the tunnel now." This statement is itself testimony to some degree of being caught up in the game, for—practically speaking—this "Go" is not really necessary. It has been firmly established and confirmed that player 1 has chosen to have his character fly down the tunnel, an action that is within the rules of the game, and thus "Go" is a little odd here. What precisely is player 1 supposed to do?

The referee, however, seems to expect something. Not finding it, he retreats at line 9 to a request for clarification for why what is expected has not transpired, asking "Are you ready?" This is too much for the group, and players 3 and 4 adamantly assert at lines 10 and 11 that it has been established that player 1 is flying. Player 3, in fact, emphasizes the flying by making a flying sound and moving his hands in a flying gesture. The referee presumably gets the message; at line 12 he says, "I've got you flying."

But still, on some level, the referee is not satisfied. While player 4 confirms once again that player one is "flying through the air," the referee again tells player 1 to "Go" at line 14. This is simply too much for player 1, who brings an end to all of this with an exasperated "Go where?" There is no more covering for the referee now. It has been made explicit that he has been overly involved in his imagination; everyone in the room (except for my camera operator) knows he meant "Go down the tunnel," and therefore he momentarily forgot that the tunnel is completely imaginary.

The referee, who is now visibly embarrassed, rather lamely tries to save face at lines 17–19 by asserting he was all along simply clarifying that the character is *able* to fly down the tunnel ("You make it"). This is implausible for several reasons, most obviously because the phrase "You make it" is used in the game when a player must roll dice to determine the success of an action, and there was no dice roll involved in this move. At this point, player 2 distracts attention from the referee's error of imagination by converting it to a demand that player 1 act out "flying." This results in general hilarity as most of the players begin to do exaggerated flying imitations, mostly based on the familiar Superman model, arms extended over the head with hands touching. This moment of playfulness, however, probably is constructed to obscure the socially embarrassing fact that one member of the group has, for an instant, noticeably crossed over a boundary.

Emotion

In the broader literature, there has been a good deal of discussion of the nature of the reader / spectator's emotional reaction to fictions, most of it in the context of the problem of how readers respond to narrative art in general. The question of how one engages a work of art entails such matters as readers' awareness of genres, how they apply their knowledge of the day-to-day world to fictions, and a number of other issues that—thankfully—I am able to sidestep here.[15] However, I cannot sidestep the directly relevant aspects of this discussion, those that have to do with players' emotional reactions to fictions.

Here I want to look at some examples of players experiencing strong emotions as they play the game. It will probably not be very surprising to readers to hear that role players seem to experience emotions as they play the game; we are all familiar with feelings of tenderness, of passion, of anger as we watch movies or television, read books, and so on. But in the role-playing game, many of the emotions the players experience are explicitly those of the fictional characters (as opposed to feelings generated by empathy with fictional characters). The player experiences the emotions of the character, but the medium for incubation of these feelings is the player's body. In the common sense of most Western societies, emotions are generated within physical individuals. How can they be generated within fictional individuals? To put it another way, how can emotions be created by proxy by a real person on behalf of a fictional character?

The first such example occurs in the Mekton game, wherein, you will remember, Ben is checking out the ship before it departs. As he announces this intention, another player says, "Oh, let you play, huh?" Ben looks the other player directly in the eye and answers: "Hey, I may not be the best pilot in the world but I attribute most of my success to the fact that I tune my vehicle to my specs." He emphasizes that last *I,* and as he speaks the word he intertwines his hands, turns his forearms outwards, and cracks his knuckles in an unmistakable gesture of pride.

Ben is not consciously setting out to portray the pride of his character here. The conventions of this group simply do not entail the possibility of portraying the character for the audience. Because Ben is not portraying pride, it follows that he is feeling pride. But he is obviously not feeling pride in himself. Nor is it really accurate to say Ben is proud of his character, the way Ben might be proud of his son when he hits a home run. This expression of pride comes across precisely as would a statement Ben might make on the basis of his *own* accomplishments. My conclusion? Ben is proud of his character as himself.[16] The nature of Ben's engagement with the fiction here is that not only is he genuinely feeling an emotion provoked not by the real world but by the fiction, but he is incorporating that emotion as a part of his ongoing subjectivity. More generally, this is the sort of emotional manifestation associated with getting caught up; what is unique here is emotion that is provoked by and experienced through strong identification with a fictional situation.

My second example is an aspect of Skip's kick, and unfortunately the relevant evidence cannot be reproduced here. The reader will simply have to take my word for the fact that at the instant Skip kicks his opponent in the fight, his face contorts into a grimace of sheer violent aggression. In this instance, and in numerous others that are similar, players clearly experience potent feelings appropriate to the characters they are pretending to be. Skip finds pleasure in experiencing some of the feelings one might have in a battle while avoiding the inconvenience and danger that actual participation in battle would entail. So he amuses himself by generating the stimulating feelings through play.

However, this case has a further wrinkle. Although I have probably observed this expression well over a hundred times on tape, I still respond to it viscerally: it provokes feelings of aggression in me as well. I have therefore been drawn into my own study and have become evidence of how observation can be a form of play. Of course, I did not set out to amuse myself by observing this role-playing game; my goal was rather to conduct research. Therefore when I feel myself being drawn into the orbit of Skip's character's feelings, I am not drawn further into the pleasures of the game; rather, I become aware of an isolated case of emotional contagion. Nevertheless, my reaction needs some further attention.

When I see the tape, I know perfectly well what is coming, yet I still react as described. I can add another bit of information about this, namely that my feelings are typically preceded by an action: I construct a facial expression similar to Skip's. One could interpret this in terms of the oddities of my personality, but I think there is something more basic going on here. It is by now well documented that human beings often imitate facial gestures, and that doing so often provokes emotional contagion. The observer actually feels the emotion appropriate to the facial expression (Hatfield, Cacioppo, and Rapson 1994).

Now we have a truly remarkable situation. Here it is not only that Skip is feeling the emotions of an imaginary character; one who observes Skip feels them as well. We have a chain of actual emotional reactions in the day-to-day world, at the bottom of which are the feelings of a fictional being. The boundaries between the various selves along this chain are more permeable than we have been led to expect by our common sense.

Many who have written on this issue would assert here that I have grievously misconceived the matter. I have assumed that the emotions the role players have as fictional characters are indistinguishable from emotions in the day-to-day world. One of the most articulate and influential of the critics who would dispute my interpretation is Kendall Walton, and because this topic is significant for my own argument it is worth attending carefully to Walton's position.

Walton (1990) offers a clear and insightful approach to the problem of specifying the relationship between the feelings we have in engaging a fiction and those we have in the day-to-day world. As part of his more general theory of what it is to appreciate a work of art, Walton tackles the matter of our psychological involvement with fictions of various sorts. At one point in his discussion, Walton (1990: 196) resorts to the sort of colorful little story for which philosophers seem to have such affection[17]:

> Charles is watching a horror movie about a terrible green slime. He cringes in his seat as the slime oozes slowly but relentlessly over the earth, destroying everything in its path. Soon a greasy head emerges from the undulating mass, and two beady eyes fix on the camera. The slime, picking up speed, oozes on a new course straight toward the viewers. Charles emits a shriek and clutches desperately at this chair. Afterwards, still shaken, he confesses that he was "terrified" of the slime.

Charles is—in my terms—caught up in the movie about the slime.[18] But Walton asks, "Is he really terrified of the slime?" and answers no. Charles cannot be afraid of the slime because he knows it is not real, so he knows he is in no danger from the slime.

How can we make sense of Charles's situation? He testifies that he is terrified, but he does not act as if he is. Is it possible to say, Walton begins, that Charles "half believes" the danger is real? No, it is not; such a formulation undervalues both his rationality and his emotion. If Charles in any degree thought he was in danger from the slime, he would surely take *some* real-world steps to avoid it. Likewise, if he only half believes the slime is real, why his all-out reaction of terror?

Walton is similarly unimpressed by the suggestion that Charles is *momentarily* convinced of the slime's reality and therefore afraid of it. His terror reaction isn't momentary at all; it may extend through the whole movie. Rejecting a number of alternative answers that have been proposed on this question, Walton steadfastly defends his contention that Charles may be afraid, but he cannot be said to be afraid of the slime. Instead, argues Walton (1990: 242), we should conceptualize the situation in this way: "It is not true but fictional that he fears the slime."

Remember that Walton uses "fictional" to designate propositions that are true in a game of make-believe. Thus it is part of a game of make believe that Charles is afraid of the slime. In the terms I am using here, it is a part of the extended imitation that Charles is engaged in. But Walton is not asking us to believe here that Charles is simply pretending to be afraid of the slime. As Walton says of Charles: "He is an actor, of a sort, in his game, as well as an object; he is a reflexive prop generating fictional truths about himself" (1990: 242). Once Charles shifts his perspective to that of a person confronting the slime, it follows—and this is typical of pretend play—that he would be afraid of the slime.

In Walton's formulation, the point about Charles is that he is both actor and prop in his game of make-believe, the game of appreciating the movie about the green slime. As a prop, he has certain reactions to the movie, and as actor these reactions impart directionality to his imagining: "Fictional truths about Charles are generated partly by what he thinks and feels, by his actual mental state" (1990: 242–243). That is, Charles has a feeling of fear, and to enrich his experience of the movie he "goes along" with the feelings his body generates. Charles savors his emotion as part of his game of make-believe, now a rich and engaging experience.

But Charles's feelings of fear are fictional because he reflects on their cause and recognizes that he is in no danger. In other words, Charles's feelings generate fictional truths rather than truths because of the way he attends to them. Thus, according to Walton Charles's fear, though real enough, is not fear of the slime. Walton refers to Charles's fear in watching the movie as "quasi fear" (1990: 246).

Walton has presented a careful, challenging, and helpful account of psychological participation, but I must take exception to his final conclusion. His argument has led him to discover an emotional experience heretofore unnoticed in human affairs, the "quasi-emotion." Without extensive exploration of just what these quasi-emotions are and how they influence behavior, one wonders how far they take us in understanding Charles's situation.[19] Furthermore, by insisting on a boundary between quasi-fear and the more familiar emotion of straight-up fear, Walton is led to underestimate the possibility of real-world effects of participation in the game. In Walton's understanding of the matter, Charles may very well experience an emotion, but Charles will not even be tempted to get out of his chair and avoid the slime, and that's the end of it. That may not be the end of it, though; Charles may have a nightmare after watching the film, for example. Some completely rational film viewers do indeed leave horror movies because they are frightened.

In my view, Walton followed Charles's situation very carefully and then took a wrong turn at the end. It is very useful to observe that Charles is two things in his game: prop and actor. Charles immerses himself in the fiction and plays with his own emotions. But the fact that he is playing in this way does not mean his emotions are not real. All of our emotional reactions are conditioned by a cognitive context, and experiencing emotions in play is no exception to this rule. Thus let's toss out the mysterious entity "quasi-emotion" and embrace the fact that Charles is indeed scared of the slime, while he is also aware that his fear is part of a game.

But if Charles is really scared of the slime, then why does he make no attempt to escape it? This is the sort of question that bothers philosophers (but not normal people). It is a well-known quality of human experience, based ultimately in the peculiarities of our nervous system, that our reactions to phenomena are complex and not always fully coherent. I may experience a strong emotional reaction to the experience of running over a squirrel with my car, in spite of my conscious conviction that such an event is neither a proper occasion for guilt nor an occasion for sorrow (if I want to reflect on the cruelty of life, there are more compelling horrors to get me going). Why do I react in the way I do? I don't know; perhaps I am suppressing a twinge of blood lust, or perhaps the squirrel's fate reminds me too graphically of my own eventual demise. The point here is simply that incoherent reactions to our experiences are a familiar part of life, and examples could be multiplied virtually without end.

In fact, there is no fully satisfying answer to the question of psychological involvement in the realm of philosophy; one must instead turn to the domain of such subjects as psychology and biology. We human beings are the product of evolutionary processes that have endowed us with multiple (and sometimes contradictory) systems for grasping the environment. Our behavior bristles with paradoxical and contradictory elements that are quite unlikely to be sorted out through logical gyrations.

In other words, a spectator's being frightened by a movie at the same time he is aware that he is in no danger is a logical problem. However, it is not a problem in practice, because human beings are entirely used to assessing their strong emotional reactions and pursuing paths of action on the basis of that assessment. This is what happens in much of the play we call entertainment, a potent form of amusement in which people provoke strong emotional reactions to enjoy its physical stimulation.

One can see this almost continuously in a role-playing game in which expert players are deeply engaged. There is so much slippage between feelings generated by characters and feelings of players that it becomes obvious it is not possible to separate feelings generated in the day-to-day world and those arising from the world of the fiction. Because much of a role-playing game is spontaneous, there is plenty of opportunity for blurring the emotions of characters and players. In one game I recorded on audiotape (but not videotape), a character shouted to another that their dire situation was the latter's fault: "You're the one who told him you were a murderer." Here the recriminations are being aimed not only at the character who said this but also at the player who made the spontaneous decision to reveal this information. Once an imaginary situation is established, it becomes a frame (Goffman 1986) within which genuine interactions take place.[20] One implication of this is, once again, that the game is only partially under the control of the players. Feelings quickly develop their own momentum.

The manipulation of feelings (and there is absolutely no need to distinguish between real and fictional feelings) is a prominent aspect of most entertainment. We players have learned to make our own emotions into a plaything such as a ball. We can largely, though not completely, control a ball when we throw it or shoot a free throw. It is the interaction between players and not-completely-predictable balls that makes for the fun and challenge of games with balls. The same is true of our own emotions. We can put ourselves in a situation in which we know we will have certain kinds of emotions, and as the situation proceeds we can influence our emotions, but they also lurch about somewhat unpredictably.

One familiar example of this is that we begin to care about the outcome of the game more than we anticipated. In the case of a romantic novel, for example (which, the reader will remember, I also classify as a sort of play or game), we may find ourselves strongly attracted to or identified with one of the characters, we may long for the couple to consummate their tragic attraction to one another, we may find ourselves reluctant to close the book and report for dinner or go to bed. Our responses are more pleasurable if we conspire with the play to suppress our awareness of the fictional character of the situation in which we are immersed. It is not that we are unable to separate fantasy from reality; rather, we choose not to do so. Once we have made that choice, it is possible for the fiction to wield a powerful grip over our emotions and physical responses.

If the boundary between a player and the character he plays is indistinct and permeable when it comes to emotion, then we need to integrate this fact into our understanding of "identifying with" a fictional character.[21] This identification is not simply, as we are prone to formulate it, that the viewer or reader empathizes with the character or can imagine herself in the character's place. Identification is also engaging in emotional play by allowing oneself to sense and feel emotions appropriate to the character, and once this project is undertaken the player does not know exactly where it will end. The conclusion is that in some respects it would be more accurate to characterize the player as taking on the role of the fictional character and experiencing events from this vantage point. Recent developments in philosophy and cognitive science can help us more fully understand this phenomenon, and it is to these I now turn.

Role Playing and Simulation

I have presented evidence that role players may create and orient to the fantasy of the game in ways that are pervasive, subtle, and not necessarily intentional. Research on children's play has established that these features are also typical of children's spontaneous pretend play. Once again, Paul Harris (2000: 31):

> When children engage in role play, they do not simply remain off-stage directors or puppeteers. They enter into the make-believe situation that they create and adopt the point of view of one of the protagonists within it. The real world recedes into the background and is replaced by the make-believe landscape and experience that would be available to that protagonist.

In addition to pretend play, I have also suggested that role-playing games are similar to improvisational acting, and to following fictional narratives. All of these phenomena depend on the capacity to take up a different vantage point from that of the day-to-day self. The player adopts the perspective of a character within the fiction and then responds emotionally and physically to the imaginary situation. Throughout this book, I assume that what I have documented here for role-playing games, and what others have documented elsewhere for pretend play, is probably very similar to what happens when people engage in other sorts of play in the realm of entertainment.

One way to conceptualize this is to say that taking up the vantage point of fictional beings is commonplace and is the basis for a variety of activities in which we use our imagination. In recent decades, a number of philosophers and cognitive scientists have developed a theory that—although it was not formulated specifically to address this issue—may offer a fruitful approach to understanding these psychological skills. A number of kinds of evidence, some of which are reviewed here, tend to support the hypothesis that humans understand the intentions of others by a process of simulation, essentially a kind of automatic pretending that answers the question, "What would I be up to if I were making those movements?"[22] As Decety and Chaminade (2005: 121) put it, "Humans come to understand the intentions of others through an introspective examination of their own mental states and processes—a kind of simulation of what it must be like to be in the 'mental shoes' of the other person." Simply put, then, the point is this: we can adopt other perspectives in play, and furthermore seem to effortlessly imagine experience from those perspectives, because of the way our minds work. Our species-defining facility in communication and learning is based in our mental capacity for simulation. Play is a way of exploiting this capacity for our own enjoyment, and—as I argue in this book—play also serves vital functions for establishing and maintaining aspects of our social organization.

It is fair to say that this *simulation theory* has been at the center of an explosion of scholarship in several disciplines. This book is, I suppose, another example of all this interest, but before I proceed I want to alert you to a few important considerations. Simulation theory touches on debate among specialists in a number of areas, notably cognitive neuroscience, philosophy, psychology, and literary criticism. As a specialist in none of these areas, my account of these debates is necessarily general, and experts will assuredly find fault with certain arguments. In compensation I attempt to refer interested readers to more specialized treatments of the issues I raise. Second, readers may well wonder how my account can depend on issues that are still controversial; if aspects of simulation theory turn out to be incorrect, does my account of becoming caught up fall with them? It is almost certainly true that my explanation of becoming caught up will benefit from further research. But it is well worth the effort to explain how role players (and the rest of us) become caught up in play; doing so offers a much fuller account for others to criticize and refine.

In the next two chapters, I build on the empirical material I have presented here, on the one hand to try to explain what is happening in these role playing games, and on the other hand to link this to broader issues of culture and action. I use simulation theory as a starting point to talk about these broader issues and place the sort of play I have been discussing in context with other fundamental human capacities, such as imitation and what I call meta-action. These concepts constitute a basis for exploring the sort of phenomena we have observed and significantly clarify just what is going on when players become caught up in the game.

5

Looking Under the Hood

SUPPOSE THAT A CLEVER BEING comes upon a complicated object that is utterly unfamiliar to her. Let's say the object is a car, and she is an alien, or maybe an intelligent person from an earlier century, miraculously transported to the present. She would surely wonder what this complicated object is. The being might recognize that an efficient way to proceed is to approach the question on different levels. Two of the most obvious approaches are (1) trying to understand the various components that make up the complicated object (this is the look-under-the-hood approach), and (2) trying to understand what sort of thing the object is, what class it belongs to. Is it furniture? an appliance? perhaps an enormous kitchen gadget? This could be called the bird's-eye view approach.

Of course, as the clever being sets to work, the approaches do not stay separate for long. The wheels and their ultimate linkage with the engine indicate movement, which suggests that the proper category is "mode of transportation." Nevertheless, adopting these two points of view—at least as an initial strategy—is a useful way to proceed in the attempt to get a grasp of what this thing is.

In this chapter and the next, I take a similar tack in looking at getting caught up in entertainment. Building on the example I presented in the previous chapter, in this one I look at the constituent components of becoming caught up. I explore the mental processes that account for the behaviors we observed among the role players: they use deictic indicators appropriate to the characters, they feel emotions and make movements that the characters might be assumed to feel and make, and they become deeply absorbed in the world of the game. Notice that this explora-tion is a preliminary, first approximation sort of endeavor. I hope to make some relevant observations that take us further into the mechanics of becoming caught up, but I have no illusion of offering a complete explanation thereof.

In the next chapter, I adopt the bird's-eye view. There I place becoming caught up in a class of similar phenomena. As that endeavor proceeds, I draw on what we have learned about what is under the hood. The goal of this exercise is to relocate becoming caught up conceptually, to move it out of the neighborhood of curiosi-ties. Its new address is as yet unclear, but I hope that by the close of the next chap-ter we will have a much clearer sense of how to think about how and why people in our society become caught up in entertainment.

Extended Imitation

Michael Tomasello, a leading proponent of simulation theory, has proposed that the distinctive characteristic of human thought enabling our species to produce complex social organizations, technologies, and language is a "very special" (1999: 5) form of social cognition. He is referring to the human capacity to recognize other humans as intentional entities like themselves. This recognition allows us to learn not just what another is doing but also to grasp the project on which another has embarked. As Tomasello expresses it:

> This understanding enables individuals to imagine themselves "in the mental shoes" of some other person, so that they can learn not just *from* the other but *through* the other. This understanding of others as intentional beings like the self is crucial in human cultural learning because cultural artifacts and social practices—exemplified prototypically by the use of tools and linguistic symbols—invariably point beyond themselves to other outside entities: tools point to the problems they are designed to solve and linguistic symbols point to the communicative situations they are de-signed to represent [1999: 6].

Human beings are able not only to embark on projects but to recognize the projects of others. Thus a human is able to join an ongoing project. Indeed, he or she can join a project that got under way millennia before his or her birth. Per-haps he or she can contribute something further to the project. Tomasello refers to this possibility as "the ratchet effect" and sees in it the most important distinction between humans and other primates, allowing the gradual building of a complex culture: "Many non-human primate individuals regularly produce intelligent be-havioral innovations and novelties, but then their groupmates do not engage in the kinds of social learning that would enable, over time, the cultural ratchet to do its work"[1] (Tomasello 1999: 5). Thus the most important implication of the form of social cognition under discussion is that humans can be socialized into an enormously complex way of life that was not of their own making.

Significantly, this ability not only appears at a particular point in the evolution of Homo sapiens; it also appears at a particular point in the development of the mind. At around nine months, human infants begin interacting with objects not just dyadically but rather in conjunction with another person. This ability is known as "joint attention." Joint attention entails the capacity to cooperate in attending to an object that one recognizes is also the focus of another's attention. Thus, for the first time at around nine months, the infant begins "to flexibly and reliably look where adults are looking (gaze following), to use adults as social reference points (social referencing), and to act on objects in the way adults are acting on them (imitative learning). In short, it is at this age that infants for the first time begin to 'tune in' to the attention and behavior of adults toward outside entities" (Tomasello 1999: 62).

Joint attention, and the various skills it enables, are key components of a role-playing game. Perhaps the most important of these skills is imitation. The relationship between the game and imitation is not immediately obvious, because in a strict sense the players cannot be imitating their characters; their characters do not exist. To address this problem, Alvin Goldman has suggested the term "extended imitation," by which he means the capacity to improvise and respond on the basis of the position of another (Goldman 2005; Harris 2000). As Goldman (2005: 91) writes, in describing not just role-playing games but any kind of play involving adopting a new role:

> I propose that role-play be viewed as a kind of extended imitation. Ordinary imitation involves the behavioral duplication of an observed action. An action is typically imitated at the same time that it is observed, but in deferred imitation, the actor imitates behavior that was previously observed and is now recalled. In the case of role play, the actor need not imitate any actually observed behavior. There is, however, a *type* of behavior the actor is familiar with and which she imitates in some relevant respects.

Such extended imitation involves not only physical processes but mental ones as well. It is based in part on "trying to duplicate in one's own mind the (supposed) mental acts or processes of another" (Goldman 2005: 92).[2] So in those cases in which the fiction or game includes images or ideas of other persons, we proceed from our understanding of their mental state. Like the role player, the child pretending to be a firefighter does not think along the lines of "First I must slide down the pole and pull on my boots, then clamber into the truck." Rather, the child in this situation imagines himself a firefighter—physically, cognitively, and emotionally—and takes it from there.

That is, in order to carry out extended imitation I must be able to simulate, along a number of dimensions, the entire experience of the fictional character. This requires what philosophers Gregory Currie and Ian Ravenscroft have called "imaginative projection," an ability they regard as necessary not only for imaginative play but also for interpretation and enjoyment of fictions. Imaginative projection is

> the capacity to have, and in good measure to control the having of, states that are not perceptions or beliefs or decisions or experiences of movements of one's body, but which are in various ways like those states—like them in ways that enable the states possessed through imagination to mimic and, relative to certain purposes, to substitute for perceptions, beliefs, decisions, and experiences of movements [2002: 11].

We humans have the ability to imagine mental and physical states that are not our actual mental and physical state. Our enjoyment of fiction and play depends on this ability. When we enjoy fictions of various sorts in this way, we do so by simulating with great subtlety and power what it would be like to inhabit this fiction. As was shown in the previous chapter, the capacity to participate in an imaginative game is based on the ability to adopt a perspective from within the game, what I called (following Harris 2000) the deictic shift. This capacity is at once extraordinarily complex and utterly taken for granted. It entails a shift away from one's own vantage point and adoption of another point of view. Role players subsequently interpret and speak from the new perspective, calculating the effects of the changed point of view instantaneously and effortlessly.

This skill, which is taken for granted in much of our day-to-day activity, becomes more visible in play situations in part because the alternative perspective is an acknowledged fiction. But it is an essential component of much of human communication. As Paul Harris (2000: 192) forcefully points out, one of the most basic advantages of human language is the user's capacity to convey information about displaced events. We do this by constructing what he calls "situation models," "a mental model of the narrative situation being described." We then typically locate ourselves within that model (we shift our deictic center). This is something we accomplish without thinking, and it occurs continuously in our play, our reading, and indeed throughout language use.

Consider, as an example, direct quotation. In English, as in most languages, there is more than one way of quoting someone else when you are speaking. You may quote someone indirectly: "He said that he hated my tie." Or, you may quote someone directly: "He said, 'I hate your tie!'" When you quote someone directly, you use *I* to refer not to yourself but rather to the person you are quoting. The technical term for the *I* that appears in direct quotation, and that refers not to the speaker but to an entity specified earlier in the discourse (here, the tie hater), is the *anaphoric I*.

As Erving Goffman (1986) and others[3] have pointed out, the anaphoric I always involves the speaker in role playing. This anaphoric I (Urban 1989) is therefore a close relative of the *I* we meet in the role-playing game. It is a momentarily adopted character understood by speakers and listeners to be the person who originated the utterance. To produce or interpret direct quotation, one must have mastered the skills of inhabiting another viewpoint. In this connection, I especially want to call attention to the fact that most speakers in most circumstances use direct quotation without any planning or conscious awareness of having done so. This shows that we have the capacity to instantaneously adopt an ephemeral role in day-to-day conversation, to act that role with aplomb, and to shift back to the day-to-day self so seamlessly that we are not even aware of what we have done.

Thus the sort of phenomena that are so obvious in the role-playing game are manifestations of human imaginative and imitative skills that we depend on in all pretending and in understanding fiction. As I will continue to show, these processes are also an important component of human interactive strategies. Indeed, they are part of the foundation of human culture. All of this has implications for how we understand becoming caught up. When a child adopts a pretend role, when a role player adopts a character, or when a fiction reader identifies with a protagonist, it is not difficult for the player to adopt the imaginary perspective and experience the world as does the fictional being.[4] If our theory is correct, such play builds on, and exploits, fundamental human cognitive characteristics. It is not surprising, then, that the role players of the previous chapter can have powerful subjective experiences of being pulled out of their own everyday perspectives. Such experiences are but enhancements of mental processes that occur continuously as we negotiate the everyday world. Probably the most fundamental of these skills is imitation, and for this reason it is useful to turn now to a more detailed examination of this topic.

Imitation

Perhaps because we so value creativity, we often dismiss imitation as mere copying. Saying, "monkey see, monkey do" about someone is not a compliment. However, our conventional wisdom is not especially wise on this point. Imitation is not only a very complex process; it plays an enormous role in important social endeavors such as learning and social interaction.

First, note that experts disagree on whether creatures with less developed brains, such as monkeys, can in fact imitate. Rizzolatti and Craighero (2004: 172) write in a recent review, "There is vast agreement among ethologists that imitation . . . is present among primates, only in humans, and (probably) in apes." However, other widely respected scientists have argued for the existence of imitative behavior among some monkeys and even in certain nonmammalian animals (see Voelkl and Huber 2000).

These arguments turn in part around the issue of how to define imitation. There is wide agreement that instances of one creature doing what another does do not necessarily constitute imitation. There are other behavioral processes such as response priming (an often cited example is the flocking of birds) that may produce behavioral congruence (Hurley and Chater 2005: 15). Tomasello and Carpenter (2005) present a careful review of the question, suggesting a clear distinction among mimicry, emulation learning, and imitation. They argue that the behaviors used as examples of imitation among nonhuman animals are better conceived of as belonging to one of the two former categories. Emulative behavior, in particular, can be quite complex and involve such activities as a chimpanzee learning to use a tool by watching another individual. However, according to Tomasello and Carpenter (2005: 134), a creature imitates only when it grasps that the model is an entity like the creature itself who is pursuing a larger project through the motions it is performing.[5]

Thus true imitation is not just a congruence between the behavior of individuals; rather it implies understanding of another agent's goals in a particular movement, something that Rizzolatti and Craighero (2004) term "action understanding." In other words, to imitate you I must, as a first step, grasp what you are up to. As a second step, I must do what you did, based on my understanding of what you were up to. The problem in grasping the nature of imitation is the difficulty for us humans to notice that when we imitate, we are without any effort at all grasping that another with capabilities like ourselves is up to something we share an interest in, and we could do the same thing. Because this is so easy for us, we assume that, say, a monkey who does what another monkey does is going through the same process. But said monkey could be simply learning how to do something by watching it get done. There would not need to be any understanding of goals, or that these are "creatures like me, except not me."

Those who use simulation theory as a way to think about how imitation occurs tend to make much of the fact that in the mid-1990s a group of Italian neuroscientists reported a set of neurons with unusual properties in one area of the premotor cortex of macaque monkeys. Neurons are individual brain cells linked in networks. Our thinking, movement, emotions, memories, and so on are all mediated through the electrochemical activity of neurons, activity that is of unfathomable complexity. Nevertheless, careful and creative experimental work by generations of neuroscientists has revealed a great deal about the structure and function of the human nervous system. This new discovery was that specialized neurons (which have come to be known as "mirror neurons") discharged not just when the animals performed certain behaviors (primarily manual grasping). They also discharged when the monkey observed the experimenter performing the relevant action. The authors of the article went on to point to indirect evidence of a similar mirror system in humans and to offer a theory about the possible role of such a system in speech perception. Giacomo Rizzolatti was a member of the research team that originally demonstrated the activity of mirror neurons. He sums up the basic point: "Mirror neurons are a particular class of visuomotor neurons, originally discovered in area F5[6] of the monkey premotor cortex, that discharge both when the monkey does a particular action and when it observes another individual (monkey or human) doing a similar action" (Rizzolatti and Craighero 2004: 169).

Although this discovery has provoked a number of interesting theories of the function of mirror neurons, it is not accurate to say there is a strong scientific consensus on the matter.[7] Another review (Brass and Heyes 2005: 489), though conceding that mirror neurons are an exciting and significant discovery, offers the judgment that "at present, direct experimental evidence for the involvement of mirror neurons" in such processes as imitation, action understanding, or language development is "relatively weak." This means I am in no position to make any final pronouncements about the involvement of mirror neurons in the process of imitation. If the experts in the field are still sorting out the functions of mirror neurons, those who depend on the experts must be very careful about asserting anything at all on the matter. On the other hand, understanding something of how the experts think about the mirror neuron system turns out to be an efficient way of highlighting the relationship between imitation and the sort of behavior we want to understand. In the end, the underlying mechanisms may turn out to be other than what simulation theorists claim; however, the relationships between imitation and occupying a position within a fiction will remain.

The central claim among those who use the new research to bolster simulation theory is that our brain represents movement of other agents through patterns of neural activation that are very similar to the patterns associated with our own intentional movements. That is, at this point there is some strong evidence that we possess an automatic "neural matching mechanism for perception and action" (Decety and Chaminade 2005: 126). We can tell what others are doing because in observing an agent carrying out an action our nervous system is activating some of the same pathways we would use in carrying out the action ourselves.[8]

Embedded within this account of imitation is an assumption about the elementary mechanisms of self-other differentiation. Our most basic forms of learning and interaction, in this view, require an understanding that we—ourselves and those with whom we interact—are in some sense agents. To say we recognize the goal of an activity is to say we are able to interpret it in terms of what Charles Taylor (1985: 259) calls a "hierarchy of privilege." That is, a sequence of movements could be described in any number of ways, and an individual could mimic those movements without grasping their purpose. We humans are agents in part because we privilege certain interpretations of meaning as correctly describing the projects of actors, as capturing what the actor is up to.[9] For me to imitate you, then, requires that you and I be oriented to a shared hierarchy of privilege, an understanding that you (and I) have the capacity to pursue a project. One implication here is that I do not so much recognize myself as an agent as recognize that I belong to a species of agents.

Again, this recognition is assumed, by many contemporary neuroscientists, to follow from the way our minds perceive and process the acts of others. Imitation, a fundamental aspect of how we learn and communicate, is an expression of our built-in capacity to simulate other perspectives. This brings me, at last, back to the matter of simulation and becoming caught up. Simulation theory posits that we understand actions of other humans by shifting away from our perspective and simulating theirs. Some neuroscientists have presented evidence that this understanding is built into the way our nervous systems process the activity of other humans. We saw that the role players easily adopt the perspectives of their fictional characters, and they speak from this perspective with such fluidity that there can be little question of their calculating every instance of "character oriented" speech. We also saw that the players make reference to time and space as they would if they were in the position of the fictional characters, and that some of their emotions were those of the characters. Among the most striking of the examples is what I began the book with, a case in which a player's motor behavior is controlled by the character he is imagining.[10]

Simulation theory offers a neat and parsimonious explanation of these strange observations: it says they are not strange at all. Rather, what we observe among the role players is simply an explicit manifestation of mental gyrations we accomplish continuously throughout the day as we interact with others. We understand others by simulating their perspectives, and therefore it is perfectly understandable if we are able to do this with little effort when we consciously undertake to do so for the purposes of our own amusement. If the speculations about the role of the mirror neuron system are in some degree confirmed, we will understand something of the mechanism whereby we accomplish simulation: it is wired into the way our nervous systems respond to at least some aspects of human action by simulating them on a neural level.

Joint Attention, Entrainment, and Mimicry

I have explained how simulation theory accounts for one of the most important aspects of becoming caught up in a fictional situation: because joint attention and simulation are built into the patterns of interaction and thought that are characteristic of our species, adopting an alternative perspective—even a fictional one—is something that comes naturally to us. We are so skilled at doing this that we can extend a perspective and imagine what many facets of experience, such as movements and feelings, would be like from this position. Such capacity has been exploited in a range of human activities, including storytelling, pretending, and playing certain sorts of games.

As this discussion proceeds, it becomes increasingly clear that the mental processes underlying becoming caught up in play are all also prominent in mediating social interaction. This is unsurprising because many forms of play are either structured interaction or are means of regulating interaction; think of the importance of play in establishing dominance hierarchies in nonhuman animals. But the matter probably goes deeper, and I continue to explore it in this chapter and the next.

A recent book by sociologist Randall Collins, *Interaction Ritual Chains* (2004), gives an account of interaction that highlights some of the mental processes we need to investigate. Specifically, Collins focuses on a range of activities he calls "interaction rituals"[11] (conversations, sexual interaction, and smoking cigarettes, to name a few). The three key components of an interaction ritual are development of a mutual focus of attention, interactive synchronization, and shared emotions and cognitions: "At the center of an interaction ritual is the process in which participants develop a mutual focus of attention and become entrained in each other's bodily micro-rhythms and emotions" (Collins 2004: 47). As this happens, a form of feedback emerges in which mutual focus and shared mood reinforce one another, with the possibility (in a highly successful ritual) of mutual entrainment and "shared emotional / cognitive experience" (2004: 48).

Note the three basic mental processes implicated in Collins's account: joint attention, entrainment, and emergence of a shared perspective. These should sound familiar; they are quite similar to the processes we have been examining that account for the human capability to grasp and embark on shared projects. Many social scientists have pointed to this capacity to adopt a perspective emerging out of interaction as the basis of human action and interaction. George Herbert Mead (1934) makes this point when he insists that formulation of the "generalized other" is fundamental to a fully human self. In introducing the generalized other, Mead (not coincidentally) discusses its development in play. He points to the child's ability to adopt an imaginary role in pretend play as the first stage in development of the generalized other. Later, as the child begins to play organized games, she develops the capability to adopt the perspective of several playmates—the perspective of the game as it were. Mead (1934: 154ff) makes it clear that although the earliest forms of the generalized other entail adopting the perspective of another social being, the fully developed generalized other consists in adopting the perspectives of groups, or what we might call cultural perspectives.

Human communication depends on a topic, an idea that participants focus on and keep afloat in conversation. This requires joint attention, the possibility of two or more persons both focusing on a common externality and both being aware they are doing so (Collins 2004: 79). Ultimately, immersion in a conversation and in a fiction depend on the same elemental cognitive function, the capacity to take up a perspective within a symbolic framework that is different from the perspective offered by the individual's sensory apparatus. As Mead (1934: 160) writes, "What goes on in the game goes on in the life of the child all the time." Without the ability to integrate a cultural perspective into one's ongoing thought, any communally shared meaning—indeed, any fully human communication—is impossible. Many animals can convey information through external signs such as calls. But, as far as we understand the matter, animals cannot participate in a shared symbolic framework. Human beings can do so, and they can do so because they are able to step outside their idiosyncratic perspectives as individuals and adopt an alternative viewpoint.

This alternative viewpoint begins as a perspective, but it quickly expands to a simulation of another's experience. In play, we have termed this expansion "extended imitation," and again Mead makes a similar point about play and its broader relevance for human interaction. "The game has a logic," he writes (1934: 158), and it is this logic we depend on to understand not only the roles played by the various positions in the game but also the attitudes and perspectives likely to be associated with those roles, and finally the attitudes of the group as a whole. Mead developed his argument in a developmental idiom, discussing play as a stage in development of the personality. I would prefer to make the same point without any implication that play is either a step along the way to forming the generalized other or an analogy to social processes. The point is rather that in both play and interaction we can observe the characteristic and species-defining human capacity of an individual to step outside of her own perspective and participate in a cultural community.

Thus what Collins calls the mutual focus of attention, the perspective shift we observe in many forms of play and in the interpretation of fiction, and Mead's "generalized other" are fundamentally similar. Each is constituted in the unique human capacity to abandon the perspective of the individual organism and adopt the perspective of another person or group. But this is only the beginning of what we need to look at. Whether in interaction or in play, the most important issue for the present discussion is what happens as other cognitive and emotional processes work to expand this perspective to encompass an "as if" world (Holland et al. 1998; Luhrman 1989: 332).

As I have already noted in quoting Collins, one very important element of this expansion is rhythmic entrainment. I will discuss entrainment together with mimicry, a closely related although separable phenomenon. Mimicry (which is not the same as imitation, as I have defined it) is doing what another person in your vicinity is doing, and there is considerable evidence that humans cannot help but mimic (to some extent) those with whom they interact (Hatfield et al. 1994: 18 ff). Entrainment refers to any sharing of "rhythms of behavior" (Kinsbourne 2005: 167), and as observers of fireflies or cicadas can confirm, such behavior occurs among organisms with much simpler nervous systems than those of humans. This suggests that some kinds of entrainment are also automatic, not intentional.

Hatfield et al. (1994) present a detailed review of research on mimicry and entrainment, breaking these processes down into a number of subcategories such as motor mimicry, vocal synchronization, postural mirroring, and afferent nerve system coordination. A great deal of research in psychology and related disciplines tends to support the conclusion that humans mimic and entrain with one another in a variety of ways (vocally, posturally, in terms of facial expressions, and so on) and that the bulk of this behavior is automatic. One of the most convincing lines of evidence in support of this comes from studies of preverbal infants. It has been repeatedly demonstrated, for example, that neonates move in patterns reproducing the rhythms of their caregivers' speech. (The classic study is Condon and Sander (1974); see Nadel and Butterworth 1999 for a recent compilation.) Writes psychologist Marcel Kinsbourne (2005: 167): "Even newborn babies assume rhythms of orienting that are complementary to those of the adult who is speaking to them long before they begin to be able to understand speech. . . . Humans are innately pre-disposed to adopt rhythms that accord with those of others."

Studies of conversation also support the conclusion that entrainment and mimicry are almost instantaneous and often take place outside the bounds of conscious intention. Much research has demonstrated that two or more persons engaged in a lively conversation quickly become enmeshed in a mutual dance of rhythmic coordination. Conversational partners can respond to one another's gestures and utterances in as little as two hundredths of a second, which is much faster than human beings can react to a stimulus intentionally (Collins 2004: 77). Conversations are more and less rhythmically synchronized, a fact that is likely to be experienced among participants as variation in how much they like (feel solidarity with) their conversational partners (Hatfield et al. 1994: 29; Collins 2004: 76; see also references cited there).

Kinsbourne (2005: 171) comments that entrainment is a powerful form of persuasion. No small part of what was classically termed "rhetoric" has to do with the importance of rhythm and imitation in effective public speaking. Speaking of the oft-noticed tendency to fall in with the activities of a crowd, he writes, "It is as though entraining with the crowd suspends personal responsibility." Another way to phrase the point is that the innate tendency to entrain and mimic can contribute to a subjective situation in which one feels one is not fully the author of one's own actions.[12] This, of course, is a source of the sense of being pulled away from the everyday self.

In Collins's account of interaction ritual, the mutual focus of attention is the prerequisite for development of entrainment. "Momentarily shared events," he writes, "involve considerable micro-temporal coordination, a condition of collective entrainment" (2004: 82). Such entrainment is powerful because of the sensitivity of our biological equipment, evolved over millions of years as social beings. The basic capacities that make close interaction and communication possible guarantee that we, largely outside of our awareness, entrain with other humans in our vicinity.

Now of course, this predisposition is considerably enhanced by adopting a shared perspective. The more we are focused, cognitively and emotionally, in harmony with others, the more this entrainment begins to carry us away: "Activities and emotions have their own micro-rhythm, a pace at which they take place. As the focus of interaction becomes progressively more attuned, the participants anticipate each other's rhythms, and thus become caught up 'in the swing of things'" (Collins 2004: 108).

Much of play may entail precisely this sort of interactive entrainment. After all, much play is based on groups of people undertaking coordinated activity with a common focus. For example, in a later chapter I discuss drinking games among college students. Typically, in these simple games an activity (drinking) is tied to a random process (such as drawing a playing card). One could almost immediately come up with a list of other examples of play and entertainment that need not entail a shift to a fictional perspective: watching sporting events (or playing most sports), dancing, competitive games, and so on.

It is worth emphasizing here that much play and interaction is unlike a role-playing game or interpretation of a fiction in that these activities do not entail a shift to a fictional perspective. However, interaction and interactive games still entail a shift of perspective; they are built on the joint perspective developed among participants. Regardless of whether attention is drawn to a fictional perspective or one created in interaction, with a shift away from the perspective of the day-to-day entrainment becomes a particularly strong possibility, and it may eventually contribute to subjective feelings of becoming caught up.

Affective Mimicry

I have discussed how the attentional shift away from the perspective of the biological individual, rhythmic entrainment, and mimicry may work to reinforce one another in either interaction or play, creating a sense of being pulled out of one's everyday subjectivity. As we learned in the previous chapter, extended imitation may also include emotions and other feelings. "Children and adults alike," Paul Harris (2000: 65) writes, "have the capacity for 'absorption' in a pretend world. . . . Temporarily, we set aside the current world with its anxieties and problems, and we live instead in the imagined world. Once we enter that state of absorption, it is the events occurring within the imagined world that drive our emotional system." This capacity is yet another component of extended imitation, the ability to adopt a vantage point other than one's own and react to the world emotionally as one in the imaginary position would.

Harris goes on to point out that from an evolutionary perspective it is anything but surprising that human beings have the capacity to react emotionally to imaginative situations:

> If simple organisms such as rats and pigeons can "generalize" an emotional reaction from one stimulus to another, similar stimulus, there is nothing very surprising about the way that human beings "generalize" their emotional reactions from a state of affairs they actually encounter to an equivalent state of affairs that they only contemplate in their imagination" (2000: 90).

Such adaptations would have been necessary in order to take advantage of the extraordinary advantage that symbolic communication offers. It is not enough for humans to be able to conceptualize a nonexistent situation; they also need to be able to react emotionally to such situations.

Our capacity to respond emotionally to imagined events is considerably enhanced in situations that entail entrainment and mimicry. Hatfield et al. (1994: 49–50) point out that both Darwin and William James argued that human emotions are strongly influenced by physical movements, and since the 19th century considerable evidence has accumulated that emotions are intensified or even born in certain gestures and expressions (Hatfield et al. 1994: 20). The general point to grasp here is this: despite the fact that in our common sense, emotions are internal states of individuals, generation of human emotions in fact seems to be closely tied to external cues. Such cues may either be an imaginary situation or the emotions of other beings. Thus as our attention and physical movement begin to be drawn to an exterior model, our emotions tend to follow.

One of the most important areas for the present work is facial mimicry. Hatfield et al. (1994: 19) offer a summary:

> Social psychophysiological investigations have found [that] the individuals' emotional experiences and facial expressions, as measured by EMG procedures, tend to mimic at least rudimentary features of the changes in emotional expression of others that the subjects observe; moreover, this motor mimicry can occur at levels so subtle as to produce no observable facial expressions.

Further, we do not only tend to mimic and entrain with the emotional expressions of others; doing so tends to make us feel the way others do, because in many cases making a facial expression associated with an emotion will cause us to feel the emotion.[13] This certainly does not imply that expressions are the primary cause of our emotions, but it does suggest that expressions may powerfully influence our emotions (Hatfield et al. 1994: 62).

Thus, as Hatfield and her colleagues point out, the "emotional contagion"[14] that is mysterious from a (Western) commonsense perspective is by now an empirically established and theoretically comprehensible process. Hatfield et al. (1992: 153–154) define emotional contagion[15] as "the tendency to automatically mimic and synchronize movements, expressions, postures, and vocalizations with those of another person and, consequently, to converge emotionally." Thus, whether in play or in interaction, it is not only that the subject may feel his attention and movements are taking on a life of their own; his feelings may also seem to originate from somewhere beyond himself. Take viewing a film as an example. It has been shown that spectators viewing video images of human faces often reproduce the facial expressions they observe.[16] This mimicry in itself may have implications for subjectivity. We may find ourselves doing things, such as making facial expressions, that we did not consciously set out to do. Further, we may begin to experience emotional states generated by our entrainment with or mimicry of fictional characters in the film.

Thus we can add another element to the list of processes that constitute becoming caught up. Following some sort of attentional shift—which may, or may not, involve adopting an imaginary perspective—the person is especially likely to mimic and engage in rhythmic entrainment with other persons or images in the vicinity. Doing so may well affect emotional experience. Once this process gets under way, these emotions may in themselves take on a life of their own.

It is fully possible, for example, that you might choose to see a horror movie so as to experience a thrill of terror but then find yourself drawn into the film through mimicry and entrainment. You may begin to feel emotions generated by the expressions and movements of the fictional characters. The emotions so generated may feed on themselves; anxiety may produce more anxiety, for example. More broadly, the autonomic arousal that is often a part of emotional experience is not entirely volitional, and furthermore it is subject to a regulatory process that may or may not be intentional. Finally, this regulation is not necessarily attenuating; it may be augmenting (Frijda 1986: 404). As a result of this, you may find you are in fact very frightened by the movie you chose to see and experience long-term effects, such as nightmares. The point here is that emotions and other feelings may be involved in complex voluntary and involuntary processes that sustain the sense of one's own activities having taken on a trajectory that is to some extent beyond one's control.

Absorption

The big questions remains: What is under the hood? We have found some systems that are undoubtedly relevant to producing the subjective sense of becoming caught up—just as in an engine we might make out pistons, a transmission, and so on—but as yet we have no sense of how these systems fit together. In this section I address the problem by returning to the matter of attention. I have noted that joint attention is a species-defining human skill, one that Tomasello (1999) argues is the foundation of our capacity to form cultural communities. The ability to simulate other perspectives, in a sense the skill to attend from numerous vantage points, is also the foundation of what I am looking at in this book, the phenomenon of becoming caught up in play (or interaction). That is, in a sense the first step toward the subjective experience of being pulled away from the everyday self is some sort of shift of attention to a different vantage point. But there is another phase of attention that is also relevant to understanding becoming caught up. As one's immersion in an alternative perspective is enhanced through entrainment and affective mimicry, one's attentional focus can narrow further. The result is a deepening of one's immersion in the alternative perspective, a subjective sense of becoming utterly absorbed in one's activity.

The experience of absorption, of becoming lost in certain sorts of activities (movies, books, conversations, and so forth) has attracted sporadic interest in social psychology and other disciplines for several decades.[17] An early attempt to provide an empirical underpinning for the topic was Tellegen and Atkinson's study (1974) entitled "Openness to Absorbing and Self-Altering Experiences ("Absorption"), a Trait Related to Hypnotic Susceptibility." The first characteristic of absorption they cited (268) is "a heightened sense of the reality of the attentional object." When one is absorbed in an activity, it assumes the status of the relevant reality. Tellegen and Atkinson established that absorption was an empirically measurable and coherent personality characteristic. Their description of the trait is "a disposition for having episodes of 'total' attention that fully engage one's representational (i.e., perceptual, enactive, imaginative, and ideational) resources" (1974: 268).

Most work on absorption has continued to investigate the topic as a personality characteristic. The kinds of questions posed about absorption are "How is the propensity to have absorbing experiences distributed in the population?" "How is this propensity correlated with other personality characteristics?" "How is openness to absorption related to family structure or childhood experiences?" (Swanson 1978).

However, there are also a number of obvious and potentially significant sociological questions one might ask about absorption. One of them is, "What sort of activities typically produce absorption, and why?" Absorption can occur in many contexts, and it need not begin in shifting one's perspective away from that of the everyday self. One could become absorbed, for example, in an important or demanding situation such as an emergency. However, it is surely no coincidence that absorption is often produced by play and intense interaction, activities often founded in a shift in attentional perspective. If one becomes deeply immersed in, say, a movie, one's attention narrows and one's emotions are fully engaged by what one observes on the screen. The film so engages us that it feels real to us, though on another level we remain well aware that we are simply watching a fiction (Campbell 1987; Walton 1990). Absorption in an interaction seems quite similar: our attention becomes focused on the content of conversation and other persons, which assume disproportionate significance relative to the rest of the world.[18]

The processes we have studied here permit at least rudimentary understanding of how this may happen. A feedback loop develops among attentional narrowing, entrainment, and emotional effects: as the experience becomes more emotionally compelling, attention is focused ever more closely on the situation one is becoming absorbed in, and as a result attention is diverted from the everyday world. If one is, say, a spectator at a sporting event, one may be galvanized, along with other spectators, by a dramatic game. As people become focused on this common interest, they may begin to imitate one another's shouts and movements, with the result that the crowd becomes even more cooperatively focused on the game. A common emotional mood may come to dominate, inflating the importance of the game, which thereby becomes an even more compelling situation in which to invest one's attention. In such a situation, the person can be powerfully pulled away from the day-to-day world and into a situation in which something external seems to be guiding the self. Ultimately, this can manifest itself as a form of ecstasy, a self-transformative experience, a standing outside of the self.

Of course, this experience is frequent not only in play but also in intense interaction. Consider what Goffman (1967: 113, cited in Collins 2004: 23) wrote about conversation: "Talk creates for the participant a world and a reality that has other participants in it. Joint spontaneous involvement is a *unio mystico,* a socialized trance. We must see that a conversation has a life of its own and makes demands on its own behalf. It is a little social system with its own boundary-maintaining tendencies."

Absorption and Trance

The mention of trance here raises the important question of how to characterize the state of being caught up. The word *trance* itself will make some readers uneasy, perhaps because it embraces behaviors associated with pseudoscientific activities such as Spiritualism. Our science does not deny the existence of trance states, but it prefers to ignore them. Ian Hacking, in his sophisticated and careful book on multiple personality, points out that trance states in general are regarded as curiosities, "isolated phenomena that fit no vision of the world" (1995: 143). Hacking (1995: 143–144) goes on to note that "Science abhors a marvel [such as trance states], not because marvels are vacuous, empty of meaning, but because they are too full of meaning, of hints, of feeling."

Though I might make some readers squirm, I am forced by the nature of the material I am looking at to consider trance, which I define (following the *Oxford English Dictionary*) as "a state of mental abstraction from external things; absorption, exaltation, rapture, ecstasy." Note that deep absorption, then, is by my definition one form of trance, although there are many others.

Probably the most familiar, and certainly the most studied, trance state is hypnosis. The heart of hypnosis is suggestibility; in fact hypnosis is often identified as suggestibility in the presence of a hypnotic induction. Psychologist Ernest Hilgard (1986), who conducted careful empirical studies of hypnosis[19] over several decades, adopts the reasonable (although by no means inevitable) assumption that most of the time waking consciousness seems to be organized by a "central regulating mechanism."[20] Put very simply, one has a sense that one can decide what to do, to plan that one will do something else later, to alter the course of one's current activity or plans on the basis of new information, and so on. It is therefore not unreasonable to assume that something in the mind is responsible for doing these sorts of things. Hilgard separates this something into separate but intertwined functions that he labels executive and monitoring functions. The executive function is concerned with planning, while the monitoring function is alert to all aspects of the environment, which it continuously scans for relevant information (signs of danger, recognition, and so on). The point here is of course not that these functions correspond to separate neural systems, but rather that we can give these labels to functions that much evidence suggests the mind fulfills.

Under hypnosis the subject turns over certain executive functions to the hypnotist, so that the subject will do or feel what the hypnotist tells him to (Hilgard 1986: 228). This sounds rather sinister, until one remembers that this happens with the subject's consent. As experts on hypnosis stress, it is not typically the case that this consent is yielded up front in the hypnotic contract, after which the subject is at the mercy of the hypnotist. Rather, consent must be ongoing; the hypnotist makes a suggestion, and the subject decides whether to go along with it. All of this can be summed up by saying that the subject gives up part of his or her initiative in hypnosis, while retaining another part.

Hypnosis affects not only the executive but also monitoring functions. Some part of the monitor must be functioning at a lower level if the subject is to accept the suggestions of the hypnotist as valid. This is the absorptive aspect of hypnosis:

the subject becomes absorbed in one sort of sensory input and sets aside others. Read, for example, this description of the hypnotized subject, written by psychiatrist David Spiegel (1990: 124–125):

> A subject becomes so fully involved in the hypnotic metaphor, for example, floating in a warm bath, that the fact that he is actually sitting in a chair at ambient temperature disappears from awareness. The logical incongruity of feeling a pleasant, warm, floating sensation or picturing pleasant surroundings recedes from awareness, facilitated by the reduction or suspension of the need to analyze the realities of the situation logically and critically. After all, the body is not really floating or any warmer than it was a moment before. Rather, the hypnotized individual affiliates intensely with a metaphor involving mental and associated physical changes.

Spiegel's formulation, that the person under hypnosis "affiliates intensely" with a suggestion while withdrawing attention to the immediate environment, is interesting. This sounds a lot like becoming caught up. This is certainly not to say that when one is caught up, one is hypnotized, for neither of these terms is sufficiently well defined to render such a statement meaningful.[21] However, the similarities between a deeply absorbed state of being caught up and hypnosis are intriguing.[22] It is not unusual at all for hypnosis to be described as similar to, or occurring in conjunction with, experiences such as becoming caught up in fictions. Josephine Hilgard's classic study *Personality and Hypnosis* (1970), for example, argues that hypnotic susceptibility is closely related to a capacity that sounds very much like the ability to become caught up:

> What we found out was that the hypnotizable person was capable of a deep involvement in one or more imaginative-feeling areas of experience—reading a novel, listening to music. . . . If we were to define this involvement, to distinguish it from its nearest relatives such as enjoyment of, or interest in, an activity, we would have to stress the quality of almost total immersion in the activity, with indifference to distracting stimuli in the environment [1970: 4–5].

There are other trance states that may entail little or no disruption of functioning in the day-to-day world; such states are often labeled "mild dissociation," or "slightly altered states of consciousness." Here I am talking about behaviors such as daydreaming and reverie, self-hypnosis, and mild experiences of depersonalization. One reason to bring phenomena of this sort into the discussion at this point is that there is some solid empirical evidence on the frequency of these states, or more accurately on how frequently these states are recognized. As we shall see, such behaviors are reported as occurring frequently, although such anomalies are probably sometimes not even recognized by those who experience them. That is, it is important to recognize consciousness as a notoriously poor observer of consciousness, so that casual reflection on one's own inner experience is not necessarily an accurate guide to the domain. As Ernest Rossi, a psychologist who has devoted a career to studying states of consciousness, writes: "The most peculiar blind spot of consciousness is its inability to recognize its own limitations and altered states when it is experiencing them. . . . Even gross alterations in its functioning induced by emotions, drugs, shock, [and] fatigue . . . are frequently misunderstood and underestimated" (1986: 97).[23]

Recent studies point strongly to the conclusion that most people not only experience trance states with some regularity but are aware of doing so (of course, this does not imply that they label these experiences as trance). These studies have sought to map the frequency of a range of relatively mild alterations of consciousness, such as hypnotic susceptibility, losing track of the passage of time or of place, of a sense of separation from one's body, and so on. A recent version of this sort of test, called the "curious experiences survey," was administered in the late 1990s to 755 adults and reported in 1999 in the journal *Psychological Assessment*[24] (Goldberg 1999). This scale consists of 31 items describing experiences ranging from the sorts of things that presumably happen to almost everyone ("talked out loud to myself") to things that presumably don't ("found myself in a place and had no idea how I had gotten there"; Goldberg 1999: 136). Respondents are then asked to rate the frequency of such experiences on a five-point scale progressing from "never" to "almost always."

As one would expect, the items in the scale that name experiences deviating considerably from our expectations about everyday consciousness are not reported by many respondents (so, for example, only 8 percent of respondents say they have ever had the experience of finding themselves somewhere without knowing how they got there). However, there are a range of items that would seem clearly classifiable as trance states that also seem to happen to people quite frequently (for example, 53 percent of respondents report they at least occasionally have had the experience that they "drove or rode somewhere without remembering later what happened during all or part of the trip"). Therefore it is not imprudent to guess that experiences of mild trance are fairly widespread in everyday life.

More directly relevant to the discussion here, one of the most reported experiences in this study was the statement "found that when I was watching television or a movie I became so absorbed in the story that I was unaware of other events happening around me," with 68 percent of respondents saying this happens to them at least "occasionally." As I have made clear, I do not think we are particularly accurate observers of our own states of consciousness; I regard this as a very conservative estimate of how often this actually occurs. Even taking a conservative estimate, then, we may conclude on the basis of this study that more than two-thirds of the population have experiences of becoming caught up at least occasionally.

Strikingly similar results are reported in another recent study titled "Altered States of Consciousness: A Comparison of Profoundly and Superficially Altered States" (Kokoszka 2000). In a study conducted in Poland, Kokoszka found that 63.4 percent of his subjects (N = 295) reported "the experience of being so engrossed in a book, movie, or television program that you were unaware of what was going on around you" (Kokoszka 2000: 172). This study also concludes that "superficially altered states of consciousness [which in this context can be equated with mild trance] are common," with 84 percent of the participants reporting having experienced at least one such state (Kokoszka 2000: 175). These findings, then, again support the notion that a reasonable estimate of the proportion of the population that is aware of experiencing trance states is around two-thirds.

These studies lead to a pair of conclusions. First, it is reasonable to speak of a range of trance states, in that subjects themselves report such experiences. Second, such experiences are common enough in day-to-day life; for example, something around two-thirds of the adult population report having noticed them, and this is probably a conservative estimate of the incidence of these states. In sum, there is consistent and persuasive empirical evidence to support the claim that trance states are a widespread and common aspect of everyday experience.[25]

It is hardly radical, then, to suggest that as a person's attention is diverted to an activity such as a game, and then is deepened through interactive processes of entrainment and affective mimicry, growing absorption may produce a light trance state. Becoming caught up, like many other mental states, is a matter of degree. One can be more, or less, caught up in an activity. To become deeply caught up is an experience that sounds a great deal like other sorts of dissociative states such as hypnosis and is likely akin to experiences that have been cultivated in ritual contexts from time immemorial.

In Sum

We human beings can become caught up in many sorts of activities. Two of the most obvious categories in which this can occur are play (including, but not limited to, play in fictional worlds) and intense social interaction. Explorations of the component elements of becoming caught up suggest that the foundation of this experience is a form of attention in part conditioned by the awareness that others like us might be (or are) attending as well. Simulation theorists such as Tomasello argue, in harmony with many earlier social scientists, that this form of attention is basic to the human capacity to build cultural communities. This ability to be aware of and react to the attentional perspective of others may well be the basis of the ease with which we can follow fictional narratives or engage in pretend play.

To understand becoming caught up, however, it is not enough to note that people may adopt vantage points that go beyond the everyday self. We must also understand, first, our facility in experiencing the world as it would be experienced from that vantage point. This is what Goldman calls extended imitation. Second, we must grasp how, either with or without extended imitation, a person can be so powerfully pulled toward that vantage point that he or she begins to feel pulled away from everyday self. Here more or less automatic processes of rhythmic entrainment and mimicry, either with other humans or with imaginary humans, are of great significance. Further, as these get under way, emotional contagion may result, furthering the participant's subjective sense that her actions are being directed by something beyond the everyday self. Finally, these processes interacting together may initiate the attentional narrowing known as absorption, resulting eventually in mild trance states.

Having learned something about the elemental components of the experience of becoming caught up, I turn now to the question, What sort of thing (or process) is this?

6

Meta-Action (the Bird's-Eye View)

AS A DROP OF RAIN takes form around a speck of dust, human social action takes shape in conjunction with a thread of culture, around which it crystallizes. Action is precipitated only in collaboration between a human being and communal conventions, although of course we humans may conform to, embellish on, or rebel against these guidelines.

Typically, the cultural ideas and practices that inform human activity remain below the level of awareness. My rebellions are limited by my being for the most part content to stay within the grooves my previous activities have worn in my path through life. I may be following the precedents my culture has established when I act and when I think, but for the most part this does not occur to me. I am too busy getting by to reflect on the fact that I am continuously reproducing the culture that has formed me.

Thus, usually the cultural patterning of our action retreats so far from our awareness that we proceed through life as if our approach to things were the only possible one. But not always. Sometimes we are aware of the conventions ordering our activity. It is not challenging to come up with examples. Consider learning a new skill such as driving a car. The new driver must master a set of rules and skills, many of which are formulated as explicit principles ("You must check your blind spot when changing lanes"). For a while, the new driver is in the uncomfortable position of having to control an automobile by keeping in mind a number of rules, but then gradually the necessary skills become what we call second nature, and driving grows to be as routinized as many other parts of day-to-day life.

Another domain in which the conventions governing activity are relatively visible is in play. By definition, play entails explicit acceptance of stipulations that establish the framework within which the play occurs. A third example of activity in which the rules governing activity are visible is a religious ritual such as the Christian Eucharist. Such a ritual, like any activity, can be routinized, but the participant does not lose sight of the fact that his or her action is a realization of an underlying set of stipulations. In performing a ritual the participant does not have the idea, "Hey, there's a more efficient way to do this." The fact that it is a ritual entails doing it in a particular way; the sequence of actions must be carried out as given. If one were to simply grab the bread and wine and head back to the pew to consume it with some cheese, one would not have carried out the ritual.

All of these cases of being relatively aware of the conventions guiding our activity are good initial examples of our being attuned to the aspect of our experience that I call meta-action; they are in a sense "action about action." When a person is acting in explicit conformation to a set of rules, he or she is doing X by following the rules that bring X about. What the person is *doing,* in the most direct sense, is not X but rather following the rules. There are many, many situations in which, as creatures aware that we act, we undertake to manipulate or reflect on or just play around with our action. These situations are occasions in which we are relatively aware that our action is meta-action.

Another good initial example of meta-action is the sort of situation studied in depth by Erving Goffman (1986), what he called keyings of straightforward activities. As he puts it, a key is a "set of conventions by which a given activity, one already meaningful in terms of some primary framework, is transformed into something patterned on this activity but seen by the participants to be something quite else" (1986: 43–44). Keys are a useful example of meta-action. One could play "going to the restaurant" with a child, in Goffman's terms a keying of going to a restaurant. Like actually going to a restaurant, playing at the activity is based on a series of highly stereotyped moves; here the goal is not to get a meal but rather to mimic the action of getting a meal.

Both of my initial examples of meta-action are activities in which people are more or less consciously following some model (such as rules, conventions, or a more primary activity). However, again these cases do not exhaust the category of "action about action." In fact, meta-action is such a broad term that it can legitimately be applied to the behavior of nonhuman animals. Thinking about this for a moment allows fuller explanation of this notion, moving closer to the heart of the matter, which is that meta-action is a way of *regulating* and *modifying* action.

Meta-Action in Animals

A well-known epiphany in the history of the social sciences occurred in 1952 at a zoo. The quirky genius Gregory Bateson was watching otters playing at fighting, and he had a flash of insight into the nature of their activity. The otters had to be communicating the message that their bites and blows were not *real* bites and blows. This could work only if they understood and communicated the notion that these actions are just signals, not tied inexorably to hostile intent. Bateson summarized the insight by saying that the otters must somehow have conveyed a meta-signal, a signal about their signals, the meaning of which was that these fighting signals are not to be taken as fighting signals (Bateson 1956: 158ff).

This meta-signaling goes beyond basic communication; it entails at least some level of symbolic behavior, because it is based on the capacity to recognize signals as signals. Here is how Bateson (1972: 178) expressed this:

> If we speculate about the evolution of communication, it is evident that a very important stage in this evolution occurs when the organism gradually ceases to respond quite "automatically" to the mood-signs of another and becomes able to recognize the sign as a signal: that is, to recognize that the other individual's and its own signals are only signals which can be trusted, distrusted, falsified, denied, amplified, and so forth.

Put another way, the point here is that humans are demonstrably not the only animals that can step out of the stream of experience and establish a marker saying in effect "Now we are going to operate on another level; our actions are going to have a special character now." Part of the special character is that the actions within this special frame have reference not only to the world in which the organism acts but also to the relationship between organisms. In the case of the playing otters, the special character of the acting sustains a playful relationship between the animals.

The ability to step out of the stream of experience in this way has implications that go beyond qualifying the character of social relationships. It is commonplace, for example, to observe that nonhuman primates use periods of play to master instrumental routines in the long period of their immaturity.[1] Although nonhuman primates such as chimpanzees do not have a way of life based on use of tools, these animals frequently use available objects such as sticks and leaves to achieve desired ends. As Jerome Bruner (1976) documented in an essay titled "Nature and Uses of Immaturity," the mastery of such forms of tool use derives from a period of play insulated from the direct pressures of survival. Younger chimpanzees practice these techniques in play, and if they do not do so, they do not fully master them (see especially Bruner 1976: 37ff).[2]

This sort of play is not about social relationships; nor does it depend on meta-signaling. Again, however, instrumental and social play are relatively visible forms of meta-action. This broader term embraces something like playing with a stick in a situation that has no direct economic implications, and playing at fighting. They are both visible because they are special forms of action, separated out from the stream of day-to-day experience, and these special forms of action serve to somehow regulate action in day-to-day experience. I use the term *regulate* to cover a lot of ground. Meta-action may entail practicing something (essentially stabilizing routines), or it may serve the purpose of introducing flexibility or innovation (Fagen 1976). It may establish, sustain, or modify social relationships.

The fact that rudimentary meta-action is already present among some non-human animals is important. For one thing, it shows us how basic this ability is. Human patterns of social interaction are obviously vastly more complex than those of even our closest relatives among the primates; nevertheless we share with these animals basic strategies that are probably innate. Meta-action is a powerful tool for regulating interaction observable among animals that cannot be said to have symbolic communication systems.

As symbolic behavior begins to appear, meta-action becomes much more complex. Consider play. As the capacity to use symbolism develops, a stick can be used not only to retrieve termites from a hole but also to stand for something else, such as an animal. What Bruner (1976: 49) says of play is also true of meta-action in general: "Once the symbolic transformation of play has occurred, two consequences follow. Play can serve as a vehicle for teaching the nature of society's conventions, and it can also teach about the nature of convention *per se*." A creature that uses symbols can recognize when it engages in meta-action, can see it as meta-action, and can therefore use it to manipulate conventions. This opens up the possibility of more or less conscious manipulation of a way of life.

In other words, because meta-action is a means of regulating the character of activity, it takes on a special importance in a species that designs its own way of life. In a sense, everything we humans do is both action and meta-action, in that all our action is informed by culture and has a symbolic character. We do not really have the option of performing an action that conveys no meaning; our activity is inevitably at once a way to get something done and an instance of perpetuating, modifying, or commenting on a particular way of life. Thus meta-action is best thought of not as a separate category of human activity but rather as a possibility that is either implicit or highlighted in all of what we do. The possibility for us to begin to focus on actions that refer (at least in part) to action is ever-present, although this possibility is often not exploited.[3]

Ritual and Play as Meta-Action

I have introduced the notion of meta-action in part because it allows following through on the plan introduced at the outset of the previous chapter. The concept of meta-action enables me to classify getting caught up in play, to identify getting caught up by understanding the category in which it belongs. More explicitly: two of the most important and interesting forms of visible meta-action are ritual and play. These forms bring us to the threshold of what surely must be considered one of the great mysteries of social science: human beings everywhere regulate action through practices of which they have little articulate awareness. It is not difficult to understand how a creature with self-consciousness might plan for a future event, such as a hunt or a dinner party. It is a good deal more difficult to understand how humans figured out ways to, say, forge commitment to the key values that regulate their social life. Long before any person was aware that human communities are built on the foundation of arbitrary conventions, human communities were doing things to make those arbitrary conventions seem eternal and unquestionable. Among the most important means of accomplishing this are the meta-action of ritual and play.

Most observers who offer theoretical accounts of our engagement with entertainment begin by classifying such engagement as a form of ritual. As I have already indicated, this is probably not the best road to take. Our engagement with entertainment is more accurately conceived as a form of play. Getting caught up in entertainment is one specific form of engaging in play; it is a type of ecstatic behavior that may be generated in play.

This classification ultimately allows introduction of a degree of clarity into the discussion of how to understand our engagement with entertainment. However, before we wade into this, it is useful to pause for a moment and survey the swamp into which I am about to lead you. Social scientists have written a great deal (this is an understatement) on how to define ritual. They have also written a great deal on their own definitions of ritual. They have come to no consensus. Indeed, it seems doubtful any consensus is possible. Ritual may refer to a Catholic Mass, a greeting routine, a formulaic courtship dance undertaken by a certain species of bird, the obsessive handwashing of a person suffering from obsessive compulsive disorder, and so on. The potential application of the term is so broad and so open to interpretation that pinning down the essential nature of ritual is unlikely.

Great minds have also struggled with how to distinguish ritual and play, and none of these thinkers has succeeded in producing a widely accepted explanation. Ritual and play are terms in popular use that took shape in an attempt to understand activities surely at least as old as our species, and they are by now inextricably intertwined with human practices and indigenous sociologies the world over. These terms bear within them arguments about religion, morality, and the very nature of humanity. No author is going to put his or her finger on precisely what they are.

Even so, let us specify a terminology that will at least allow me to explain my perspective as clearly as possible. One of the confusing tendencies in the literature on ritual is that the term is often used both to refer to a category of religious action and as a synecdoche to designate broader sorts of meta-action. There has been widespread agreement that the prototypical ritual is a formulaic religious ceremony such as, in the Christian tradition, a baptism. But writers often go on to argue that there is an *essential* similarity between a ceremony such as baptism and secular ceremonies that (like baptism) mark a change in social status. Thus a high school graduation or a fraternity initiation also becomes a ritual. Or the argument can take the form that there is an *essential* similarity between a sequence of prescribed vocalizations or actions (such as a baptism) and any other sequence of prescribed vocalizations or actions. Thus, reciting the pledge of allegiance or performing one's morning routine of ablutions becomes a ritual.

It is understandable why some authors have taken this approach, because for some purposes it is effective. If you want to point out that the cleanliness routines of the American middle class have a certain magical quality to them, this is a good way to go. As noted earlier, similar motivations are probably behind some theorists' decision to label entertainment activities as rituals. Doing so provokes insights about how entertainment activities may be more important than we casually assume, that such activities may reflect key values (as religion does), and so on.

However, adopting a wide definition of ritual is less appropriate for other sorts of investigations. If we want to move to more detailed and specific insights about the implication of our engagement with entertainment, it begins to be clear that an expansive conception of ritual is a rather dull tool to bring to bear. Above all, it starts to become apparent how useful it might be to consider how entertainment activities are quite *different* from prototypical rituals. So, in this book, I would prefer to use the word *ritual* in a conservative and fairly restrictive sense; *a ritual is a religious ceremony of some sort.*

Entertainment activities, then, are better construed in the terms in which the participants themselves usually understand them: *they are forms of recreation or play.* Indeed, entertainment activities often look similar to religious rituals, but this is because entertainment is of the same genus as ritual (that being visible meta-action); it is not the same species. To spell out the advantages of understanding entertainment activities as play, I now want to explain some of the distinctions between these two species (ritual and play). However, I am not going to try to be comprehensive. I will say enough about the relationship between ritual and play to get me through the present argument, but without anything approaching a complete discussion of this relationship.

I noted in the introduction that as a general rule of thumb ritual is serious and play is not serious. [Humphrey and Laidlaw (1994: 68) choose just the right words when they write "ritual is in earnest" (and play is not)]. I do not deny that play may be approached in earnest or that ritual is sometimes approached with light-heartedness; my point is rather that we completely take for granted that in general play is about fun and ritual is not about fun.[4]

This dichotomy may seem suspiciously obvious but in fact it encapsulates some important wisdom. As I will discuss below, generations of social scientists have demonstrated how rituals reinforce basic social values. Play, on the other hand, often reinforces desires and ideas that must remain subterranean, largely inarticulate.[5] This is why we think of play as fun, irresponsible, separated from the serious businesslike world. Now, the practices and ideals formed and reproduced through play, though they are devalued in official discourse, are nevertheless often vital and significant in our social life. The clearest example of this is probably just the case I am talking about in this book. We live in a society in which it is very important that people sustain two rather contradictory streams of motives. There are the motives of the daylight—those of work, production, and responsibility—and the motives of the night—those of leisure, consumption, and enjoyment. We might be inclined to call the former stream of motives values and the latter stream desires. What I have been saying here is that, roughly, as an initial generalization these desires of consumption are often reinforced through play.

One might object here that desires, by their nature, would seem not to require reinforcement. Who needs to be reinforced in attraction to a vacation at the beach or a passionate romantic liaison? The question indicates the effectiveness of our methods of naturalizing our values of leisure, of rendering them unquestionable. Although it is fair to assume that most humans beings are attracted to tasty food, no one desires tasty food. People desire whale blubber or risotto with truffles or a Big Mac; our desires may be based in widely shared human characteristics but they always manifest themselves in particular, culturally shaped, configurations.

Returning now to the differences between ritual and play: another manifestation of the "play is not serious" theme is the observation that in play we openly recognize the artificiality of the conventions establishing the play, while in ritual the conventions—even if they are understood to be conventions—are at the same time considered not as artifice but as truth, not as contingent but as eternal. Notice this is another way of denying legitimacy to the values associated with play; they can be dismissed, because after all they are associated with a social situation we all acknowledge to be unreal. However, the argument I am developing here is that as people become engaged in play activities, the artificiality of the play situation recedes from consciousness. So the participant may well arrive, via an alternative route, at the same place that the ritual participant does. He or she may have an experience in which some significant commitments for the real or the day-to-day world are generated out of the artificial world of play.

Bradd Shore (1996: 90) has said, in discussing this distinction, "In games, the structure of play is taken for granted, receding into the background." That is, play is often more improvisational and engaging than ritual is. The frameworks of ritual and play are very similar; speaking loosely, we begin with a formula, a cultural object that stipulates some rules for activity. However, in ritual there is typically considerable emphasis on carrying out those rules. In play, the emphasis is more on the activity; as the activity gets under way the rules recede and the focus is on following the trajectory they have set in motion.

This is important because the free and improvisational character of play is, broadly speaking, the means whereby the subterranean values of play are called to life. To say play is fun is to say that through it we often realize the possibility of expressing desires that often remain suppressed in the day-to-day world, or of letting go of the physical restrictions required in our everyday routines. Play is not associated with the rigid constraint of action precisely because so often it is about expression and reinforcement of commitments that dwell outside of explicit social rules and values.

In sum: ritual and play are two forms of meta-action, activities through which human beings take a step back from and do something to or about their own action. Meta-action, as I have noted, is a means whereby humans (and even nonhuman species) regulate their patterns of action and interaction. Many social scientific theories can be seen as arguments about how certain forms of meta-action are used in communities to create and sustain a social order. Think, for example, of the study of kinship terms or political rhetoric or economic systems; each is an indigenous form of meta-action used to shape alliances and conflict, to organize distribution of valued resources, and so on.

I have been arguing that the meta-action of play, though quite similar to ritual in a number of ways, has some unique features. In play, stipulations are used to create a special framework within which the player may improvise in ways that allow expression of possibilities that the complexities of day-to-day life do not allow. Play creates a microcosm that is in some way an ideal, a framework within which something enticing can be brought to life and experienced.

This linkage between ideals and meta-action is reminiscent of one of the most well-known and influential statements on the meta-action of ritual, the argument advanced by Emile Durkheim (1995, original 1912) in his *Elementary Forms of*

Religious Life. I summarize this argument briefly here because by doing so I can take several steps toward specifying how becoming caught up in the play of entertainment works to regulate social life in contemporary society. My stated goal in this chapter is to specify the nature of becoming caught up: What sort of "thing" is it, and what else is it like? The best way to do this is to answer another question at the same time, the question of what becoming caught up does. Turning to the question of meta-action and ideals takes us a long way toward answering this question.

Durkheim's Theory of Ritual

Durkheim (1995) proposed that a society's most important symbols—those that are shared in common and allow a group to function together—are valorized in collective rituals. It is through collective rituals that cultural ideals are established. For Durkheim, the mechanism of this valorization was collective effervescence, the excitement generated through the synchronized (we might say entrained) thought and activity of a group.

> It is by shouting the same cry, saying the same words, and performing the same action in regard to the same object that they [individuals] arrive at and experience agreement. . . . The individual minds can meet and commune only if they come outside themselves, but they do this only by means of movement. It is the homogeneity of these movements that makes the group aware of itself and that, in consequence, makes it be [Durkheim 1995: 232].

The intense collective emotions that constitute collective effervescence are generated in processes of physical synchronization and entrainment. In collective effervescence, people become "tightly focused on their common activity," and as that proceeds "they experience their shared emotion more intensely, as it comes to dominate their awareness" (Collins 2004: 48).

The ethnographic observations that support Durkheim's theory have been seriously questioned, but as a general account of the efficacy of ritual the theory remains compelling and powerful. It continues to guide empirical investigation into ritual and religion and to inspire further theoretical innovation. Furthermore, note that Durkheim finds in ritual some of the same mental processes that in the previous chapter I showed contributing to becoming caught up.

In Durkheim's account of ritual, it is emotional convergence that is harnessed to valorize the cultural ideals that make communication and solidarity possible in any society. This occurs because ritual makes these symbols sacred; it imparts to them a valence, and they seem to partake of something beyond the familiar world of the day-to-day. This valence is generated from the effervescence, the delirious social arousal created ultimately by entrainment and contagion. Of course, the ritual participants do not recognize this; they attribute the power they sense to the sacred objects prominently displayed at the ritual. Those sacred objects (in the specific cases he discusses, they are the *churingas* of the Australian aborigines) represent both the key social groups and the fundamental cognitive categories making communication possible.

One way of summarizing all of this is to say that Durkheim sought to explain how a surplus of social energy, fundamentally emotional in nature, could be generated and then associated with certain objects or ideas thereby coming to seem compelling in a way that transcends day-to-day experience. His explanation turns on feelings of self-transformation. The ritual participant feels that something extraordinary has changed her into a new being dwelling in a new environment:

> It is not difficult to image that a man in such a state of exaltation should no longer know himself. Feeling possessed and led on by some sort of external power that makes him think and act differently than he normally does, he naturally feels he is no longer himself. It seems to him that he has become a new being. . . . And because his companions feel transformed in the same way at the same moment, and express this feeling by their shouts, movements, and bearing, it is as if he was in reality transported into a special world entirely different from the one in which he ordinarily lives, a special world inhabited by exceptionally intense forces that invade and transform him [1995: 220].

My answer to the question, "What does getting caught up do?" is probably now clear. In contemporary society, our ideals are generated through processes very similar to those Durkheim describes. Although in the normal course of things there is little shouting and moving in unison, we do experience entrainment, emotional contagion, and ecstatic states. As I have noted, Randall Collins expanded Durkheim's theory by documenting how everyday social interaction may generate the kind of effervescence Durkheim locates in collective ritual. Such emotional energy is continuously created in closely coordinated social interaction, "in which participants develop a mutual focus of attention and become entrained in each other's bodily micro-rhythms and emotions" (2004: 47). The emotional excitement generated in this sort of interaction—which Collins at times describes as becoming caught up in interaction—infuses individuals and ideas and endures over time, producing effects such as stratification, solidarity, and commitment to ideals.

Now, I want to expand the same point even further by pointing out that similar processes of attention, entrainment, and self-transcendence may occur as people engage the culture of entertainment and are caught up in these activities. Again, the effect of these practices is valorization of important cultural ideals. The culture of entertainment in contemporary society is complex and serves many social purposes, but one of the things this culture accomplishes is to render certain ideas and practices powerful, perhaps even unquestionable. Entertainment does this by creating a subjective sense that these ideas and practices have the power to take over our consciousness and compromise our everyday capacity to direct our action. Experiences of becoming caught up in the play of entertainment are the moments when we experience this power. Note, then, that ultimately the explanation I propose here follows Durkheim in tracing the efficacy of certain powerful forms of meta-action to experiences of ecstasy.

Subjectivity

Durkheim had this to say about the distinctive feature of human consciousness: "The animal knows only one world: the world it perceives through experience, internal as well as external. Man alone has the capacity to conceive of the ideal and add it to the real" (1995: 424). Ultimately, Durkheim holds that these ideals are formed in collective rituals, experiences through which the excitement created by entrainment and emotional contagion comes to vitalize the most important social symbols and categories. This view, formulated more than a century ago, is not incompatible with simulation theory, which also locates human distinctiveness in a fundamentally social form of cognition. Simulation theory assigns paramount important to our ability to adopt a perspective on action that is other than our own.

Both of these theories point to the distinctiveness of human modes of perception and conception; they point out that human perception is conception.[6] As Durkheim and simulation theorists recognize, this form of conception entails self-consciousness. Our perception carries with it a duality of perspective that renders our understanding of much of the human activity around us automatic, and this in turn entails a certain grasp of our own action. If we inherently understand alternative perspectives on action, then action is not an unreflective stream of movement; we can always step back and see that it is action.

This in turn entails the capability to comment on or regulate action, at first in very basic ways and then, with growing symbolic capacity, in very complex ways. The point here is that humans—perhaps because of the way their minds react to the motor behavior of other humans—locate themselves within their activity so as to entail self-other differentiation and orientation around goals. We do not just do something. Rather, we do something with an often implicit but there-to-be-activated awareness that we are doing something and are separable from the doing. To activate this awareness is to become aware of engaging in meta-action. This means that to see meta-action is to understand that one's perspective is just a perspective; there could be another view of things.[7]

Here I have pointed out that engagement in entertainment activities is one form of meta-action, a category of the sort of meta-action we call play. I have argued that this engagement, though not ritual, has social effects in some ways similar to those described by Durkheim and Randall Collins (2004). Play experiences are designed to be an opportunity to express and experience possibilities of interest to us. As we become engaged in play, we may well become caught up in the activity and experience a form of ecstasy similar to what Durkheim and Collins find in intense social interaction. The effects of this ecstasy are also parallel to those outlined by Durkheim and Collins; the key features of the play frame are valorized, and felt to have the power to create self-transformation. In this way, cultural ideals are created through the processes of becoming caught up in entertainment activities.

Ritual and play are, at the most general level, forms of meta-action necessitated by a way of life based in culture. It is a tremendous advantage to be able to adapt one's behavior immediately so as to maximize the possibilities of success, and pass these adaptations between generations. But there is also a downside to this ability to stand back from action and manipulate behavior, interaction, and social organization.

To understand the fact that one's way of life can be manipulated is to understand that one's way of life is contingent. Thus it is not surprising to find that human beings have invented ways to, in a sense, overcome their knowledge of what they are up to. As Bradd Shore (1996: 115) puts it: "I suppose it is no coincidence that the playful primate, the master of games, is also the primate who had to face the great evolutionary paradox of having constantly to invent a life world while attributing to that world the character of both structural and moral necessity." Ritual and play, in different ways, are sophisticated meta-action technologies for transforming conventions into certainties. In this way we expand the boundaries of the taken-for-granted. We set up situations and then, aided by mental processes that are to some extent automatic, we experience the realities of these situations so deeply that we successfully forget we set them up.

This can occur because in play, as in ritual and intense social interaction, the participant may experience a sense of ecstasy. Such experiences may suggest (in the proper context) the operation of powers beyond the mundane experience of the day-to-day world. In ecstatic experience, the characteristic quality of human consciousness—that is, its self-consciousness—collapses (at least in part). With collapse comes compelling evidence of a dimension of existence lying beyond the imperfections and doubts of the day-to-day. This is surely one reason trance experiences are so often sought out; in trance, we can experience a level of certainty and unity that is elusive in everyday consciousness. More broadly, human beings throughout history seem to have hit upon powerful forms of meta-action that render the contingent outside of human control, render it transcendent. Becoming caught up is one version of such a mental technology.

However, there is a downside to these techniques as well. Losing track of the contingency of the conventions ordering our lives is comforting on an individual level and a powerful source of order on the social level. But in contemporary society the practices and ideas that are rendered powerful through the mechanisms we have discussed are often produced by powerful commercial interests investing considerable resources into enhancing their efficacy. This point has relevance throughout our social order: for economics, morals, our communal life, and politics.

Contemporary Western societies such as the United States place tremendous emphasis on the rights and freedoms of the individual. Our commitment to these rights and freedoms is a significant part of the moral foundation of our society. But in practice one of the most significant of our freedoms is the possibilities we have for pursuing entertainment, including entertaining consumption. The processes I have outlined in this book suggest this creates a paradox, for in entertainment activities we may have experiences that infuse certain ideas, practices, and substances with a remarkable power. Indeed, these ideals can seem to have a potency that overwhelms us. In the next chapters I increasingly emphasize this point in the context of the culture of entertainment: Many practices, ideas, and substances that are valorized through the play of entertainment come to have such power that they are seen as having the capacity to override the will of the person. In a way, we in contemporary society have designed such potent practices of valorization that we have begun to see ourselves as prone to being overwhelmed by the stimulating experiences we seek out. In extreme cases, we apply the concept of addiction, but the issues implicated here extend beyond addiction, and have to do with how we understand ourselves and our purpose.

7

Romance and the Romantic

AMONG THE CLEAREST EXAMPLES of romantic realism in our society is the romance story itself, whether embodied in a novel, a film, or some other genre. When we engage a romantic story we enter a world in which we glimpse the possibility of a perfect love relationship, we despair over the obstacles in the way of its realization, and in the end we experience a thrill as those obstacles are overcome. Romance holds particular interest for me in this book in that it is a good example of a cultural form seeming so close to our day-to-day world that at times we feel it spills over into mundane reality. This distinguishes the romance from many other varieties of romantic realism. Few of us will ever experience anything approaching being in charge of an intriguing murder investigation or leading a band of adventurers on a quest. But most of us will experience a romantic relationship that contains all the elements of the romantic story: unfulfilled longing, erotic attraction, obstacles to fulfillment, and moments (however brief) of perfect union.

In this sense, the romance offers a useful opportunity to examine one of the central ideas of this book, the notion that there are strong affinities between becoming caught up in play and becoming immersed in interaction with other people. After all, the word *romance* can be used to refer either to a kind of fiction or to one kind of intense interaction in the day-to-day world. What are the implications of this overlap?

Perhaps the most obvious question to ask about the overlap between romance and romantic fictions is whether engaging the fictions has any influence over our actual approach to romantic relationships. (If it does, just how does this happen?)

In this chapter I take romance as a case study and see if it is possible to be more specific about how playful engagement with romantic fictions and romantic relationships in the day-to-day world intersect.

Which Came First, the Stories or the Behavior?

Scholars have long debated the relationship between romantic fiction and romantic behavior. Take as an example a book review written in the *Nation* in 1887 by William James; James was reviewing a bombastic treatment of romance that saw it as a recent development in the evolution of the human species.[1] He was unconvinced that romantic love was a recent phenomenon: "So powerful and instinctive an emotion can never have been recently evolved" (1887: 237). Rather, said James, romance became the object of literary attention, especially during the Romantic period, but this does not mean that it had not existed before that time: "But as well might one say that chiaroscuro did not exist in nature till Rembrandt's time, as say that romantic love did not exist in human breasts till a couple of generations ago" (1887: 238).

The problem with this position is that no sooner has one distinguished between an emotion and how we describe and evaluate the emotion than one begins to understand the distinction will not stand. This is because how we conceptualize an emotion influences our experience of it. By a later paragraph in the review, James has moved in this direction and hence more or less contradicts his earlier position, admitting the delicate mutual interaction between stories and realities:

> No doubt the way in which we think about our emotions reacts on the emotions themselves, damping or inflaming them, as the case may be. Literature reacts on life; but just how much, it is hard to say. The love-drama is so complex, and contains so many acts, that it is likely that reflective interest in any one of them will alter the proportions of the play. But how much and for how long? is the question. . . . [1887: 238].

I cannot improve on William James, but the scholarship of the last century has clarified this picture to some extent. Most of those who have studied the matter would be more inclined to agree that romance and the romantic influence one another than that romantic love is an instinctive emotion. As Lawrence Stone (1988: 16) has written, "Historians and anthropologists are in general agreement that romantic love—this usually brief but very intensely felt and all-consuming attraction towards another person—is culturally conditioned, and therefore common only in certain societies at certain times. . . ."

How this cultural conditioning takes place is the matter of concern here. One cannot assume, for example, that romance is the primary phenomenon and romantic stories the secondary one. No one has ever demonstrated that romantic stories are, either logically or historically, preceded by romantic experiences, that once upon a time someone had a romantic experience and an observer subsequently told a story about the experience. From a historical point of view, the opposite seems closer to the truth. As Denis de Rougemont (1956: 75) argued in his classic study *Love in the Western World*, the basic conventions of the Western version of romantic love originally took shape in the poetry of the troubadours of Languedoc in the 12th century. (This 12th-century outbreak can itself be traced back to sources outside Europe, especially in the Middle East. See also Zeldin 1995: 76 ff.) We do not necessarily know that the poetry preceded the romantic antics in aristocratic courts that appeared around the same time, but we do know the practices and ideals of romance were in "flat contradiction" with prevailing norms in the society (de Rougemont 1956: 76–77).

To jump to a later period, it was only after the development of the mass market for romantic fictions that arranged marriages gave way to love matches in European society: "It was not . . . until the romantic movement and the rise of the novel, especially the pulp novel, in the nineteenth century, that society at large accepted a new idea—that it was normal and indeed praiseworthy for young men and women to fall passionately in love" (Stone 1988: 19). There is at least as much reason to believe, then, that our ideals and practices of romantic love are an imitation of our stories as that the stories are an imitation of our behavior. Of course, once people start behaving like the stories, art can imitate life, and vectors of causation become too complex to trace.

A glance at some recent sociological studies of romance and romantic fictions points us in another direction and adds further complexity to the picture. At least initially, these studies suggest that for contemporary men and women the familiar contours of romantic fictions are false and misleading, and no proper guide for behavior in intimate relationships. Perhaps it is premature to conclude that romance and the romantic are deeply intertwined.

Do People Really Buy into the Romantic Myth?

Sociologist Ann Swidler (2001), in a study of how Americans think about love and romance, reports findings that would seem directly relevant here. Her informants, for the most part white and middle-class, are typically explicit about rejecting the "happily ever after" love-story version of what makes a successful long-term relationship. They have enjoyed romantic novels and movies since they were young, but they have for the most part figured out that the notion of meeting a perfect partner and dwelling forever after in bliss is a myth. Rather, the adults Swidler spoke with often organize their thoughts about love around an approach she labels "prosaic realism": love requires hard work; love is often accompanied by other, more ambivalent, feelings; and so on.

Eva Illouz (1997) reports similar findings from another interview-based study of romance. She writes of her interview subjects that "most respondents do not believe in or subscribe to the idea of love at first sight" (1997: 158) and instead express the conviction that love involves hard work and compromise over a long period of time (1997: 160–161). She summarizes the point: "Realist models of love are systematically opposed to 'fantasy-based' ('Hollywood,' 'story-like') models" (1997: 161).

Right off the bat, then, my investigation into the relationship between romantic fictions and actual behavior seems to have run into an inconvenient fact. When sociologists actually ask people whether they accept the ideas and values expressed in romantic fictions, people respond with a very clear *no*. But perhaps Swidler's and Illouz's interview subjects were insufficiently steeped in romantic fictions. Perhaps the results would be different if we queried people who are avid consumers of such fictions. Conveniently, there is a study that directly targets such a group, Janice Radaway's well-known book (1984) on readers of romance novels, *Reading the Romance*.

Radaway's study remains one of a very few empirical discussions of how people use romantic fictions. One of her central questions is simply, "Why do women read these novels? What do they get out of them?" If there is a dominant theme in the responses of her subjects to this query, it is that romance novels are valued because they provide "escape" (1984: 87–88). What this word means, in the first place, is that these novels are effective in so stimulating readers' imaginations that they feel they are transported away from the physical and social environment in which they are reading and into the story itself.

In one sense, this harmonizes beautifully with my argument in this book. It is precisely the experience of becoming caught up that makes these novels so effective as escape literature. Becoming caught up in a fiction is what enables us to forget about our surroundings and focus our attention so closely on the world of play. But in another sense, the appeal to escape points in a direction that continues to be inconvenient for my argument. What Radaway's subjects state very clearly is that they read romances because of the pleasures reading them brings. They most certainly do not read romances *because* these fictions shape their real-world romantic behavior.

Of course, the readers may read for pleasure but find that the experience also influences them in ways they had not foreseen or intended. To the extent there is evidence for this in Radaway's study, the results seem to amount to more bad news for my thesis. Radaway's interview subjects do emphatically attest that women who read romances are changed, although the change does not entail behaving more romantically. It consists instead in a greater degree of individualism and self-assertion in relationships. That is, a woman who reads romance novels is likely to begin to assert her own needs, as the heroines of the novels so often do (1984: 101 ff).

Happily, we are not playing baseball, because this is my third strike. The authors of these three respected studies, who together have interviewed more than 150 people about romance and romantic fictions, unambiguously report that these interview subjects draw an explicit and clear line between fictional romances and behavior in real romantic relationships. I am not the only one who must regard this as bad news; the notion that those who engage romantic fictions are more likely to conduct their actual relationships in accord with the values of those fictions is widespread among intellectuals and the public in general.[2] As Illouz (1997) points out, in recent decades this notion became something of a pet topic for postmodern theorists who saw in it the possibility of supporting their contention that under current social conditions fictional models have taken precedence over daily reality.

But we have just learned that in fact people are not at all confused about the relative status of romantic fiction and romantic reality. What is remarkable about contemporary culture is in fact that we can be so awash in compelling romantic realist fictions and retain such a firm fix on the distinction between the day-to-day and the worlds in which we play.

However, this does not necessarily imply that engaging romantic fictions has no effect on people's thinking and behavior. In the first place, note the finding that people maintain a bright line between romantic fiction and their actual behavior and beliefs about romantic behavior; this is utterly consistent with what I reported earlier about role players. They are not confused whatsoever about the fictional and imaginary nature of their game, in spite of the fact that they consistently and subtly orient to the game on physical, emotional, and linguistic levels. This in turn is consistent with research on children's imaginative play; even preschool children typically maintain a firm distinction between reality and make-believe (Harris 2000: 65).

At the same time, whether we are talking about role players, children's imaginative play, or adults engaging fictions, there is also consistent evidence showing that play may influence emotions and action beyond the play situation. Some of this evidence has been presented in earlier chapters. This is what can account for people maintaining a clear distinction between the sorts of things that happen in romantic fictions and the course of their actual romantic relationships yet at the same time letting those fictions influence their thinking and behavior regarding romance in the day-to-day world.

Thus if we return to our three studies of people's ideas about romance, we discover that people can explicitly reject the "movie image" of perfect love while at the same time continue to hold it up as an ideal. For example, Swidler found that those who explicitly rejected romantic idealism also returned to it again and again as they talked about their relationships: "The same interviewees who reject the 'movie image' of love use it repeatedly in their own thinking" (Swidler 2001: 111).[3] Illouz also found that the same respondents who dismiss an exemplary romantic story as a myth regard it as more interesting and compelling than more realistic stories of love. Indeed, they regard a "love at first sight" story as expressive of "genuine romantic sentiment" (1997: 164). Furthermore, Illouz's interview subjects consistently cited examples of the movie image of love when asked about the most memorable moments from their own romantic lives.

Thus in both of these books, the finding that people explicitly reject the movie image of romance does not by any means imply this image has no effect on them. This is the case in Radaway's study as well. Her subjects say that reading romances affirms their hope and faith in romantic perfection. The world of the romance is one in which a hero makes an eternal and unquestioning commitment to the heroine:

> It seems highly probable that in repetitively reading and writing romances, these women are participating in a collectively elaborated female fantasy that unfailingly ends at the precise moment when the heroine is gathered into the arms of the hero who declares his intention to protect her forever because of his desperate love and need for her [1984: 97].

The readers say that although they know this sort of commitment to be atypical in the day-to-day world, they also know it is not impossible (1984: 100). In short, then, the perfect romance of the novels they read does indeed shape and sustain their faith in the idea of pure romance.

So all three studies find that people recognize formulaic romantic stories as unrealistic and naïve while continuing to seek, in the day-to-day world, the values such stories express. Why should this be? Swidler's explanation—and I think it is valid—is that for most people it is obvious that the myth of romance (you will meet the right person, fall madly in love, and then live forever after in bliss) is utterly false. However, there is an enormously powerful institution in our society—called marriage—that is based on the notion of two people falling in love, making a commitment, and then spending the rest of their lives together. Thus people need to retain the mythical formulation in order to make sense of their own behavior in getting married and staying married.

I would add something to this, however. Swidler's argument explains why the persistence of the mythical notion of romance is adaptive in a society where marriage remains normative, but it does not really explain where people's deep commitment to this necessary idea comes from. It is important to pause here and reflect on a point easily lost track of: our commitment to romantic love is an element of faith so profound it is difficult to imagine a parallel. If you doubt this, think for a moment. We attribute to romantic love the power to transform our lives, and finding the fulfillment this love is expected to bring is for many the very purpose of life. Both our fictions and our lives support the view that we hold love to be, as Denis de Rougemont (1956: 24) says, "stronger and more real than happiness, society, or morality." In what other area of life do we remain firmly committed to an idea that our experience consistently argues against? In fact, the finding that people so frequently deny their faith in the ideal of romantic love only makes this mystery more striking. *Where* can our faith in romantic love dwell if we explicitly deny that we believe in the idea?

In part the answer is that our faith in ideal romance is a matter of feelings; we all recognize we can be drawn in different directions by (as we put it) the mind and the heart. But to say so is only a partial answer to the question at hand, because it assumes an overly clear distinction between thought and emotion. Where is the emotion that doesn't include some sort of thought? Furthermore, in point of fact, much of our faith in romance is stored in complex thoughts such as fantasies. A better answer to the question of how we retain our faith in romantic love is that although most of us recognize the romantic ideal does not describe a realistic romantic relationship in the day-to-day world, it is not irrelevant either. The label says it all: the romantic ideal describes an *ideal* romantic relationship.

Now we have returned to more or less where we left off at the close of the previous chapter, where I argued that becoming caught up in entertainment is a means by which certain of our ideals are created and sustained. In fact romance is just the sort of ideal that would be sustained through playful activities, for as its origins and continuing record make clear, romance is not a dependable pillar of the status quo. Rather, romance is one of our rogue values, often working in practice to disrupt marriages and other stolid institutions. Romance is a passion difficult to sustain in an enduring relationship, and a force that may well drive individuals to actions so disruptive of the routines of the day-to-day that they verge on madness. Thus if my thesis has any merit, this is precisely the sort of ideal that would be created and reinforced in experiences of becoming caught up. Can we find any evidence of this?

Falling in Love, and Stories About It

To review: romance offers an opportunity to investigate whether becoming caught up in romantic realist fictions has any repercussions for activity in the day-to-day world. Empirical studies in this realm support a paradoxical conclusion: people deny that the conventions of romantic fictions provide useful guidelines for their intimate relationships, but they nevertheless judge and evaluate intimate relationships in terms of these conventions. That is, the conventions of the prototypical story of romance continue to be held as ideals even though people recognize these ideals are not likely to describe on-the-ground intimate relationships.

Durkheim argued that ideals are generated in collective rituals through processes of what he called collective effervescence. I have suggested that what he describes entails processes very similar to the cognitive and emotional processes constituting becoming caught up: attention shifts away from the perspective of the day-to-day world, and entrainment and emotional contagion develop, perhaps issuing in deepening absorption. The question, then, is whether these processes can be observed in the play of romantic relationships, whether fictional or real.

The experience of actually entering a romantic relationship is well described in literature and in social science research, and on top of that many readers are familiar with this process from their own personal histories. I will make no attempt to paint a nuanced picture of the experience here; I am more interested in the mythic version, our prototypical narrative of romantic love. From a subjective point of view, the basis of romantic love is the utter perfection and desirability of the object of one's love; let us follow along with everyone else and call her or him "the Other." The lover is unable to drive the Other from his mind: "The lover is lost in contemplation of the Other, and obsessed with the minute shifts, the ups and downs, of their relationship; love intrudes upon every moment of waking life (and many of sleep)" (Person 1989: 13).

The lovers experience or at least strive for an unprecedented intimacy. To quote the graceful psychoanalyst Ethel Person again (1989: 14): "It is precisely the lovers' leap out of objectivity and into subjectivity that signals the liberation of love. If it is true that the greatest breach in nature is between two minds (as William James suggested), then we must acknowledge the magnitude of the emotion that allows us to bridge such a chasm." This stepping outside of one's own perspective is, of course, the attentional shift described repeatedly in these pages as the first step toward becoming caught up. It is also in itself a powerful component of the sense that one is a participant in something beyond one's individual boundaries and will.

This shift in attention is also a familiar aspect of engaging romantic fictions. Radaway (1984: 93) summarizes the experiences of romance readers this way:

> Romance reading . . . so engages their [the regular readers who were her interview subjects] attention that it enables them to deny their physical presence in an environment associated with responsibilities that are acutely felt. . . . At the same time, by carefully choosing stories that make them feel particularly happy, they escape figuratively into a fairy tale where a heroine's similar needs are adequately met.

As happens with role-playing games, readers adopt a perspective within the book and then deepen their experience of this perspective through extended imitation. For example, they are very likely to experience emotional reactions to her (the heroine's) situation.[4]

This is also likely to be the case with romantic fictions presented through visual media such as movies or television. In this case, it is easier to show that entrainment and affective mimicry may help to generate the participants' feelings. Such media can present images laden with basic human emotional and physiological information. As was mentioned in Chapter Five, it has been shown that spectators viewing video images of human faces often reproduce the facial expressions they observe. Now consider the imagery in a dramatic television production such as a soap opera. As many have commented, close-up shots of human faces are one of the most obvious characteristics of the genre. These close-ups provide detailed information and cues that have repeatedly been shown to provoke almost automatic engagement and mimicry, and thus it is not difficult to see how emotion is generated in cases of this sort.

Entrainment and emotional contagion are also central to actual romantic interaction. Romantic relationships usually entail some sort of physical dimension. Take as an example a particularly strong form of physical interaction: Randall Collins discusses sex as an interaction ritual and points out that the basic components we have been talking about are all fully present in sexual activity. There is the development of a mutual focus of attention ("the awareness of contact with each other's body"; 2004: 231), rhythmic entrainment, and generation of emotional energy. In sum, the passion of a romantic relationship can be multiplied through sexual interaction, and the same sorts of processes of entrainment and mimicry already present in the chaste interaction can be intensified.

Of course, the generation of emotion that seems to come from beyond the boundaries of the self is also obvious in romantic interaction, where we call this version of becoming caught up falling in love. The experience is often described in such terms: "The lover feels caught up in a great emotion, literally swept away, and he rides the crest of that wave of emotion with a feeling of exultation as long as there is either hope of reciprocity, or a clear signal of love from the beloved" (Person 1989: 38). The lover feels powerless in the face of love, which so overwhelms him that he feels all of his experience has been transformed. It is this experience of being overwhelmed, constructed from the various processes we have discussed, that ultimately lends credence to the feeling and thought that romantic love is such a potent force.

In sum, a person might have an experience of self-transformation in either a romantic experience or playing with a fictional account of a romantic experience. The mechanisms of doing so are similar in the two cases, reflecting the workings of mental and physical processes very similar to those I have claimed characterize both intense interactions and play. The experience of self-transformation that can be created either in a romance or in a story about a romance may well convince the person who undergoes it of the power of romantic love to transport one into a realm beyond the day-to-day. Thus it seems as if the question with which I began is not the correct one; the question is not really one of how immersion in fictions influences action in the day-to-day world. The question instead has to do with how the day-to-day world and that of romantic realism intertwine. How are they (as Clifford Geertz 1973: 90 once said in a somewhat different context) each sustained "with the borrowed authority of the other"?

On the Boundaries Between Fiction and Reality

The results of this inquiry into romance and the romantic remind us that the conventional distinction between the fictional and the real as its opposite is considerably overdrawn. Our fictions are full of reality and our realities are full of fiction. As was illustrated in the study of role-playing games, a fiction may be thoroughly interpenetrated by realities. One occupies a fictional perspective, but then once one has done so one quickly converts it to a new reality. Likewise, our realities are less real than we imagine.

Romance, for example, can with considerable plausibility be considered a game. Romance is a form of spontaneous pretend play based on the stipulation that the other is the perfect match and that one's union with the person will be blissful perfection. Kendall Walton (1990) says one could, while walking in the woods, pretend that tree stumps are bears, and the distribution of stumps in the world then prompts one's imaginings in particular directions. A romantic relationship is not so different from this. The other, like a stump, prompts one's imaginings in certain ways, and not in others. The other becomes a prop in the game, a game played to stimulate pleasurable fantasies and feelings such as longing and erotic tension.

More broadly, there is a playful element to many of our romantic interactions. Much of Goffman's work can be seen as an argument for the close kinship between those interactional situations we take to be fictional (such as theater) and those we take to be real. It is sometimes said that Goffman uses the stage as a metaphor for things like self-presentation and conversation, but this is insufficient to an understanding of what he was up to. The world of the stage and that of the day-to-day are not qualitatively different. Goffman's 1986 book *Frame Analysis,* for example, devotes entire chapters to explaining how theatrical orientations interpenetrate our day-to-day action in the world.

Once one begins to think about this, then, it is no surprise that the lines between romance and the romantic begin to blur. Nor is it particularly difficult to understand that essentially the same feelings can be generated in either genre. Radaway speaks directly to the question of what readers of romance novels feel, suggesting that their reactions are very similar to what one might experience in an actual intimate relationship:

> Although the readers are themselves reluctant to admit this on a conscious level, romance reading seems to be valued primarily because it provides an occasion for them to experience good feelings. Those feelings appear to be remarkably close to the erotic anticipation, excitement, and contentment prompted when any individual is the object of another's total attention. In effect, romance reading provides a vicarious experience of emotional nurturance *and* erotic anticipation and excitement [1984: 105].

We can now begin to grasp the potency of the cultural technology that valorizes romantic love. The real point here is not that reading stories might have an influence on how people act in the day-to-day world. Rather, it is this: throughout human history societies have played on the fact that human beings are capable of experiences of ecstasy to endorse particular ideas and practices. All that is needed is activities to produce feelings of transcendence and an ideological framework to explain the nature and genesis of these feelings.

Romance is a particularly fruitful opportunity for this sort of arrangement, because both the ideological framework (stories of love) and the activity (falling in love) can generate strong feelings of transcendence. After all, we have noticed that both playful immersion in fictions and interaction can produce such feelings. When one factors in the possibility that the fictions may be interactive, and the interactions may be playful and informed by strong cultural conventions regarding romance, one begins to understand that really what we have here is a circle. In romantic stories, we learn the conventions of romance, and we may well have the same sort of feelings and experience we have in a romantic interaction. In a real-world romance, we bring the conventions of romance into an emotionally and physically charged social interaction and discover the power of those conventions. Taken together, these experiences reinforce the notion of the power of love to overwhelm us.

Regardless of the medium, even though I have balked at classifying engaging a romantic fiction as a ritual, the mechanisms whereby such engagement influences actual behavior is remarkably similar to the process Durkheim describes. A player becomes caught up in a fiction that shares significant features with her day-to-day world. As with Durkheim's ritual participant, she becomes convinced that both she herself and her situation have been transformed. Again, in a direct parallel to Durkheim's account, she attributes this transformation to the power of the most prominent aspect of the context, something she knows to be a tangible part of the real world: romantic love itself.

Control and Release

"A culture," wrote Ruth Benedict (1934: 46) in *Patterns of Culture*, "is a more or less consistent pattern of thought and action." In contemporary anthropology, the stress is definitely on the "less." Ethnographers of Benedict's era, and the theorists who built on their work, probably overemphasized the unity and cohesion of cultural systems. It turns out—and this should have been anticipated—that most cultures are no tidier than our own; groups and individuals compete for the power to define reality, knowledge is unevenly diffused throughout the society, things change.

Among the significant sources of inconsistency in culture—and for some reason this has not been a prominent theme in recent writing on culture—is the fact that different, sometimes contradictory, things need to get done. Love must be made and war waged, people must work and enjoy themselves, and so on. Thus societies usually require diverse and even contradictory sorts of behavior from their members. Your role as son may require emotional and cognitive resources different from those of your role as husband; in fact, throughout the day and throughout the life course, consistency is more likely the exception than the rule.

This situation has a psychological dimension, in that the conflicting tasks required by life must be inscribed in people as motives. The result of this is that people may, as Max Weber wrote, "have within themselves a series of motives, each of which, if separately and consistently followed through, would have stood in the way of the others or run against them head-on" (Gerth and Mills 1946: 291). Oftentimes, however, these contradictory imperatives are not perceived as such. In the first place, human beings are flexible, and thus (for example) the need to adopt a deferential demeanor in one context and an air of assertive authority in another may not be experienced as particularly demanding.

There are other time-honored techniques for minimizing the psychological effects of contradictory social demands. Sometimes motivations and social orientations are separated by time or place or social context, so that no directly contradictory demands are actually felt. Or there may be a sort of division of labor assigning some social work, with its associated values and motives, to particular groups, certain stages of the life course, and so on.[5] This chapter offers an example of another possible approach to the problem of conflicting motives, and indeed in a sense this approach has been illustrated throughout this book. This is the possibility of sustaining two somewhat contradictory cultural realms, each with its own motives, logic, and means of valorization. In our society these realms can be roughly indexed by oppositions: work versus play, articulable principle versus hidden desire, discipline versus leisure, control versus release. What Radaway, Illouz, and Swidler found is a compelling example of this general principle. They all conclude, in one way or another, that our notions of how to proceed in intimate relationships are organized in two rather contradictory systems of ideas and practices. Part of becoming an adult in our society is to leave fairy tales behind and acknowledge the limitations and difficulties of day-to-day life, and nowhere is this more important than in the realm of intimate relations. Most of us would say that a woman who wants a long-term romantic partnership but is unwilling to settle for anything less than a knight in shining armor needs to grow up. Yet at the same time most of us never abandon our faith that the kind of acceptance and passion and nurturance we see in romantic fictions is an actual possibility. Thus on the one hand we have the realm of our rational and practical principles, and on the other there is the realm of feeling and desire, emerging in our behavior and our fantasies but explicitly denied in our talk.

More broadly, the point is once again that getting caught up in fictions is often (among other things) a means for encoding motives at odds with certain of our articulate principles. In contemporary society, the efflorescence of opportunities for entering into narratives in this way can be traced above all to the contradictory demands placed on us in the economic realm as we are required to fill the roles of producers and consumers. That is, those of us who dwell in late modern society are (as many have observed) subject to two very powerful social imperatives that are often in direct contradiction, those of consumption and production. One's role as economic producer, something close to the core of personal identity in many parts of our society, likely demands self-control, deferral of gratification, and obedience. These are very different personal qualifications from those required in one's role as consumer, a role understood to bring us close to the very purpose of our existence: to enjoy life, to find pleasure. Here, one should ideally display impulsivity, self-indulgence, and hedonism.[6]

Anthropologist Robert Crawford (1984) described the contradiction between producer and consumer ethics in a classic article titled "A Cultural Account of Health: Control, Release, and the Social Body." Every society, he points out, "organizes releases from its normal renunciations" (1984: 90), often in the form of collective activities such as celebrations, holidays, and games. Such occasions are, among other things, an opportunity for release of tension generated by the renunciation demanded in everyday life. "In contemporary American culture," he writes, "release is . . . the indispensable creed of . . . [the] economic system" (1984: 90). Contemporary society has hit upon the possibility of selling opportunities for release, creating the somewhat perverse situation of a spiral between the demands of the two realms: the harder I work, the more tension I create, the more I need leisure, the harder I must work in order to obtain it, and so on.

Crawford labels the conflicting imperatives of this system as "control" and "release," and he points out that these fundamental directives are literally embodied:

> Americans find themselves astride two opposing mandates, one calling for self-control, the other for release. Both mandates appear as specific historical forms.

Both mandates are internalized in varying degrees and are variously experienced depending on person and context. And both are central to our ideas of personal well-being [1984: 94].

This embodied cultural contradiction is evidenced in many ways. One of the most striking (mentioned by Crawford and developed more fully in Nichter 2000) is dieting, a cultural practice that furnishes clear evidence of the inability to resolve the tension between the desires to consume and control consumption.

Without motivated producers and frenetic consumers, the economic growth that sustains our way of life would stagnate. Thus, rather than resolve this contradiction our culture offers means to deal with the tensions it generates. Consider, for example, the marking of time into realms of control and consumption: the hours of work (punctuated by breaks for consumption of food or stimulants such as tobacco or caffeine), the hours of leisure, the cycle of holidays tied to consumption, and so on.[7] There are also, of course, well-established structures within which higher consumption is associated with particular stages in the life cycle or with particular gender roles (Campbell 1987).

Ephemeral experiences of getting caught up in fictions—romantic ones, for example—are among the most important social mechanisms whereby the motives of release are generated and sustained. Such experiences are, almost by definition, moments of isolation from the broader context. When we say someone is caught up in a fiction, we mean that the person has to some degree ceased to attend to her surroundings. Thus such experiences may serve as a cultural technology for creating and sustaining networks of motives that dwell, metaphorically speaking, below the level of full consciousness and clear articulation.

That is, because experiences of getting caught up are insulated, set off from the day-to-day world, they have an experiential plausibility that influences us quite separately from our rational understanding and evaluation of the images involved. I may understand perfectly well that the actress I spot in the airport is a human being just like me, but if I was once deeply absorbed in her performance as a ravishing romantic heroine, I may very well react to her as a person with an almost otherworldly allure. Likewise I may understand that no car will change the contours of my life, but if a TV ad showing a man driving through the mountains has briefly provoked a reverie of escape and freedom, an association may have been created at an inarticulate level.

Although I have used the term *valorization* to refer to the process whereby certain ideas about pleasure and consumption are reinforced, the term is inaccurate in one sense. In fact, typically we do not recognize the values of leisure as values; they are more likely to be understood as desires. Desires are associated with dark forces we neither completely understand nor control; they are manifestations of the body, often at odds with the mind and the will. The power of our desires may surprise us, and when we are guided by them we may find ourselves behaving in ways we do not completely understand.

Classic social science has focused more on the role of values in undergirding the social order, while more recently attention has been given to the role of desire. The vast complexity of the social system is held in place not only by what we admire and value but also by what we want and long for. My argument has been that as people engage various forms of entertainment, emotions are harnessed to strengthen key ideas in our high-consumption society. But this is less a matter of setting up consensual values than of forging the conviction that certain forces are powerful and inexorable; they are desirable.

The argument I have presented here suggests that as a person becomes caught up, he or she undergoes an experience of self-transformation and attributes this experience to the power of the central symbols he or she has engaged. Such symbols may be forms of amusement such as games or television; they may be ideas such as romance, or they may be substances such as food or drugs. It is not only that these symbols come to be understood as powerful. Because of the way this power is manifested in subjective experience, as a sense of not being entirely under the control of the day-to-day self, it is also felt as something mysterious and inexorable.

Thus it is not only that our cultural dynamics create a situation in which we are likely to both experience romantic feelings and understand them as powerful. These powerful feelings are also mysterious, for they manifest themselves in ways not seeming to fit our ordinary language and experience. This, after all, is a good part of what makes these feelings so appealing. In this way, a value is constructed that is not a value. It is subterranean and potentially disruptive; it is inexorable and beyond our capacity for control. It is, again, often understood not as a value but rather as a desire. It is no coincidence that in the archetypal romantic legends such as Tristan and Isolde love is generated by a magic potion. Love is not a rational process; it is something that controls us.

The combination of a potent force, shaped through experiences of transcendence, and the notion that this force is in conflict with a society's day-to-day values, sets up a particular sort of situation with regard to our capacity to direct our own action. This means if I understand that I am controlled by some force I do not fully understand, and it causes me to do things that from a social perspective are not entirely in my own interest, then a paradox is created. We are confronted with a realm of behavior in which people do things they do not seem to choose, because in our understanding they are at times making self-destructive choices. Yet they seem to be unable to do anything else; they seem overwhelmed by the power of some practice or substance.

In contemporary North American society, this situation is often understood in terms of the concept of addiction. Addiction is important for my argument here, not so much in terms of actual addictive processes but rather as an idea. One could say that the ideology of addiction is important for the argument of this book, in that this ideology is in part a means of understanding the contradictions brought about by the cultural processes we have been examining. These contradictions center on the idea of freedom; we regard our freedom as the very basis of our quest for self-realization, but our self-realization often lands us in a state of profound desire that seems to compromise our freedom. In the next chapter I turn to exploring this matter.

8

Play and Agency in Legal Drug Use

IF WE ARE LIKE MOST of those whom sociologists have talked to, we do not take the conventions of romance very seriously as a pragmatic guide to our intimate relationships. However, we treasure the romantic when it occurs in these relationships, and such moments work to vitalize our ties to those we love. The implication is that we make judgments about our experience based on its conformity to the formulaic conventions of romance. It is not only that we make *judgments* about our experience in this way; probably even more significant is the fact that we expect our intimate relationships to *feel* like becoming caught up in romantic fictions. In this way, our experiences of becoming caught up create certain expectations for the level of stimulation in our lives.

Romance, of course, is not the only ideal that affects us in this way. More generally, we aspire to having our experience measure up to the standards of entertainment; we hope that our lives can be as engaging and stimulating as becoming caught up. If our minimal requirements for entertainment embedded in the day-to-day world are not met, we are likely to diagnose our situation—particularly when we are young—as boring. I turn to the topic of boredom in the next chapter. In this chapter I focus on how we avoid boredom and pursue stimulation through consumption. In looking at this topic, we also find the same unfortunate tendency that appeared as we closed our study of romance: our techniques of stimulating ourselves sometimes turn out to work too well, and we begin to develop the notion that our stimulating experiences can overwhelm us and force us to act in ways we do not fully choose.

The example I study in this chapter is consumption of the legal drugs tobacco and alcohol, but of course these are not the only things one can consume to enhance experience. Other options include food, music, electronics . . . the list could go on. There is no reason to suppose that broader practices of recreational consumption are the same as the routines of drug self-administration I describe here, but the interpretations I offer may be a useful starting point in augmenting our thinking about other sorts of consumption.[1]

The material I present here is a qualitative study of early-phase tobacco users that I carried out in conjunction with two colleagues, Mark Nichter and Mimi Nichter. The study was based on repeated interviews, over about a year, with first-year college students who were also low-level smokers. In this part of the study, 55 students on two campuses were interviewed between one and five times (a few students dropped out of the study after the first interview) during the academic year. The intent of these interviews was to place tobacco use in the context of the student's broader experience, and so over hours of interviewing we touched on a range of subjects: academics, social life and relationships, family and religious background, and so on.

Although it may initially seem odd to consider early smoking and drinking as forms of play, it should be kept in mind that in contemporary North American society people very often begin using intoxicating drugs for recreational purposes.[2] This does not mean that all early-stage routines of drug self-administration are playful, but the material I describe here suggests that some are. When I say routines of drug use may take the form of play, I mean that the actual practices of ingesting the drug and experiencing its effects are embedded in broader routines that are themselves playful. Generally speaking, if a drug is taken for the primary purpose of entertainment or stimulation, and if the practices associated with its ingestion tend to create a social sphere outside the day-to-day world, then this activity clearly meets one of Huizinga's central criteria for being play: it creates— and proceeds within—boundaries separated from the everyday world. That such routines are also governed by rules and are absorbing (these are Huizinga's other criteria) will be demonstrated as we proceed.

To take an example of the sort of play I examine here, a beginning smoker might light up a cigarette at a party to play at being a sophisticated socialite. (This activity would be classified as mimetic play in Caillois's classification.) She might become engaged in an engrossing conversation with a group of fellow smokers with whom she was not previously acquainted. Here the cigarette is an important prop or component of a broader playful context (see Stromberg et al. 2007). In early-stage alcohol consumption routines, the case is especially clear. On college campuses consumption of alcohol is often explicitly structured as play, in the form of drinking games. As noted in a recent review (Borsari, 2004: 30), such games "have emerged as a considerable influence on college alcohol use in the past 20 years." Borsari goes on to note that several studies have found a high rate (between 47 and 62 percent) of students reporting participation in drinking games in the past month.

More broadly, to the extent that any drug use is undertaken in order to produce alterations in consciousness, it certainly fits under Caillois's rubric of ilinx (play undertaken to induce vertigo). What I ask the reader to consider is that even though calling any part of legal drug use play probably seems somewhat incongruous, overcoming this hesitancy may allow us to use some of the insights from earlier chapters to enhance our understanding of legal drug use, and of recreational consumption more generally.

The enhanced understanding I offer is along these lines: apart from any consideration of the physiological effects of drugs, or the actual utility of other sorts of consumables, people can have reactions to practices associated with acquisition and use of these consumables. More specifically, I argue here that people can become caught up in the play of these practices. This is one reason they come to regard consumables as potentially powerful sources of transformation, and why in some cases people develop ideas about addiction to substances or practices. The early-phase practices of self-administration of alcohol and tobacco that we learned about in our study are good examples of this.

But Isn't It All About the Chemicals?

To make this argument, I must first address an obvious point: probably most people understand both the behavioral effects of drugs and the dependency they can foster as simply the result of certain chemicals acting on the body. In this view, the arbitrary conventions that govern the use of a drug in a particular culture have nothing to do with the drug's effects. However, it is not so. A venerable finding of the anthropology of drug use is that the same drug may have effects varying with the cultural context. In some cultures, alcohol is thought to render a person passive, but in others the result is hungering for violent confrontation (MacAndrew and Edgerton, 1969: 17). The Pacific drug kava is believed in some areas to render the user incapable of motion, while in other areas it is consumed in preparation for particularly demanding manual labor (Knauft, 1987: 92–93).

The most prudent conclusion in light of such observations is that drugs produce physiological arousal that is diffuse and may be interpreted in many ways.[3] This point does not reflect the carping of anthropologists operating on the margins of mainstream research on alcohol and drugs; it is a commonplace in the mainstream. In a commentary published recently in the journal *Experimental and Clinical Psycho-*

pharmacology, Rudy E. Vuchinich (2002: 99) writes, "All this basic and applied research [in behavioral pharmacology and psychological substance abuse research and treatment] obviously indicates that the effects of drugs . . . depend critically on the behavioral-environmental context of drug use." The effects of drugs emerge out of an interactive system comprising a number of components: setting, expectations, emotions, physiological responses to the chemical, and routines of drug self-administration. (The latter are the aspect of the "behavioral-environmental context" I will look at here.)

No wonder, then, that drug use is often associated with rituals and other relatively invariant routines that in effect cue appropriate responses and interpretations (Knauft, 1987). These conventions are a necessary part of the drug-consuming experience, because they offer a framework for channeling arousal into something more particular and interpretable. No wonder too that for many users of drugs (including those using powerful substances such as heroin) situational cues for use—in the absence of the substance itself—can partially replicate the effects of the drug (DiClemente, 2003: 15). Such issues as the conventions for taking drugs and the expectations regarding their effects, then, can strongly influence both the effects of the drugs and one's understanding of their long-term properties.

Just as the context of drug use has repeatedly been shown to shape how the effects of drugs are experienced, context has also been established as an important factor in the growth of dependency. I discuss dependency more fully below, albeit briefly. The most important points can be simply made: chemicals (such as opiates) can create significant long-term physiological effects such as tolerance and withdrawal, but in spite of oft-repeated claims in popular and even some scientific literature, most experienced researchers agree that no chemical is inherently addictive. That is to say, no chemical will reliably produce addictive behavior among all, or even almost all, users. Furthermore, in spite of widely publicized research linking drug use to certain genetic configurations, genes alone will never completely explain dependency. A simple example of this is that if a person is genetically prone to alcohol abuse yet adheres to strict religious beliefs prohibiting use of alcohol, this person will not become addicted to alcohol.

In practice, dependency develops out of interaction among the characteristics of the nervous system, the characteristics of chemicals, and environmental factors. Another simple point in this regard: many developmental processes (in humans and other animals) entail complex interactions over time between a genetic program and aspects of the environment. Developmental results depend on the environment, even in basic processes such as, say, limb development in the human embryo (Tomasello 1999: 50). Complex phenomena such as addiction will never be reduced to genetic predispositions or chemical properties alone, in spite of the fact that the interaction between chemicals and the nervous system is an extraordinarily important aspect of the development of dependency.

Because cultural expectations and practices contribute to this dependency as well, it is important to understand as much as possible about this topic. Really, it is not addiction per se that is the target of my inquiry here. Rather, I want to look at the ideology of addiction. For reasons I discuss, in our culture prototypical addictions such as alcoholism have emerged as an extraordinarily fruitful metaphor for understanding why people act the way they do. As this metaphor spreads, it comes to shape addictive behavior. That is, the behavior of North American alcoholics reflects, in part, ideas about addiction that were fostered in reflections on alcohol dependency but that subsequently developed a life of their own. My goal here is to study, and hopefully better understand, the role of play and becoming caught up in shaping the ideology of addiction. It is in this spirit that I now turn to a description of the conventions of play we found among young men and women who were in the early stages of learning to use legal drugs.

Play in the Early Phases of Alcohol Use

The two drugs that have the most important health and behavioral consequences in contemporary Western societies are alcohol and tobacco. As I have noted, cigarette smoking sometimes takes the form of play, perhaps especially among less experienced smokers. But this is even more obviously the case with those who are beginning to establish patterns of alcohol use, because as noted earlier this use often takes the form of explicit games.

The rules of the games vary widely. All are sets of conventions that order activity and create a temporary frame for activity outside the realm of everyday routines and responsibilities. Of course, the activity that the games order most noticeably is drinking; inevitably the point of these games is to tie compulsory consumption of alcohol to some other ongoing activity (such as a test of competence, a card game, or simply the passage of time). Thus, in terms of Caillois's classification, drinking games combine agon or alea with ilinx.

The simple and profound point about drinking games is that they structure use of an intoxicant through a game process beyond the control of the individual participant. It is the rules of the game, not the decisions of the drinker, that determine the pace and level of consumption. As one becomes emotionally engaged in the competition of the game, one's drinking is patterned by its trajectory. It may seem incredible to suggest that the familiar and simple act of entering a game could sufficiently transform an agent such that she makes choices she knows to be irresponsible. Yet this is precisely what happens. Consider this description, taken from the testimony of a college freshman (pseudonym Megan) interviewed in the tobacco study described here:

> *Megan:* I still drink quite a lot [laughs], to be honest [laughs[I got drunk last night. Um, cause like there's a couple who didn't have finals, so I went over to the X house and there were like, six of us playing a drinking game. Which was fun, I mean, you know, we're just like, good friends, and we're just like, hanging out.
>
> *Interviewer:* What game?
>
> *Megan:* We played, like, Connections
>
> *Interviewer:* How do you play that?
>
> *Megan:* That game is DANGEROUS. It was my suggestion, and I don't know why I suggested it, I'm an idiot. What you do is, you just deal out a deck of cards to people, and they flip over, and like if you, you have to connect to the person next to you, like either by suit, like if it's both like diamonds, or by, um, number, like if it's both like 4's or something. And you have to drink that number of drinks. So if it's like 4 you drink 4, if it's an ace you drink 13. . . .
>
> *Interviewer:* SHOTS!?
>
> *Megan:* Just drinks of beer. Oh, God, shots?
>
> *Interviewer:* I was just, like
>
> *Megan:* Oh, my God, I think I would die! No, we don't, we drink, we play with beer. And um, anyway, I always just get so screwed, for some reason, like I always get the high card, and then I always connect . . . and you just have to keep drinking, keep drinking, keep drinking. It's a fun game though.

What does Megan mean when she says the game is dangerous? Why does she say she is an idiot for suggesting this game? These remarks offer a clear view of the contortions of the will that can be associated with play. At the outset of the game, Megan is unwilling to make a straightforward decision to engage in heavy drinking. She decides instead to play a game that may or may not lead to this outcome. She goes on to describe this game and its effects ("I always get so screwed"). The process of her being forced to drink is described as an undesirable outcome, yet Megan suggested the game and is freely participating in it. But it is the game that is responsible for the irresponsible drinking, not Megan, or not the Megan of the everyday world.

Note that the basic mechanism producing these effects is entrainment, in two senses. Most directly, Megan is entrained with the rules of the game, which is also understandable as a form of absorption. But Megan is also entrained with the other players, who are consuming alcohol in a highly structured and regulated format.

Once a decision to engage in this kind of a game is made, one's enjoyment of the play depends on one's capacity to surrender to the fiction of the game. I have pointed out that once this process is under way the surrender may deepen to the extent that the player feels pulled along, even controlled by the game. Megan knows all this. One could argue, then, that the game provides an excuse to drink. But it is also true that Megan is rehearsing cultural practices engrained in her as a member of contemporary society. We learn to play in ways that reinforce our conviction that the substances and objects and experiences available for consumption have mysterious powers to transform and even control us.

This pretense of being utterly bound by the rules of the drinking game is not unique to Megan. Here is Jessica, describing a game called "century club."

> *Jessica:* Sunday night I think was girl's night. . . . We played century club, like some of us girls, so we ended up very, very drunk that night also
>
> *Interviewer:* What's involved in that game?
>
> *Jessica:* Um, that would be taking a shot of beer every minute for a hundred minutes. . . . In that game you can't miss a minute, so we'd like have to go in turns to go smoke
>
> *Interviewer:* Oh, right
>
> *Jessica:* And you'd try to smoke as quickly as possible because you had to go back in and take the drinks you missed

Here again, the rules of the game are taken to be inviolable and to dictate alcohol consumption regardless of the situation of the player.

For Megan and Jessica, and for many who play drinking games, the game is about willingly entering into a social arrangement wherein they will give up a degree of responsibility for their own actions. This is especially true of an alea game such as connections. After all, when Megan agreed to play the game, it was not certain she would draw high cards, or connect. This simple-sounding point has some broad implications. Throughout this book I have called attention to how cognitive and emotional processes operating outside the realm of intention can contribute to a powerful subjective sense of self-transformation in play activities. But even apart from the operation of such processes, to enter into the frame of play is always to modify the conventions guiding the self, and in this sense to modify the self. Vygotsky (1978: 100) captures this point in his comment that in play there emerges a "fictitious I," a psychic entity that is oriented only partially to the everyday world, and in part to the framework in which the play occurs. In the case under discussion here, the *I* of the drinking game is a slightly different person from Megan, and as the game proceeds it is understandable if the two grow further apart.

For those who play drinking games, the emotional starting point of the play is ambivalence. We know, for example, that Megan suggested the game—she wants to play, and to drink—and she is a self-classified idiot for doing so: drinking in this fashion is irresponsible. The game, however, is fun; we have Megan's own word on it. This emotional transformation is, of course, typical of play. There is no ambiguity about Megan's or Jessica's initial choice to play the drinking game. They choose the game. Having done so, however, they are well aware that the game takes over and allows them to experiment with a drug by removing a degree of their responsibility for drinking. Already, in doing this, they meet the first criterion established in the American Psychiatric Association's diagnostic manual (*DSM-IV*, 1994: 178): "The individual may take the substance in larger amounts or over a longer period than was originally intended."

When young people play with a strong intoxicant such as alcohol, they enter a world of entrainment, transformation, and altered subjectivity before they experience any of the physiological effects of the drug. It is easy, in our cultural environment, to take the symbolic qualities of alcohol at face value and attribute to alcohol alone all of these effects. This, after all, is presumably what the young people playing these games do. In doing so, they create anew the cultural conviction of alcohol being a substance that can override the will of the drinker. This cultural process can also be observed, albeit in a somewhat subtler form, in tobacco consumption practices.

Caught Up in the Play of Smoking

Beginning smokers on college campuses are overwhelmingly likely to use tobacco primarily at social gatherings, which are of course a break from the everyday routine. Furthermore, they are likely to conceptualize this tobacco use as "not serious," or a form of play. Students repeatedly told us that smoking allowed them to alter their everyday identity, to become someone mysterious, or sexy, or tough. The cigarette was explicitly understood as a way to take on an identity different from one's everyday self. That is, cigarette smoking is mimetic play, a form of imitative pretending.

In this connection, it is useful to conceive of the cigarette, especially for younger smokers, as often being what Vygotsky (1978) referred to as a "pivot."[4] A pivot is essentially a prop used by a child to enter a world of play. Vygotsky uses the term because the object is the armature that facilitates transformation between the world of the everyday and that of play. The cigarette is symbolically salient in any number of ways—a marker of independence, rebellion, an often admired willingness to take risks, and so on—and is very useful to adolescents and young adults as they engage in mimetic play. The cigarette can quickly transform a situation and (as I have already commented) the person in the situation.

In sum, we found that many students like to engage in pretend play at social gatherings, and they find a cigarette a useful prop (Walton 1990) in so doing. Any form of pretend play, of course, entails a deictic shift; one pretends by imagining oneself to be in a different position than one occupies in the day-to-day physical and social world. Several of our informants told us, in some version, that at parties they became somewhat different people (see Stromberg et al. 2007). Smoking cigarettes is analogous to dressing up in a costume, a useful prop for temporarily assuming a role. Here is one woman we quoted in the earlier paper:

> I think that if you're smoking you look like so mysterious . . . so much more deep down inside yourself, and I think a lot of people when they're talking to somebody, if they're not drunk they're trying to get to know that person, and if the person seems mysterious, then obviously you're going to be much more intrigued [Stromberg et al 2007: 16].

To extend the point, consider this from a male smoker:

> I started smoking just to watch and witness how being a smoker changed me into all these different groups and people. So I'd be a smoker . . . and I'd be at a party and someone would come up to me and ask for a cigarette or I'd go ask someone for a cigarette and we'd just start talking. It was kind of interesting how that would work, how being a smoker kind of helped me meet people [Stromberg et al. 2007: 16].

These students could not be more explicit about how smoking cigarettes allows them to pretend to be other people. As could be expected from previous chapters, this shift in perspective is also accompanied by imitation and entrainment. I have just noted that early-phase smoking is often highly imitative, based on models drawn from the smoker's social acquaintance or on the widespread imagery of smoking. Smoking and its associated conventions are also potentially entraining. These activities draw the smoker into a situation in which the trajectory of the play may begin to guide activity, perhaps especially mental activity such as imagining. Entrainment in these activities (which may include, for example, intense conversation) can lead to powerful experiences of becoming caught up, in which the passage of time seems to collapse[5]:

> Whenever I go outside in the evenings especially, there are always other people that I know out there lighting up too and we tend to get into these big, long discussions about stupid things and before I know it an hour has gone by. Even when I mean to just smoke half a cigarette or one cigarette, sometimes I'll smoke more just because when you see someone else light a cigarette, you get this urge to do the same.[6]

Here is another low-level smoker on the entraining aspects of both drinking and smoking: "Like when it comes to drinking, and then with everyone around you smoking, I guess it just makes you want to smoke that much more."

Another noteworthy observation about cigarette smoking is that it is often used for emotion management, and this amounts to an especially fruitful opportunity to observe that the chemical effects of tobacco are not the whole story. After all, the potent chemical nicotine is a stimulant, and in American society cigarette smoking is often seen as a relaxing activity, an effective way to manage stress. More broadly, we heard that smoking is useful for management of emotions such as anger, stress, and depression. These themes emerge very early in the first phase of cigarette use.[7] Even those who smoke only sporadically often report that cigarette smoking relieves stress, and college students who have begun to smoke more regularly are very likely to use smoking as a way to manage boredom (Stromberg et al. 2007; I return to this in the next chapter).

For established smokers, tobacco use becomes a routine that is in itself soothing, which can be craved in its own right:

'Cause just sitting here and flicking a cigarette is just . . . it's so satisfying to me. I, you know, that's a large part of it. It's just that it's in my hand—*Yeah*—and then I can put it in my mouth when I need to, and it just satisfies those fixations that I have. And that's also, I mean, not only is it a physical addiction, like it's a mechanical addiction. . . . I'm just so used to doing it all the time that I feel almost, like empty if I'm not doing it.

I noted earlier that the player caught up in a game stands outside of normal experience of agency. The processes I have discussed—the deictic shift, imitation and entrainment, and emotional transformation—all have the capacity to foster a subjective conviction that one is being carried along by something beyond the conscious choices of the everyday self. As these processes interact, the conviction deepens. As a result, as the player becomes caught up in the world of play, a form of subjectivity may emerge that is different from the self of the everyday world.

More generally, I have shown that among the early-phase users of alcohol and tobacco of our study, such use is sometimes structured as play and users may become caught up in this play. How does this perspective enhance our understanding of agency in legal drug use? To the extent that becoming caught up in play—and the subjective sense of transformation that it can yield—is implicated in such use behaviors, then certain conclusions follow. First, it is the very point of play that the new self, the fictitious *I* of play, proceeds without continuous intervention from the everyday self.[8] The fictitious *I* of play may make decisions that are somewhat different from those that would be made by the day-to-day self. For example, this new social being may decide to continue to play longer than the day-to-day self would, a point of considerable relevance if one is playing with an intoxicating substance such as alcohol or tobacco. In the midst of this experience, or reflecting on it later, the player may well form the impression that something beyond his ordinary self was directing his action.

Second, such an impression harmonizes with the subjective sense of self-transformation that becoming caught up in play can yield. The player was not only doing things she might not ordinarily do, but she had a sense of being someone slightly different than who she is in the day-to-day world; indeed, this was cited as one of the reasons for engaging in this play in the first place. Third—and this point simply combines the conclusions I have just reached—the player may be left with a strong sense of being swept along and overwhelmed by the activities of drug use. This sense is not for the most part attributed to the practices of play. Rather, the compelling nature of smoking or drinking practices is likely to be understood as a feature of the power of the substance itself. Already at this point then, the young smoker or drinker has experiences in which her own agency seems to be overwhelmed, experiences she may understand—in conjunction with broader cultural notions—as a part of the capacity of alcohol or tobacco to foster dependency.[9]

Dependency

Although drug use is an area of human behavior that has been much studied and reflected on, debate still rages over some of the most basic questions about this behavior.[10] One of the most obvious areas of contention has to do with the causes and nature of dependency. In such a situation, there can be no suggestion that the analysis offered here sweeps away the confusion. But it is possible that this approach could prove to be a useful tool in trying to understand in new ways how the ideology of addiction is sustained.

I have shown how, in early alcohol and tobacco use that takes the form of play, the legal drug user may become involved in a process that yields a subjective sense that his everyday control over his action has been overridden. As one begins to play with an intoxicating substance, an interactive process starts to emerge. Involved in this process are a complex mix of cultural conventions, emotions and other physical feelings, and attentional narrowing. As occurs in any sort of play, the player may become caught up in the activity, and the activity may therefore seem to develop its own momentum. Playing with this momentum has its own challenges and appeal, and the player may begin to yield herself to the play. It is this delicate mutual adaptation between a player and the trajectory of the game that makes play a potent force in shaping human behavior, because as the player becomes more caught up, a subjectivity emerges that is different from the self of the everyday. In the particular cases examined here, the changes of subjectivity and agency are likely to be attributed not to the process of becoming caught up in play but rather to the efficacy of the drug itself. Such experiences are one contributor to the broader cultural notion that intoxicating drugs can overwhelm the agency of those who use them.

I said earlier that it is a well-established point in the literature on drug use that the effects of drugs on the body are conditioned not only by the chemical properties of the drug but also by the cultural assumptions, expectations, and routines of use associated with use of the drug. The argument I am making here offers one more example of the point, especially as concerns expectations and routines. The expectation that alcohol and tobacco have the capacity to overwhelm the user's will is a conviction certainly rooted in part in an individual's physical response to habitual use of a substance, but the role of cultural factors should not be underestimated here, either.[11] The playful routines of legal drug use may in themselves create a strong subjective sense that the user's capacity to control her action has been overridden.[12] As one established smoker in our study put my point, "It's not tobacco I'm addicted to; it's smoking cigarettes."[13]

The neophyte drug user may experience this overriding of everyday agency in the play associated with legal drug use prior to any physical dependence on the drug. In this way, certain of the routines through which legal drugs are self-administered work to valorize the notion that these drugs have the capacity to compromise the agency of the user and foster dependency. When this happens, ideas about the potency of certain substances, activities, or symbols are reinforced.

My point here is twofold. First, under some circumstances a drug user may undergo a process of becoming caught up in this activity, a process we have seen in other sorts of play. To become caught up is to develop a subjective sense of being immersed in an activity that is unfolding, to some extent, beyond the control of the everyday self. This subjective sense may in itself contribute to the player's sense that his authorship of his own action has been in part compromised. Further, this process of becoming caught up may proceed to the point where the player begins to feel his self and situation have been transformed. At this point, the player may look for a cause of this sense of transformation, and in this case he is likely to locate the drug itself as the cause.[14] To reiterate, the point here is not to deny the role of the chemical properties of the drug in transforming consciousness; it is rather to point out that in many cases this may not be the only relevant factor. In the end, the drug user's consciousness has been transformed, and the user is therefore confirmed in her impression of the capacity of the drug to overwhelm her ability to act independently.

The Ideology of Addiction

Early-phase routines of legal drug consumption help to infuse the substances themselves with the power to override the user's capacity to choose. These routines work to endow the substance with what Sedgwick (1993: 132) calls a "surplus of mystical powers."[15] This example is intended to illustrate a much broader and more diverse set of practices whereby products and services are rendered desirable, even irresistible, in contemporary society. The playful practices through which we engage in what we call entertainment and consumption have communal effects not much different from the rituals described by Durkheim in *The Elementary Forms of Religious Life*; through them our communal symbols are created and sustained.[16] As people become caught up in the playful routines of entertainment and consumption, they feel, on a level that transcends mere cognition, the power of the ideas, objects, and substances that make up important parts of our culture and shape our way of life.

But these practices also have implications at the level of the individual and our ideas about individuals. As we closely consider the process of becoming caught up, we are required to think in new ways about the nature of the self and its choices in play. At the most global level, the point is that one who is caught up in play experiences a subjective sense of being guided by something beyond his or her everyday self.[17] Indeed, this is in one sense the very point of the play, for play gives enjoyment by offering mock challenges and satisfactions, and those challenges and satisfactions are more savory when the player colludes in forgetting their artificiality. The player is assisted in this by some convenient facts about human physiology and culture. There are indeed aspects of our behavior that we control at best incompletely. They include some of our emotional responses, our tendency to imitate, and our tendency to entrain. I have also pointed here to the importance to the cognitive process of absorption. In absorption, we focus our attention so closely on some activity or framework that our actions can come to seem dictated by the activity, with no conscious direction by the self.

Conventions of play have developed over millennia to exploit these possibilities. In a consumer capitalist economy such as our own, it is no surprise that human ingenuity has been directed to enhancing the opportunities for and gratifications of play experiences. Such experiences are appealing and fun (thus people are willing to pay for them) and over time play activities may foster the conviction that the ideas and substances implicated in such experiences have the power to overwhelm the self. What better way is there to generate profits than to cultivate people's conviction that their appetites are beyond their control?[18]

As I have noted earlier, this conviction of the potency of such cultural symbols is strengthened by the often underground nature of the desires reinforced through our play. In the particular example I have considered here, consumption of alcohol and tobacco is often valued; the businessperson may value a drink after a long day, the college student may value the keg at the party, "I need a cigarette," and so on. But it would be at the very least odd to consider this valuing of alcohol and tobacco as reflecting explicit "values"; alcohol is on nobody's list of American values. In official discourse, consumption of these substances is routinely discouraged. Therefore it is all the more likely that their consumption will be understood as a desire that dwells somewhere beyond the boundaries of the familiar, the comprehensible, the easily controlled.

Thus the practices of valorization through becoming caught up in play are an important means whereby choice is transformed into compulsion. Through these practices many ideas and products come to seem not only desirable but to have the power to overwhelm the human capacity for choice. If such processes work in the ways I have outlined here, then they may constitute more evidence that there are some flaws in the popular understanding of our capacity for autonomous action in this society.[19] Officially we celebrate the strength of the individual, but there are plenty of hints that the contemporary self—like contemporary forms of community—is in some ways fragile. In the next chapter I want to look at another form of this fragility, boredom.

9

The Oscillation Between Boredom and Stimulation

Life in Australian societies alternates between two different phases. In one phase, the population is scattered in small groups that attend to their occupations independently. Each family lives to itself, hunting, fishing—in short, striving by all possible means to get the food it requires. . . . The dispersed state in which the society finds itself makes life monotonous, slack, and humdrum.

THIS IS HOW DURKHEIM (1995: 216–217) described the life of the Australian aborigines in those times when they are forced by limited resources to dissolve larger residential units and spread out over the desert in search of food. It is also a part of the foundation for his argument that human existence is, in its very nature, dualistic. All people dwell within a physical world, but all people are also self-conscious beings who continuously invest the physical world with meanings and in doing so transcend the merely physical. Durkheim felt that the Australians' way of life amounted to an especially stark example of this duality. This is because their calendar was separated into times when the struggle with the physical world was nearly overwhelming in its monotony, and times when the exuberance of their social gatherings was equally overwhelming, suggesting in a particularly noticeable way the power of the ideal in human existence.

You will note that Durkheim's observations are laced with unforgivable stereotypes. For example in describing the excitement of their ceremonial phase he asserts that the simple minds of the Australian natives easily become caught up in the excitement of their ceremonies, as "the emotional and passionate faculties of the primitive are not fully subordinated to his reason and will" (1995: 217). Such claims are recognized as racist in our day, but they were, unfortunately, virtually universal among European intellectuals up to about a century ago. If one separates Durkheim's underlying argument from his racist discourse, however, what remains is worth considering. He is arguing that for the Australian native, on-the-ground experience entails a tangible manifestation of a contrast intrinsic to human cognition, the distinction between our experience as individual beings and our experience as social beings. It goes without saying that for all practical purposes these two levels of experience are inextricably intertwined. But Durkheim would argue that nevertheless, at certain points in our lives, the two poles of our dual existence emerge into our awareness.[1]

Here I agree with Durkheim: human existence is indeed characterized by an inherent dualism, linked to our nature as self-conscious beings. This brings me back to Chapter Seven, in which I discussed subjectivity and meta-action. Throughout this book I have worked from the assumption—one that is shared in much recent work by observers in several disciplines—that we humans orient ourselves in the physical and social world by continuously supplementing our own perspectives with those of our fellows.

Boredom in Contemporary Society

In making his point that the duality of human mentality is incarnate in experience in the two phases of Australian life, Durkheim emphasized not only the effervescence of the ceremonial period but also what we would call the boredom of life outside that time. Although we in contemporary society do not need to disperse into smaller groups in the dry season, we are quite familiar with the contrast between times of boredom and times of excitement. In fact, this duality is such an important part of contemporary life that one might well wonder whether Durkheim's emphasis on the "monotonous, slack, and humdrum" quality of the Australian's life during times of dispersal is a projection of modern Western expectations upon a non-Western society. Historians who look into the matter generally reach the conclusion that finding parts of everyday life to be boring is not something that troubles all the inhabitants of all times and places. Our expectation that experience should be engaging and interesting is a relatively recent development.[2]

Patricia Meyers Spacks (1995: 6), for example, argues that our notion of boredom cannot be found in literature or private writings before the second half of the 18th century. Certainly this does not prove people never felt bored before that time, but it probably does suggest a growing tendency to attend to and think about such feelings during this period. Of course, the second half of the 18th century is a time we have discussed in earlier chapters. This is the period associated with early

Romanticism, the rise of the novel and the modern fashion pattern, the beginning of the Industrial Revolution. It is perhaps of particular relevance that during this time the idea of leisure as a domain separated from work began to take shape (Spacks 1995: 16). To feel bored is to compare one's experience to periods of engagement and stimulation, and to find the present moment insufficient.

The idea that boredom as we conceive it is not necessarily universal, that it may in fact be associated with the changes that came with Romanticism, is highly congenial to my argument in this book and to my version of common sense. In an earlier chapter, I signed on with those who see contemporary patterns of consumption not as universal—not as a response to goods and services that any human beings would quickly fall into—but rather as a culturally conditioned response. My common sense holds *not* that everyone will behave just like a member of contemporary society if only given the chance, but rather that people everywhere typically orient their activity around the values, ideas, and desires that are endorsed by those around them. Usually the values of most people in a society turn out to be suspiciously coherent; people often hold that the right thing to do is precisely what supports and facilitates the institutional arrangements of their societies. Our powerful lust for consumer goods seems to us like a manifestation of human nature, but both reflection and the available evidence suggest that in some societies being acquisitive is neither adaptive nor held in high esteem. Similar reasoning tends to persuade me that boredom, like our versions of competition and consumption, is associated with the rise of consumer capitalism; what better way to fuel frenzied consumption than to foster nagging feelings of emptiness and discontent whenever one is not being stimulated by something new and exciting?

However, it is also conceivable that times and places engender their own versions of boredom, and it is an error to assume our version is the only one.[3] Something like this is the conclusion of a recent study of (conveniently enough) a group of Australian natives, the Warlpiri. The author of that study, Yasmine Musharbash, agrees that prior to contact with Westerners the Warlpiri probably were not much concerned with boredom (2007: 310). But she also resists the conclusion that boredom is necessarily a reaction to Westernization, pointing out that the sociocultural context in which boredom is generated among the Warlpiri of today is quite different from what provides the background for boredom in, say, the United States. In spite of her insistence that local varieties of boredom are likely to reflect local conditions, Musharbash also formulates a more universal definition of boredom, a notion of what we would be comparing from place to place. She writes (315), "Boredom arises when values and circumstances fail to correspond, when ways of being in the world and the world jar."

In conducting the research for this book, I spoke with and observed three groups of people who were engaged with forms of entertainment and consumption: early-phase tobacco users, role players, and fans of the television (and movie) series "Star Trek." People in all three groups talked about boredom, and what they described was usually consistent with Musharbash's formulation. Boredom occurs in situations of what Peter Conrad calls "alienation from the moment,"[4] where the self and the situation are at odds.

There are echoes, in this formulation, of what Victor Turner called "liminal situations." Building on the earlier work of Arnold van Gennep (1960), Turner pointed out that rites of passage—initiation ceremonies—typically consist of three stages: separation, limen, and aggregation. The first of these stages separates the initiates from the rest of the group, and the third stage entails their reintegration into the group. But Turner's interest was especially drawn to the middle stage, the liminal, because oftentimes this phase is characterized by symbolism that expresses the condition of the initiate as neither what he or she once was nor what he or she will soon become. Logically, the initiate—who is being transformed from one social state to another—must pass through a social moment when he or she is "betwixt and between" social states, unclassified.

In many societies, what is unclassified and therefore unknown is typically considered powerful, and even dangerous. The symbolism of the liminal is often an attempt to give some sort of shape to this moment of standing outside the social order. Thus it is common to find in rites of passage imagery of androgyny, birth, death, or other processes that represent ambiguity or transition between states.

In later work, Turner pointed out that liminal symbolism is not confined to rites of passage but can often be found in association with other sorts of social transitions, such as those occurring in pilgrimage or the calendar (think, for example, of New Year's Eve, or the weekend). In fact, once one is alerted to liminal symbolism it can be located in so many parts of the cultural realm that the analytic usefulness of the term begins to fade; in practice the term quickly becomes overly broad.

Although this puts me in danger of compounding the problem, I will point out that boredom is a liminal state. Boredom occurs in transition, when one falls out of synch with the march of the culturally defined situations and frameworks we seem to need in our activity. In such moments, no prefabricated social response is available, and the actor must resort to his or her own resources to find the way back to the stream of everyday action. In a sense, boredom is generated when the person is confronted by an impasse in the everyday process of yoking the self to the ongoing projects that are embedded in the stream of the everyday. The expected ease of inhabiting a situation breaks down, at least for an instant, and something intervenes between the person and the social context. It is, again, "alienation from the moment" or a clash between the world and ways of being within it.[5]

As I mentioned in the previous chapter, in studying young persons who were beginning to experiment with tobacco we[6] noticed the prominence of what we started to call "the rhetoric of boredom."[7] This discourse is laced with a liminal vocabulary: boredom is in the first instance described in terms of nothingness (nothing to do) or emptiness. Boredom may also be characterized by the imagery of death, as in "killing time" or in the description of a situation as "dead." Another feature of the rhetoric of boredom is the construction "just [verb phrase]." Young men and women describe the negativity of boredom as being "just" some activity. The point is not that these activities are repetitive and therefore actively boring, but rather that these pursuits simply do not count as activity ("I didn't do anything all week. I just watched a lot of TV. . ."). Common examples of this formulation are "just sitting [or laying] there," "just sitting [or laying] around," "just doing nothing," and "just passing time."

These activities are characterized by passivity. Watching TV is more active than "just sitting there," but even this endeavor can be effectively pursued with little engagement or input. Thus in saying one is "just doing X," one reports a dearth of structure or demand for activity in the situation. Another situation in which the college-aged student is likely to encounter this threatening lack of structure is in breaks in the schedule, between classes, or a vacation or a weekend. Here is Carol (a young woman who furnishes several of the examples here) talking about her summer break:

> *Carol:* Over the summer I didn't have anything to keep me busy. That's pretty much what it is. That's why on the weekends you smoke more, except for smoking more when you drink. Just the fact that you have nothing to do.

Passive boredom, this lack of structure, is not necessarily generated by a complete lack of available structure. There are often things you *should* do, but you don't *want to* do them. Thus passive boredom is sometimes conceptualized in a vocabulary of avoidance. One of our interviewers pursued the issue in this exchange from a group interview:

> *Interviewer:* Is boredom ever something like, like that where you have stuff to do, where it's like—
> *Group member:* Not something you want to do?
> *Interviewer:* Not necessarily like, you know, there's times when you really have nothing to do and you're just bored—
> *Group member:* Yeah
> *Interviewer:* But is there other times where you have stuff to do, you just don't want to do it so if you're, if you're bored?
> *Group member:* Oh yeah, oh yeah
> *Group member:* There's never any time where you have truly nothing to do. Like you could always, like they were saying, clean your room, or. . . .

Group member: Study. . . .

Group member: Read some chapters or something

Group member: Yeah

Here the group confirms that you may be bored not because you lack things to do but because you lack things you want to do. You are bored because you are avoiding something you need to take care of. Again we find that boredom is defined in terms of a not, and it entails lack of engagement with a task that would impose a structure on activity.

Closely related to this matter of the boring situation is the slightly different problem of boredom and the self. Boredom, in this age group, is often associated with being alone. We heard repeatedly that not being engaged with others is in itself boring and unsettling; as one young man says, "When I'm not doing something with friends then I'm usually bored." It was common for our subjects to explicitly associate boredom with loneliness or to try to work out the subtle distinctions between the terms.[8]

Allow me to summarize the rhetoric of boredom in terms that have been developed earlier. One becomes bored when there is nothing in experiences that engages you, nothing that pulls you into an activity with its own momentum. The most prominent engaging activities are a form of playful entertainment or intense interaction. These young persons seem to be saying, then, that when they are bored they lack the stimulation that has been shown to characterize intense interaction and play. This stimulation involves becoming immersed in cognitive and emotional processes that catch one up and carry one away, at least to some degree. In sum, an awareness of and sensitivity to boredom is a correlate of having and wanting to have compelling experiences of being at least somewhat caught up in play or interaction.

Marginal Situations

One useful way to summarize all this is to note that in discussions of boredom the word *engaging* frequently functions as an analytical primitive, a concept that is often used but rarely explored. For example (my emphasis throughout):

> Sometimes *disengagement* is pleasant, as when we rest, relax, or just "chill out." But if the *disengagement* is a disconnection to what is going on, if the activity continues without our making a connection with it, we can feel bored [Conrad 1997: 471].

For the Warlpiri, "The boringness of a place is created by the absence of people ('not enough people') and a lack of social interaction and engagement ('nothing happening'). . . . Events that fail to emotionally engage run the risk of being labeled boring" (Musharbash 2007:310).

Of course, I have used the term myself several times in my description of the rhetoric of boredom.

Suppose, then, that we take a closer look at the term *engagement* itself. It is clearly used as a contrast to boredom in these quotations; engagement is precisely what boredom is not. This makes sense in terms of the various formulations of boredom I have offered: boredom occurs in the face of a breakdown of the machinery that gears self to the guidelines of a situation. Becoming caught up, by contrast, occurs when a situation and the self mesh so completely that the boundaries between self and situation fade, and the self merges into the situation. One becomes caught up. Engagement is in this sense a mild version of becoming caught up, and either of these terms can be contrasted with boredom; engagement, and becoming caught up even more so, are the opposites of boredom. This suggests that the solution to boredom is to seek out an experience of engagement or becoming caught up, and in this sense feelings of boredom are signs that prompt the person to seek engagement at some level.

This formulation would be broadly consistent with the arguments offered by both Durkheim and Turner. For Durkheim, the lassitude of dispersal is the opposite of the effervescence of the gathering, just as in contemporary society the monotony of boredom is the opposite of the stimulation of becoming caught up. Further, Durkheim argued, it is in the exciting phase that social ideals are generated and valorized. Turner's approach, though formulated in quite different terms, shares with Durkheim's the contrast between a state of withdrawal from full social engagement and a state of reintegration with now revitalized cultural values, what he (1967) calls "the basic building blocks of culture."

I offer these remarks on the theories of social scientists from an earlier generation to point out, first of all, that what we see in contemporary society is a local version of some widespread forms of meta-action. Disengagement, a gap in the expected relative harmony of self and situation in the stream of experience, is responded to by action that adjusts this disruption in the flow of action. Second, I mean to call attention to the fact that just as this society is not so very different from others, neither is the explanation I am offering here. This chapter suggests an adaptation of an approach formulated, in somewhat differing versions, by a number of social scientists over the years. The general idea is that human life naturally oscillates between phases of engagement with cultural and social routines and phases of relatively less engagement, brought on in any number of ways: periods of uncertainty or rapid change, transitions between social states, or perhaps just not much to do. The latter phase is uncomfortable, and it may even be experienced as dangerous.

Why does it feel so disconcerting to be left adrift, apart from engagement? As far as I know there is no research that bears directly on the question. I can speculate on the basis of the earlier discussion of the social character of human cognition. To engage with a situation is potentially to experience demands and challenges, but it also permits the comforts of participation and relative certainty. The liminal condition of lack of engagement entails being left outside the project, missing the reassurance and certainty of falling easily into a situation. Thus, like other nebulous, liminal situations, lack of engagement is associated with a particular sort of symbolism that gives some shape to this lack of definition.

The theory has it that these naturally occurring phases of life are both manifestations and expressions of the deeper quality of human experience. "Man is double," as Durkheim (1995) says. We are at once biological individuals and participants in a vast cultural project. As the project begins to fade from our awareness, even a little, as we become aware of the contingency of the vast systems through which we engage the world, we confront the abyss. The words of sociologist Peter Berger are apposite here, if we understand that boredom is an example of what he calls a "marginal situation" (1967: 24–25):

> The marginal situations of human existence reveal the innate precariousness of all social worlds. Every socially defined reality remains threatened by lurking "irrealities." Every socially constructed nomos must face the constant possibility of its collapse into anomy. . . . This chaos must be kept at bay at all cost. To ensure this, every society develops procedures that assist its members to remain "reality oriented" . . . and to "return to reality."

In our society, one of the forms of meta-action through which we can reestablish our engagement with powerful and unquestionable cultural frameworks is what we call entertainment.

Our society is unusual in that the resources whereby this transformation is accomplished use our equipment for interaction but do not necessarily call functioning communities into being. As I have shown in earlier chapters, we have perfected techniques for using fictions to induce some of the same sorts of mental and physical processes that occur when people become immersed in intense interaction. These processes can create powerful feelings of self-transcendence and may be a means whereby the person can reenter the stream of events with a stronger appreciation for the power of cultural ideals. On the other hand, as we shall see, responses to boredom often also take the form of convening of social groups. Let us now look at one particular set of practices that young people resort to in confronting boredom, practices that have to do, again, with the consumption of tobacco.

What to Do When You Are Bored

I always want to smoke. It's just something to do. Yeah, it comes down to that a lot. It takes up like three minutes of your time when there's nothing going on. So you're kind of like, "I could go smoke a cigarette, and after that I'll figure out what I want to do."

The link between having nothing to do and smoking exemplified in this young man's speech—call him Art—is a theme we heard about again and again in our interviews. To combat the nothing, one must rely on a something, a positive that can fill the emptiness. The cigarette "takes up like three minutes of your time when there's nothing going on." Art repeats and expands the point in another interview:

> *Art:* To me, besides like the smell and all that, a cigarette is kind of like a length
> of time to me. It's like an activity that takes that long.
> *Interviewer:* Right.
> *Art:* And it's kind of nice like that. I mean, it's a disgusting habit, but it's. . . .
> *Interviewer:* I mean, why is it nice to have that length of time? Is it a time to get
> away from it all?
> *Art:* Usually. I mean, you can have your serenity smoke or whatever, I just made
> that up.. . . . Or, you know, like if you want to go out and have a cigarette,
> you know it's only going to take you that long. Driving in the car, it's just
> something to break up the monotony. Like, take this much time to do
> something, I don't know.

Cigarettes are a response to boredom first, then, simply because smoking a cigarette is something to do. When one is confronted by what one understands as emptiness or monotony, the thing to do is to change the situation, and a cigarette is one way to do so. Recall the young man quoted in the previous chapter who said, "I'm just so used to doing it all the time that I feel almost, like empty if I'm not doing it."

"Emptiness" is a prominent term from the lexicon of boredom. Of course, I do not intend to claim that the cigarette is the only possible response to emptiness; there are many ways to fill one's time. My point is simply that if one is confronted with the threat of emptiness, smoking a cigarette is an appropriate way to dispel the threat.

One can respond to a boring situation not just by filling it with the routines associated with smoking itself but much more broadly, with a range of social practices that surround smoking. There are, for example, the activities entailed in acquiring cigarettes, or the well-developed social interactional routines that have taken shape around smoking. Consider, for example, Carol's story about returning to her natal home, where her parents are caring for an infant, over spring break:

> *Carol:* Dead at nine o'clock. Nothing whatsoever. Because my sister who's 17, her room's in the basement, so, she's down there doing whatever. She's awake. . . . But she doesn't have anything to do with the rest of the house. And my five-year-old sister, she's got school, so she's in bed by 8:30 or 9:00 or whatever. And my parents, who usually would be up, are in the bedroom with the baby trying to, you know, my mom's feeding her, or she's napping. So at like nine, all of the lights in my house are out, and I'm just like, "I feel like my parents are 90."
>
> *Interviewer:* [Laughs]
>
> *Carol:* So I'd be like [whispering], "I'm leaving, Mom." I'd knock on her door and whisper at her. I'd leave at nine, we'd go pick everyone up, and go, "What do you want to do?" "I don't know, what is there to do?" "I don't know." "Well I gotta go get gas and cigarettes." "All right, let's go get gas and cigarettes." So, we'd go to a convenient, get gas and cigarettes, and then we'd drive around some more. And then we'd call people: "What are you doing?" . . . "We're just sitting around at our house." Okay, so there's like four of you sitting here, four of you sitting there, we'll just drive around some more. And Jennie will smoke some pot. She'll be like, oh it's so funny, because her and Lauren are the only two of my good friends still at home, so they've gotten real close. So they have a whole system where Lauren packs a bowl for Jennie, because she's driving. . . . So, we drive around, someone holds the steering wheel for Jennie while she smokes. And then we go to Denny's, or Steak-N-Shake, or somewhere around there, and smoke and eat and talk. And then we go home, at 1:30, because that's Lauren's curfew. If not we'd stay at Denny's a lot longer.

Note first of all the role of the rhetoric of boredom in this vignette. The first word is "dead." Carol characterizes the nothingness of her natal home in the following lines of her story. She meets up with friends and asks "What are we going to do?" They are "just sitting around." All of these phrases are markers of the rhetoric of boredom. Carol and her friends are faced with a sort of anomie; there are no particular social requirements imposed on them. Away from the structure of college, and no longer fitting into the structure of her natal home, even the peer routines of her high school years are no longer operational (she says elsewhere that in high school she would attend parties in this sort of situation). She really has little to work with—the car, a group of similarly anomic friends, late-night restaurants, marijuana, and cigarettes.

In this situation, Carol and her friends devise something to do, something that might initially seem—even to them—random but in fact is anything but. Because they need cigarettes, they must acquire them, which entails obtaining fuel for their car. They have a project; they are off and running. They call others to join in the project. They travel, their activities structured by the ingestion of another drug, to the smoking section of a restaurant, where they spend the evening hours.

In this story, we also observe something that was often commented on in the interviews with young smokers, the point that smoking combats boredom by instigating social groups. This brings us back to the earlier point about the relationship between boredom and loneliness. Here is another young woman commenting on the relationship between smoking and the lack of any immediate social connections: "I'm just bored walking on campus, like there's nobody to call and I don't have to return any phone calls and I don't want to talk to that person anyways, so just wasting your time, like you have 10 minutes and cigarettes take like six, so. . . ."

The subjects in this study often told us that to be outside of a functioning social network is boring, and thus a reason to smoke. Here a small group of students discusses why they started smoking immediately upon arriving on campus:

> *Speaker 1:* When we first got here, it was basically boredom that—
> *Speaker 2:* Yeah—
> *Speaker 1:* Caused it.
> *Interviewer:* Boredom, [that's?]—
> *Unidentified speaker:* [Because] we didn't know anyone either. . . . It's not like you can be like, call people up, "Hey, what're you doing?"

Or consider this exchange from a group interview:

> *Interviewer:* What about this whole boredom thing? Like when you're driving, like is there other times that boredom sets in?
> *Subject:* School. Yeah, every night. . . .
> *Subject:* Yeah, there's nothing to do.
> *Subject:* See, during the day we don't ever really smoke unless it's after lunch, but at night we're all back at the dorm and all of us are doing random things, but everyone can stop and take a cigarette break. And when somebody is bored, it just sounds like a good idea to go with them.
> *Interviewer:* So is it just to do something, just to break the drone?
> *Subject:* Yeah, almost. Like, hey I'm bored, I'm going to go smoke.
> *Subject:* Because we'll be sitting in our separate rooms, them in their room and me in my room, just playing on the computer, you know, doing nothing, kind of flipping through the TV. They'll come over and be like, "Let's go smoke." "OK."
> *Subject:* Nothing better to do.

Smoking not only structures the unstructured; it brings people together into a group that interacts.

To summarize: first, smoking fills empty time; when one is smoking a cigarette, one is doing something. Second, the various routines associated with smoking—acquiring cigarettes, getting to a place where one can smoke them, the local interactional traditions that include cigarettes, and so on—give further shape to unstructured time. Finally, cigarettes combat boredom, in its guise as loneliness, by bringing people together.

I have been using cigarette smoking here to represent an enormous range of entertainment and consumption activities that boredom may provoke, activities such as eating, fiction reading, shopping for pleasure, watching television and movies, surfing the Internet, playing games, and so on. All of these activities share some basic features with cigarette use: they entail routines that structure time—both in carrying out the activities themselves and through ancillary activities—and they often bring together temporary communities. They may also foster opportunities for becoming caught up. But here again, a problem arises. Precisely because entertainment activities may be very effective in creating the kind of stimulation that banishes boredom, they may be in some sense too appealing. Once again, we approach the borders of the phenomenon we call addiction. This can be illustrated by looking at the situations of two of the Star Trek fans I interviewed.

Chris

I turn now to two brief case studies, studies not intended to represent any group but rather to allow me to further explore the relationship between becoming caught up and boredom. I contacted both of the young men I describe because they were self-identified fans of Star Trek.[9] It began as a television show, but over a period of three decades it blossomed into several TV series, a book series, movies, role-playing games, fan groups, and more. Probably in part because it is a science fiction show, Star Trek fans are heavily involved in role-playing games on the Internet.

In recent decades, technological innovations and social currents have combined to encourage and make possible a range of participatory fan activities in increasingly detailed fantasy cultures. During the 1970s role-playing games such as Dungeons and Dragons, Renaissance Fairs, science fiction conventions, and so on offered participants increasing opportunities to assume an identity in a fictive world for entertainment purposes. Today similar phenomena are prominent on the Internet, where participants may spend hours, days, or lives playing variants of role-playing games.[10] As a result, being a fan of Star Trek does not necessarily just mean liking to watch the associated television shows or movies; it may entail a range of other activities as well and can become a prominent feature of a person's way of life, even if the fan is balancing this interest with other commitments such as work and family.

Both of the young men I describe here are reflective and intelligent, and neither displays outrageous behavior that would make him stand out from millions of other fans of sports teams, musical groups, and so on. Yet both of these fans are very clear that their attraction to phenomena such as Star Trek, role-playing games, and television in general has at times been so strong that they have felt powerless to resist it.

My first subject is Chris, a likable and intelligent man in his midtwenties who is having trouble finding himself. By this I mean that he has entered and dropped out of college several times, has pursued professional goals with enthusiasm for a while but then given them up, and left his parent's home but established no permanent home of his own. In Erik Erikson's sense of the term (1968), Chris is still working to finalize his *identity*; he hasn't found a sector of the social landscape with which to identify. He is locked in a transitional situation (there it is again) that he regards as typical of his generation, between childhood and adulthood.

Chris is also a Star Trek fan. He is typical of many of his compatriots in his somewhat tongue-in-cheek approach to the whole business; he is deeply immersed in the world of Trek but at the same time speaks with mild disdain of those who, in his view, are unable to recognize the difference between the Star Trek world and the real one. But it is an open secret that Chris has himself been subject to this confusion at some times during his life.

I met Chris at a Star Trek convention I attended as a part of my research into the fans of the phenomenon. He agreed to do an interview, and we talked for a little over two hours in two sessions. He grew up in a small town in the South in a region where he has hundreds of identifiable relatives. After graduation from high school, Chris was desperate to leave town; being known by virtually every person in his hometown meant he was enormously restricted by others' expectations. Even now, when he returns to visit, he says he quickly becomes another person, someone he recognizes but no longer feels comfortable with.

Not surprisingly, then, Chris blossomed when he moved away to attend college. "I developed my own personality in college; until then I didn't have one," he says. But although he learned who he was during these years, he could not puzzle out what to do. He went through a number of phases in which he would find a major, pursue it with enthusiasm, and then eventually give it up as not really what he wanted to do. Here he describes one of these phases:

> I was trying to be this conser—, this good little boy, I was in, I was majoring in journalism and public relations. And I was going full force, I was in organizations, I was doing all this, I dressed nice, I was, you know, an A crowd type, you know. And I met all these people, and at first I, you know, I was trying to be so fake— and that was not me at all—that I blended in well. And after a while though, I saw

some differences, I suddenly realized that these people were serious, and that this was just something that wasn't me.

Realizing he had immersed himself so fully in something so foreign to his nature evidently shocked Chris, and he dropped out of college to spend some time sorting out his priorities. Since that time, he has reenrolled and dropped out again, worked a number of jobs, and generally just drifted.

In the year following his first exit from college, Chris felt that nothing lay before him except a series of "pathetic" jobs. By his own assessment, he was depressed, and he immersed himself in role-playing games such as Star Trek and Dungeons and Dragons. Chris says he would spend sunny days inside working on aspects of the games rather than getting out and enjoying the world. Looking back, he regards this as dangerous; he says he knows many people who are "scary" because they are so deeply involved in role-playing games.

When I pressed Chris to explain what he meant by this, he said he continues to participate in role playing games with many who would rather "work on their characters" than work out problems in their real lives. Role-playing games offer the opportunity to build particular characters over a long period of time, and Chris is suggesting that some role players have given up on their real-life personae in favor of their fantasied characters. He also implies that there was a time when he too would have fit this description.

At the time he spoke to me, Chris was no longer immersing himself in role-playing games to a degree he considered inappropriate. But neither had he managed to become fully engaged in any of the pursuits more conventionally considered to be a part of the real world. There was evidence of still being caught up, right there in our interview. Listen to how Chris introduces his discussion of an episode of a "Star Trek" program called "Deep Space Nine":

> The Bajoran civilization, eight hundred years ago, it was a myth, a rumor that they'd built these solar sail ships. And this is, eight hundred years ago, I mean humans were, you know, in the middle ages almost.

The second sentence is an aside, a moment when Chris pauses in the telling of his story to say something directly to the audience (in this case, me). Thus it is particularly striking that here and in an earlier reference Chris uses the word *ago* to point to the time framework not of the present but rather of the Star Trek world, four centuries in the future. That is, Chris intends the phrase "800 years ago" to refer not to the 12th century but to the 16th.[11] Chris is narrating not from the perspective of the time period he and I were mutually occupying. Rather, this story is being presented within the time frame of the Star Trek world.

Furthermore, the Star Trek world subsumes this one. Because the world of Trek is imagined to take place in the future, anything about the present world is included within the world of Trek. Thus Chris easily integrates a fact about actual European history into his tale, making something real into part of a fiction. In the terms I have used throughout the book, we see evidence here of a deictic shift and imaginative pretending; Chris is locating himself in a position in the fiction as he narrates, and then embellishing the fantasy in terms of this imaginary perspective.

So, Chris has left behind compulsive role playing, but he is still caught up in Trek and dissatisfied with his day-to-day life: "The biggest problem with me, and I will tell you now, is that my total confidence is shot. . . . I have *no* confidence." I asked Chris to tell me about some of his favorite episodes from the television series, and the first episode he described had to do with a civilization that had—as a whole—lost confidence. This story carries a message with considerable emotional impact for Chris, because the plot centers around how members of this civilization rediscover a part of their history and in so doing experience a boost to their confidence. Because Chris is explicit about his own loss of confidence, it is not difficult to speculate about what this story means to him on an emotional level.

All of this goes to show that throughout his life Chris has been able to find not only considerable pleasure but also deep emotional meaning in Trek. He has become caught up in Trek and role-playing games; there is evidence of it even as he speaks in the interview. Chris's situation in some ways exemplifies a widespread condition in contemporary society, one I discuss more fully in the next chapter. He takes his independence and uniqueness very seriously and looks to realize himself in part by pursuing his interest in the world of Trek. In fact, he is so interested in the world of Trek that he is continuously tempted to lose himself therein. In one way, this creates a problem: his accomplishments in this world are not the basis for a firm identity and sense of self-confidence.[12] Another Trek fan, code named Douglas, is very explicit about this.

Douglas

Douglas is a college student majoring in engineering, and anxious not to be identified as a person who is so involved in Star Trek that he confuses the show with reality.

> I don't want you thinking I'm running around going to conventions, you know "Oh Spock, you were so good. Now just exactly how did you save the ship from these people? How did you do that?" I mean, I don't want people thinking I live in a fantasy world and we're really concerned about how a character saved the ship by using something that doesn't even exist.

He starts to characterize these overly involved fans as the type of people who have Trek posters in their bedrooms, but he withdraws this characterization when he remembers that in fact he has such posters in his bedroom. He jokes that I will use this as evidence against him when I conduct his "Trekkie trial," presumably an inquiry into the question of whether he is hopelessly lost in the world of Star Trek.

For my part, I must say I have talked to dozens of Star Trek fans who raise the issue of being overly involved in the world of Trek and who cite anecdotes about others who have this problem. I have never spoken to anyone, however, who actually seems to be confused about the boundaries between Trek and reality. This does not mean such people do not exist, although my suspicion is that if they do they are quite rare. At the very least, such fans are not nearly as common as the anecdotes would suggest. Rather, I think this widespread concern about loss of a clear sense of the boundaries of reality testifies to something other than the existence of a group of fans who have lost their grip.

Specifically, I think people tell these stories about others to reassure themselves and their listeners that their experiences of becoming caught up are not pathological. Star Trek fans recognize they may become deeply emotionally involved in the world of Trek, and the realization sometimes scares them. They have thus developed a mythology about Trek fans who are insane, who are unable to distinguish their fantasies from reality. The fan who is merely emotionally involved is thereby confirmed as normal, in contrast to the fan who is crazy.

However, even fans such as Douglas who are careful about not giving any signs of what I would call being caught up often betray their own situation. Douglas repeatedly expresses his disdain for Star Trek fans who are so immersed in the program that they seem to believe it depicts a reality. He jokes: "I think some of them are gone. They've gone where no man has gone before." Yet in describing the events depicted on an episode of "Star Trek" called "The Next Generation," he says, "It showed a different Star Trek past than what really happened." Does this mean Douglas is actually confused about the status of Star Trek as fiction? Certainly not. But in using this phrase, Douglas too shows evidence of a deictic shift into the framework of Trek.

Douglas gets it right when he describes highly involved fans as people who are "really concerned about how a character saved the ship." That is, being deeply involved in the show is a matter of what one is *concerned* about. For all practical purposes, no fan is so deeply involved in the object of delight that he loses the rational capacity to distinguish it from reality. Rather, they may come to *care about* what they idolize more than many aspects of their everyday lives (Campbell 1987).

Many fans with whom I have spoken are uncomfortable with the way they arrange their own priorities. Douglas's words on watching television could be applied to other sorts of activity as well:

> As the summer goes on it's like, well, it's hot. If I study I'll sweat all over everything. We'll sit here and watch TV for a while. We'll just watch a little more. Well, we like that show. Well, we want to see if that dog really bites that guy. And when "Star Trek's" over it's 11:00. We have to get up at 5:00 in the morning. I'm not going to watch "Cops." I cannot stand that program. And they're making money. Watching these people do nothing. Which is what I'm going to have. Let's go to bed.

Douglas repeatedly says, when talking about television watching, that at the end of an evening watching television he has nothing. By this he means he has done nothing to enrich himself or further his goals as a person; he has simply wasted his time. For this reason, he does not want to watch TV, yet—as the quote indicates—he repeatedly finds himself drawn into a full evening in front of the set:

> I spend too much time watching TV. I don't spend enough time reading, studying, doing other things. Therefore I call the TV evil. But yet, if you want to find me, there's a spot in front of the TV that you can find me.

One could argue that in expressing doubts about aspects of his own caught-up behavior, Douglas is merely echoing an elitist critique of popular culture that has managed—in spite of the well-known American distaste for elitism—to garner widespread visibility.[13] But such an interpretation itself smacks of elitism, in denying that Douglas can accurately describe his situation without being swayed by his obeisance to the snobbish intellectuals who look down on Trek and TV. Furthermore, to say only elitists question the depth of immersion in entertainment activities represents a woeful empirical error; such doubts are an almost universal aspect of discussion of this topic with people from all walks of life.

Douglas's feelings here are indigenous, and related to a pervasive American understanding of what human life is ultimately about. TV is evil, Douglas says, because it entices him down a path that ultimately diminishes him as a person. For this reason, he compares television to an addiction; he is compelled to watch TV by a craving that seems not entirely under his control.

Weakness of the Will

Chris's and Douglas's situation is sometimes characterized as entailing "weakness of the will," a phenomenon that has been of central concern to Christian thinkers and to professional philosophers as well.[14] When people do things they claim they do not want to do—have another piece of cake or a cigarette, pursue an ill-advised sexual relationship, strike someone in anger—we are confronted with behavior that challenges our understanding of the basics of human agency. The complex and meaningful qualities of these acts make it clear they are not simple reflexes, but neither are they intentional and chosen. The commonsense explanation of this situation is that this is a matter of desire overwhelming reason.

It is indisputable that this explanation can be of use in an ethical system, because it provides a neat answer to a potentially complex problem: Why do people do things that they deny full responsibility for? However, as Donald Davidson (1980) has pointed out, on an intellectual level the "desire overwhelming reason" explanation is a facile solution to the problem of weakness of will. It is to say there is really no problem here, and weakness of will is simply a case of people being misled or dishonest about their true preferences. John said he wanted to stop smoking, but he had a cigarette; therefore although he may very well want to stop smoking, he wants to have a cigarette even more, and there is no paradox here. But Davidson resists this dismissal of the problem, and I agree with him. It is a woeful error to refuse to listen to what people actually say about their desires in many realms of their experience: we are, just as we say, often torn between alternatives.

Douglas tells me he often watches television all evening, though he says he does not want to do so. We can say, "Douglas misleads us and perhaps himself when he asserts that extended TV watching is not what he wants to do. If he really wants to stop, all he has to do is punch the remote." I disagree with this on both empirical and theoretical grounds.[15] I was there when Douglas said this, and I judge him to be sincere; he really would prefer to spend less time watching TV.

The argument that I have presented in earlier chapters is the basis for another approach to this problem. I have shown that practices of becoming caught up in play infuse the symbols of such play with power. But in thinking about this question of choice, I find it especially important to think about what sort of power these symbols have. The *processes* whereby this infusion of power take place are important. Mental processes such as entrainment and emotional contagion have the effect of displacing a person's subjectivity, especially regarding the authorship of his or her behavior. As I enter into a fiction and begin to experience the world from an imaginary perspective, as I begin to imitate and feel in harmony with the new perspective, I may feel that unfamiliar powers have manifested themselves in my experience. These powers are mysterious—I do not understand their nature or origin—and they seem able to transcend the workings of my day-to-day capacity to direct my own action. Thus the ideals created and endorsed through becoming caught up in play are not only rendered potent but constructed as subterranean, beyond rational understanding, inexorable.

Rather than speaking of weakness of the will or of desire overwhelming reason, we could look instead at how adaptive boredom and feelings of powerless are in our socioeconomic order. Our society, built on values of control and release, puts people in the position of having desires that seem overwhelming and inexorable. In the most radical case, we attribute to these desires a mysterious potency that we are powerless to resist. Cases like these of the two Trek fans are less extreme. When these young men talk about their lives, they articulate a diffuse sense of dissatisfaction. They attribute this dissatisfaction, at least sometimes, to the strength of their attraction to entertainment and their lack of interest in the day-to-day world. Their capacity to choose seems compromised, and in this way perhaps they are representative. Balancing the allure of entertainment with the demands of the day-to-day world is a struggle most of us face at times.

To speak broadly, I can say both Durkheim and Turner call attention to the fact that social ideals are often highlighted in an experiential contrast beginning in a phase of social disengagement and proceeding to the ecstasy of reintegration with communal symbols. The rhetoric of boredom is a local example of the phase of disengagement, and like all forms of liminal symbolism it at once labels a threat and points toward a solution. As Kenneth Burke put it, the essence of rhetoric is to move people to particular sorts of action. "The basic function of rhetoric," he writes, is "the use of words by human agents to form attitudes or induce actions" (1952: 41). To characterize a situation as empty, dead, and boring is to suggest certain kinds of action in response to the situation, namely action that imparts structure and stimulation. In this way boredom, is the initial phase of a humble sequence of meta-action that pervades daily life in contemporary society. The familiar oscillation between boredom and becoming caught up in the play of entertainment begins with a threat of anomie and ends (optimally) in powerful engagement with cultural symbols rendered vital in their experienced capacity to meet the crisis.

This oscillation between the mundane and the ecstatic is nothing new in history. However, as anthropologists are traditionally[16] fond of reminding their readers, generalizations about human beings always take shape in variations stamped by the peculiarities of a particular locality. Our particular version of the phases of life has some significant consequences for the nature of the self. I have already pointed out that our ideology of the strong and rugged individual fits rather uncomfortably with the fact that we evidently regard ourselves as so easily overwhelmed by stimulating experiences. Boredom reveals what is in a sense the opposite side of the vulnerability of the contemporary self; it turns out we are also easily overwhelmed by feelings that we have nothing to do. Damned if we do, damned if we don't.

This difficult situation makes sense if we keep in mind that our society demands of us an extraordinary level of flexibility and openness to change. This flexibility in turn requires that the self not be defined by firm and unvarying commitments and values. We are socially constructed to be receptive to the trajectories of the imagination entailed in its play. Little wonder, then, that we can be pulled in unanticipated directions by unacknowledged powers. Little wonder too if, like the men and women of other times and places, we sometimes understand ourselves to be helpless in the face of these powers, at their mercy. Keep in mind that it is a rhetorical rather than a scientific claim as I say that our ideas about addiction are a form of worship.

Thus, in a sense our capacity to enjoy the range of entertaining activities and substances available to us entails that we feel empty without them.[17] Yet when we are in their presence, we sometimes feel overwhelmed by their power, helpless to resist. In the next chapter I further explore the implications of this situation for how we understand ourselves.

10

Entertainment and Our Understanding of the Self

AMONG THE MOST CONSEQUENTIAL QUESTIONS in social science is, How do collective symbols motivate and organize human activity? We know that human beings can cooperate in building what they need in order to face the challenges of an often harsh world. Perhaps even more miraculously, they can collaborate in sustaining a day-to-day world in which they feel more or less at ease, in which anxiety and hopelessness are usually held at bay, in which most of the time they feel like getting up in the morning. All societies do this, and no one really fathoms how it is done. However, as I have argued in earlier chapters, new ideas such as simulation theory can contribute to fresh ways of thinking about questions of this sort and may therefore offer the opportunity of refining our understanding. Here I have tried to synthesize some of these newer ideas with parts of the classic social scientific approach to the question of how a group of people create and sustain a communal order.

As was discussed in Chapter Six, Durkheim developed the concepts and line of argument that first directly addressed the question of how collective symbols organize commitment to society's ideals. He argued, in *The Elementary Forms of the Religious Life*, that the effervescence generated in collective rituals can be captured in symbols that sustain allegiance to these ideals beyond the actual performance of the ritual. The generations of social scientists following Durkheim

---

Parts of this chapter appeared previously in an article published in the journal *Ethos* (Stromberg 2000).

have criticized and refined his approach, but today it is for the most part taken for granted that collective events such as rituals play a vital role in forging meaningful cultural symbols.

Many have commented that Durkheim was looking backward at the French Revolution for his model of how commitment to symbols and ideals is generated (Lindholm 1990: 28, 30; Lukes 1973: 422). Broadly put, it is in the crowd that history is often made: "Suffice it to think of the night of 4 August, when an assembly was suddenly carried away in an act of sacrifice and abnegation that each of its members had refused to make the night before and by which all were surprised the morning after" (Durkheim 1995: 212). The assumption here is that at the heart of an effective ritual there is social interaction, quintessentially the sort of interaction that occurs in an excited crowd. This energy of interaction undergirds the social order in that it can become associated with, and vitalize, enduring symbols, institutions, moods, and attitudes.

Ironically, however, the French Revolution is one of the icons used in broader contexts to represent the origin of a society in which public gatherings and physical interaction no longer play a dominant role in generating collective symbols and identities.[1] This transformation has occurred gradually over the last two centuries; by now it is fair to observe that power is overwhelmingly channeled through symbols generated by interests that are, in the broadest sense, commercial.[2] In contemporary society people are far more likely to be influenced by widespread print media and by their radios, televisions, and computers than they are in large-scale collective gatherings.[3]

Thus one of the challenges of social science in the century since Durkheim has been to adapt his model to a society in which public gatherings are no longer the site at which commitments and meanings are most likely to be generated. Sociology and anthropology have responded to this challenge only sporadically. The topic has gone in and out of fashion, and no strong subdiscipline or consensual theoretical frameworks have emerged around what Horkheimer and Adorno (2002) called the culture industry.[4] Even today, work on the institutions of entertainment and advertising tends to be located outside the core social sciences of anthropology and sociology (in disciplines such as marketing, communications, cultural studies, film studies, and the like). Thus, as John Thompson (1990: 1–2) has written, "Despite the growing significance of mass communication in the modern world, its nature and implications have received relatively little attention in the literature of social and political theory."

The situation will be corrected one small step at a time, and this book is intended as one of them. Here I have offered evidence and argument—held together with a few assumptions—that in contemporary society some of our most important commitments and desires are sustained not in collective rituals but rather in activities of play, recreation, and leisure. I began by calling attention to the phenomenon of becoming caught up in play. When we become caught up in a book, a movie, a game, we suspend our disbelief and enjoy these fictions if we were, for a few moments, dwelling in the world they represent. Doing so, it turns out, entails some of the same cognitive and emotional processes that occur when a person is engaged in high-intensity social interaction. In particular I have signaled the importance of attentional processes, entrainment, and emotional contagion; singly and in combination, these processes can create powerful experiences of self-transcendence.

The potential significance of such experiences becomes clear if one considers just how many aspects of our culture can be described as playful fictions. In addition to the enormous apparatus of entertainment proper (movies, television, print, the Internet, spectator events . . .), there are all of the aspects of our culture that become ever more entertaining in order to attract attention: advertising, the news, candidates for political office, any public presentation, textbooks, and on and on. Then there are those romantic realist fictions of all sorts (including images) that surround us, perfecting our reality while depicting it. In contemporary society, entertainment opportunities are ubiquitous and constantly expanding. Through these opportunities, people may be drawn into ecstatic experiences that have enormous cultural significance, for in these experiences people see and feel the power of certain ideas and values, ideas and values that turn out to be central in sustaining our way of life.

Perhaps I need to pause here to tie together and make explicit what is entailed in this process of infusing power into our values, ideals, desires. What is it, specifically, that gets valorized? The place to start in answering this question is with the examples I have given. I discussed, for example, romance, an important idea in our relationships, and in a variety of forms of entertainment. Obviously, the idea is so central in songs, movies, novels, and so on because it is important in our relationship histories. Just as obviously, it is important in our relationship histories because it is important in so many genres of entertainment. The idea of romance is valorized in the sense that romance emerges from this dialectic as a force of overwhelming power. Not only is romance endlessly fascinating to us, we understand that those caught in its grip may be completely under its sway. They may abandon their reason, their commitments, even their families when under the grip of romance.

Another of my examples is equally striking. The drugs alcohol and tobacco are also understood to overwhelm people; alcohol, like romance, often destroys established lives. I do not for a moment deny that the power these drugs assert is a matter in no small part of chemistry, but I do deny that this is the whole story. I argued that, as is the case with romance, experiences of becoming caught up in play with these substances contribute to our conviction that they can overwhelm us. More broadly, I want to suggest (fully acknowledging that at this point I am moving from what has been demonstrated to what seems likely) that the machinery of entertainment and advertising work in similar ways to valorize other tangible substances, services, and objects. As I have mentioned earlier, many advertisements take the form of romantic realist fictions in which a product plays a starring role. The product becomes what creates the fantasies that occur as the viewer becomes caught up in the minifiction, and thereby the product becomes desirable.

But what of role-playing games? What of the vast array of pleasurable activities they can be taken to represent, activities that are not obviously tied to a particular idea or substance? These are activities that are undertaken because their participants find them to be amusing. Games of all sorts, many genres of both visual and print fictions, spectator sports . . . the list could go on. In these activities, there is no idea or concept with obvious social significance, no substance with peculiar properties. There is, primarily, fun and enjoyment. Therefore the activity itself is valorized as desirable. It is very simple. A great deal of what is valorized through the processes I have discussed is simply activities that people then come to desire, and often to do so they must purchase things. One could write a book on the economy of amusements, although that is not the book I have written.

Instead I have directed my interest to the significance, on a general level, of becoming caught up in the play of entertainment. In that spirit, in this chapter I want to consider one more target for valorization, perhaps the most important of them all. This is the very notion of the flexibility of the self.[5] It is difficult to talk about our conception of the self because unless one has thought carefully about this topic, one will not even recognize that we *have* a conception of the self. One of the distinctive achievements of our culture is the extent to which how we think about the self has been naturalized, rendered unquestionable and almost invisible. We *know* what the self is, so there is no need to reflect on it, to try to understand why our conception of the self is historically peculiar. Mary Douglas (1992: 41) observes that "in our western industrial culture, knowledge of the person and self is deliberately sunk into one of those areas of protected public ignorance." This ignorance serves to insulate our ways of thinking about the self from any scrutiny or doubt, and it thereby protects the architecture of ideas and values that are founded in our conception of self.[6]

So, first I want to point out that we who live in contemporary society have certain ideas about what a person is, as do people in all communities. Again like everyone else, our ideas about what a person is are not random, but rather they mesh—often in very complex ways—with our beliefs and ideas about other parts of life. For example, ideas about what a person is have immediate implications for what a person should do, and thus for ideas about morality and meaning. Because of this, the concept of person turns out to be a central legal and political concept, as well as being directly tied to the cosmologies outlined in religious systems. The concept of person is often closely tied to even such seemingly distant conceptual realms as time, as Clifford Geertz (1973) famously demonstrated for the Balinese. Because a concept of self is often part of the foundation of a social order, such concepts can be difficult to see, much less to talk about. Such is frequently the case with our most basic assumptions.

I also want to remind readers that a society's most basic assumptions have been repeatedly shown by social scientists to be rendered potent, even unquestionable, through rituals. Randall Collins (2004: 25) writes, "Rituals do honor to what is socially valued, what Durkheim called *sacred objects.*" He continues, "In modern societies, the foremost of these is the individual self."[7] Throughout this book I have argued that social scientists would do well to look carefully at play as another means of cementing our most important commitments. Through play we often forge commitments that clearly shape our behavior but that we are reluctant to acknowledge openly. As a result, if one looks closely, in many realms we seem to have two, somewhat contradictory, systems of values. Now I want to point out that this is also true of the self.

In fact, our conception of what we are as human persons, as selves, is patently contradictory. Individual autonomy is surely near the top of any list of articulated values in contemporary society. Writes Nikolas Rose (1996: 1), the "ethic of the free, autonomous self seems to trace out something quite fundamental in the ways in which modern men and women have come to understand, experience, and evaluate themselves, their actions, and their lives." Americans in particular pride themselves on their individualism and autonomy, counting freedom of choice among the most cherished of political and cultural values. It is through this freedom that we are able to bring into being our own version of the sacred, the unique features of each self. Central to our ethics is the conviction that each person is understood as the incarnation of an inimitable blend of characteristics that should be treasured and cultivated.

Why then should the United States be a hotbed of what Eve Sedgwick (1993) calls "addiction attributions"? In spite of our conviction that ours is a culture of free choice, we evidently regard ourselves as profoundly vulnerable to being controlled by our involvement with certain substances or activities. Even casual observers note that by now one can be said to be addicted to just about anything: eating, dieting, sex, exercise, the Internet, work, and so on. This suggests that rather than being rugged individuals, we are all too easily overwhelmed by any number of environmental factors that seem able to seize control of our will.

So which is it? Is the contemporary self an amalgam of free will and a unique essence capable of shaping the very course of history? Or is it a fragile wraith buffeted by potent forces that are a continuous threat to its capacity to direct its own action? It is both. Men and women in our society—in all societies, actually—must often sustain contradictory streams of motives. I have argued that our not-to-be-taken-too-seriously entertainment system actually does the serious cultural work of sustaining some of the motives that we are likely to deny or discredit, motives that are nevertheless vital to our economy and our entire way of life. In the contradictory ideas we hold about the self, we encounter perhaps the most striking example of this principle. There is a culturally acknowledged self, the one we claim, the free and unique individual. There is also a malleable self, capable of deep immersion in the fantasies of entertainment and the stimulation of ubiquitous play opportunities, yet vulnerable to being controlled by its craving for stimulation. I should be careful here because my language might suggest the understanding that the self is some tangible thing, perhaps analogous to an organ in the body. But in fact, the self to which I refer is an idea, or a system of ideas, about what a person is. It should also be kept in mind that once people accept a set of ideas about what the self is, those ideas may well function for all the world like a tangible object. They will control behavior with extraordinary consistency and efficacy.

The flexible self is a set of ideas (actually held as much in the form of feelings as beliefs) that influence people's expectations and understandings, and that therefore influence their behavior.[8] In a culture in which individuality and autonomy are celebrated, there is also an undercurrent that pulls people into conformity and eagerness for stimulation, and brings them to cultivate their capacity for transformation. My argument here is that this flexible self is valorized and sustained through entertainment activities.

I have noted that when a person becomes caught up in an entertainment activity, he or she may trace the power of this experience to a particular source such as a game, a drug, or an experience. But now I also want to point out that cumulatively, as a person has such experiences, he or she is repeatedly learning a theory about what sort of being he or she is.[9] As experiences of becoming caught up become more powerful and frequent, the participant develops the sense both that his experiences can transport him to a higher plane of excitement, and further that the ecstasy he feels in play is a standard that other parts of life should meet. These beliefs and expectations can powerfully shape the person's ongoing activity.

Thus, in spite of our conviction that we are an individualistic people, our culture conducts an ongoing and rather successful campaign to encourage development of a self that finds pleasure by suspending its commitments and throwing itself into stimulating experiences of entertainment. Awash in experiences of the flexibility of the self, the person comes to expect and finally to embody flexibility. I now want to return once more, albeit briefly, to our history in order to seek some clue as to the origins of this strange situation.

The Self-Defining Subject

Historians are agreed that the modern period, beginning very roughly around the time of the Reformation, ushered in significant changes in social character. One of the most significant implications of Reformation theology stems from its vehement rejection of the medieval Catholic view that the sacred is concentrated in particular domains (in the activities of the sacraments, the officers of the church, religious holidays, saints, and so on). In the thought of the reformers, the mediator of God's grace became the individual believer, and this principle is one of the most important sources of the emerging tendency to conceptualize human beings as autonomous individuals. But it also follows from the rejection of the older view of the sacred that the ordinary life of the believer comes to be sacralized; the reformers all urged versions of the general principle that the sacred interpenetrated day-to-day life (Taylor 1989: 217). Eventually, this conviction spread beyond Protestantism and became a component of the modern Western worldview. The culture of entertainment—with its oscillation between boredom and becoming caught up, its ubiquitous opportunities for stimulation—is a manifestation of this principle, transformed over centuries. We now live in an order in which the sacred is woven into the fabric of the everyday, and indeed an order in which the sacred may or may not be conceived in religious terms.

An important factor in the development of this situation was the emergence of the literary genre we call the novel. I referred to the novel in an earlier chapter as reflecting a shift in the conventions whereby narratives are grasped; rather than looking for the meaning of the narrative in a preexisting transcendental scheme, the novel reader looks instead to the relationships established within the structure of the story.

This change in conventions of narrative also reflects a change in the relationship of the person to the wider world. Puritans, to quote Watt (1957: 85), had "an intensely active conception of life as a continuous moral and social struggle; they all . . . [saw] every event in ordinary life as proposing an intrinsically moral issue on which reason and conscience must be exerted to the full before right action is possible." The same is true for the increasingly secularized Puritan heirs of the 18th century, except that they sought these meanings in the course of their lives. The novel comes into existence once it is accepted "that individual human beings . . . were allotted the supreme role on the earthly stage" (Watt 1957: 84).

As noted earlier, the novel represents a shift in interpretive practices, from seeking meaning on the transcendent plane to looking for it in the framework provided by the trajectory of a life. This is one dimension of the epochal transformation that Charles Taylor (1975: 6) has referred to as the birth of a "self-defining" subject. "The modern subject," he writes, "is self-defining, where on previous views the subject is defined in relation to a cosmic order."

If the subject is self-defining, then the meanings that ground the subject on the earth and locate her in the cosmos are not given, at least not in any easily discernible way. The self-defining subject must figure things out by patching together symbolic resources from many sources (Stromberg 1985). In the world of the self-defining subject, symbolic resources multiply and become the medium through which struggles for economic and political power are waged. What I have called entertainment is one arena in which the self-defining subject seeks grounding meanings, although very often the person does not conceptualize their engagement with entertainment in these terms. (As I am trying to show, ironically the most consistent and perhaps most powerful of these grounding meanings is the notion that the person is ungrounded.)

Within this general context, the development of a culture of entertainment can be seen as the emergence of a realm in which symbolic resources enter the economy and the broader social order. There is power (often manifested as money) available through purveying those resources subjects use to define themselves. In this situation, the increasing instability of the self is in the interest of power holders; those who are trying to find themselves can be counted on to be avid consumers of symbolic resources. Many observers have argued that in contemporary society we have just such an organization of personhood, a form of subjectivity that is highly flexible and context-dependent.[10] Here I follow those who maintain that this form of subjectivity, in its very essence unstable, began to emerge starting in the late 19th century. This form of subjectivity renders inhabitants of the contemporary social world especially receptive to the charms of becoming caught up in entertainment, because not only do such experiences stimulate and excite, they also constitute a form of certainty in the midst of ever-fluctuating everyday life.

The Ideal of Character

One can pick several starting points in telling the story of the new form of social character that had begun to emerge in American society by the late 19th century. In an earlier chapter, I looked at how related ideas in the realms of theology, art, and economics prepared the way for the contemporary concept of self. Another important force shaping our concept of self, especially in the 20th century, has been rapidly changing forms of community. Although the stability of rural communities must not be overstated, it is nevertheless safe to offer some generalizations.

The growth of large population centers entailed that many people were spending their lives in social contexts that were quite different from those their parents and grandparents had experienced. In rural settings with relatively low population mobility, one is likely to know one's neighbors, and families may have remained in one area for many generations. By contrast, in the city one may encounter and need to make judgments of many unfamiliar people in the course of a day.[11] The great urban migrations of this period thus typically entailed not only that one began to encounter more people every day but also that, compared to an earlier era, it was less possible to evaluate persons on the basis of long-term knowledge of them and their families. This situation encourages development of the capacity to both send and interpret the kind of signs of personhood that can be produced in ephemeral encounters.

A well-known summary of the change in notions of person that accompanied the large-scale urbanization of the late 19th century in American society is by historian Warren Susman (1984). Throughout most of the 19th century, the relevant term for conceptualizing individual human beings was "character." When human beings are understood in terms of character, the essential thing about a person is how he or she conforms to widely accepted ideas of virtue. A person with character is a person who measures up to a standard, who exemplifies certain widely agreed virtues such as courage and honesty. Today we demand that people be authentic, that they somehow discover what they really are and then struggle to achieve it. Today we advise people that nothing is more important than fulfilling their potential. Such admonitions are meaningless in a world where people are understood in terms of character. In the world of character, what is admired is behavior that adheres to accepted values rather than what reflects something hidden within each individual.[12]

The ideal of character, and the forces that began to change that ideal, can be illustrated in any number of ways; one particularly clear example is the history of courtship.[13] As Beth Bailey (1988) points out in her book *From Front Porch to Back Seat*, the idea of the "date" is relatively recent. The word originated among prostitutes in the late 19th century; a "date" was a set time for a prostitute to meet a client. At the turn of the century, courtship in most parts of middle- and upper-class America still took place through the system of "calling." A man would come to call on a woman, and they would socialize in her home. In some urban areas, however, this approach was beginning, by the turn of the century, to be replaced by the system we are more familiar with today, in which the man (at that time it was expected to be the man) asked the woman to go "out" with him.

The significance of the difference between these two forms of courtship is that in the calling system the interaction of the couple is for the most part under the control of the woman's parents. It is the woman's mother or perhaps father who decides whether to accept the man into her home, and her decision is typically based on the man's social standing. If he is a member of a family into which the parent could imagine her daughter marrying, she will accept the caller. If the caller is not accepted, the courtship is over before it begins. The dating system represents a considerable loosening of familial control over courtship, because in this case the decision to engage in courtship activities is no longer made for a woman more or less exclusively by her family. In the dating system, the woman involved has more autonomy in deciding what a suitor's chances will be.

In one sense, what is going on here is a shift toward greater freedom. The couple has wider latitude out in the anonymous public than they do sitting in the parlor with mother. Even more important, the suitability of the man has become more a matter for the daughter to judge than for her parents. But there is something else to notice here as well. The shift in *who* makes a judgment about a suitor is also a shift in *what* the suitor is judged on. Although the daughter is likely to know her suitor's social standing and to be capable of reading the signs in his behavior that betray the standing, she is much more likely than her mother or father to be swayed by his personal characteristics: his charm, his looks, his romantic fervor, and so on. In the shift between the calling system and the dating system, one can observe a change in how the person is defined; in the first system, a man is significantly defined by the group he is born into and by the behaviors signaling his association with that group. In the second system, he is increasingly defined by certain of his individual characteristics, by what was starting to be widely known as his personality.

The point here is not that individual characteristics were considered unimportant prior to the late 19th century. But which characteristics were significant, and what they were thought to signify, did change around this time. Many authors have pointed out that these changes may have economic roots; ideas of character, which stress rigid adherence to values such as thrift, industry, and piety, are well suited to a developing economy oriented toward building of economic infrastructure (Lears 1983). Both entrepreneurs and workers need to exhibit such characteristics for an economy to work. However, as industry becomes bureaucratic and consumption of consumer goods becomes more important, these very qualities may begin to impede development. If the economy depends on mass consumption, thrift and industry must be supplemented by impulsiveness and pursuit of leisure. Bureaucratic organization demands not rigid adherence to principle but rather a willingness to be flexible in meeting changing goals and getting along with others (Susman 1984, Lears 1983). The system of mass consumption ultimately depends on a form of behavior that entails a willingness, indeed an eagerness, to continuously try new products and ideas in the quest for fulfillment.

Thus the turn of the 20th century was a time of fascination with the new notion of personality, the conception that each person should develop his or her own charisma, the capacity to be popular, unique, and appealing (Susman 1984). It is interesting to note that this transition in the conception of self was accompanied by a wave of uncertainty and insecurity, especially among the middle classes, as people confronted the contradiction between what they had been raised to be and what they were expected to be now. One index of this social bewilderment can be found in the domain of public health. This age seems to have been characterized by a virtual explosion of emotional disturbance among the middle classes.[14] During the latter part of the 19th century, increasing attention was focused on a disease called "nervous exhaustion," or neurasthenia (Lears 1983: 7). The symptoms that characterized the malady, though undoubtedly all too real for its sufferers, sound diffuse and even vague: exhaustion, insomnia, phobias, chronic pain, drowsiness, and so on. In terms of modern diagnostic categories, probably much of what was termed neurasthenia would today be classed as depression or anxiety disorders. Whatever the precise diagnosis, there was a widespread public perception that mental instability was on the rise, and a corresponding level of alarm about this possibility.[15]

What was wrong? Looking back from the perspective afforded by the last century, it seems that people were trying to understand themselves and their experience in terms that were no longer adequate to their day-to-day lives. The self-mastery that was, according to ideas about character, the key to a virtuous and successful life was beginning to be less relevant to everyday experience. People were being steered toward ideals that were corrupt in terms of ingrained notions of character, and they needed a new way to think about themselves and their lives.

The general social uneasiness was not limited to the level of the individual. It is important to remember that, in spite of widespread optimism about the future course of industrial and moral development, the late 19th century was a time of considerable social turmoil. Labor unrest continued to grow in the first two decades of the 20th century, and there was a significant and increasing gap between the lives of the middle and working classes. The recurring economic cycle of expansion and depression generated widespread unemployment and attendant suffering. Society's divisions were plain to see, and their existence fit poorly with articles of faith such as the perfectibility of the social order, the universal possibility of self-improvement, and the availability of technological solutions for all problems. Middle-class people began to lose faith in the beliefs that had guided the lives of their parents, and where that faith had been they felt an ominous threat from below.

When people's lives do not make sense in terms of received values, categories, and expectations, they are prone to develop the kinds of emotional and physical symptoms that are typical of extreme stress: addictions, depression, debilitating anxiety, apathy, and so on. It is such situations of widespread disorientation that social scientists have shown to be associated with the development of millenarianism (Wallace 1956). Indeed, this period was marked by an efflorescence of millenarian and quasi-millenarian ideologies, articulated by prophets such as Phineas Parkhurst Quimby, Mary Baker Eddy, and in the mid-20th century "positive thinkers" such as Dale Carnegie and Norman Vincent Peale (Meyer 1980).

Lears has also called attention to the consolidation, during this period, of a "therapeutic ethos," a blend of values and institutions that stressed the possibility of vitality and fulfillment in everyday life and new means of attaining them. In addition to positive-thinking religious prophets, this was the period in which our contemporary practices of psychotherapy began to take shape, health-food enthusiasts such as the Kellogg brothers promoted packaged breakfast cereals as the foundation for a life of regularity and vitality, and of course modern forms of advertising emerged. Lears notes that Americans were used to the humbug of entrepreneurs such as P. T. Barnum, that they regarded exaggerated claims for products or spectacles as a part of their entertainment value. He (1983: 28) goes on to describe the inflated advertising of the day in terms that harmonize with the themes I have developed in the present work:

> No doubt many ordinary Americans refused to embrace this world literally, but they were drawn into it for its entertainment value—the sensual appeal of its illustrations, the seductiveness of basking (however briefly) in the promise of self-realization through consumption. Many advertisements took their place alongside other mass diversions—the amusement park, the slick-paper romance, the movies. None demanded to be taken literally or even all that seriously; yet all promised intense "real life" to their clientele, and all implicitly defined "real life" as something outside the individual's everyday experience.

There are three points here I would like to highlight. First is the idea that self-realization occurs (in part) through consumption. Second is the observation that advertising, and entertainment more generally, is not taken seriously. Third is the somewhat contradictory point that nevertheless the images of entertainment are the dwelling place of real life, life as it should be. Together, these points add up to the dominant version of the therapeutic ethos: the conviction that a finely tuned individualism could be the salvation for each person and the offer to furnish this through conformity to mass-produced symbols.

In short, the solution to the cultural disorientation of the turn of the 20th century turned out to be the growing faith that happiness and purpose could be realized in the fulfillment of the self, and the culture of entertainment was among the most important cultural systems taking shape to offer this fulfillment. Today we learn that the most important thing in life is to unravel the mystery that is yourself. You are unique; indeed, the uniqueness of the self is the highest value.[16] Although this is typically interpreted as a celebration of individuality, I urge caution about this judgment. We can develop ourselves only after we get some advice as to what our selves might be.[17] Today—and what a fortunate convenience this is!—we live in a world in which any number of institutions exist to tell us what we should want and how to get it. Thus our individuality is mixed with a good deal of conformity and suggestibility.[18]

The contradiction between our unique individuality and our socially ensured dependence on external powers has continued to develop in recent decades. Particularly since the 1970s, American society has seen ephemeral epidemics of new emotional disorders that seem to testify to a level of cultural confusion not unlike that of the late 19th century. In addition to the enormous expansion of addiction attributions, one can point to spectacular growth in diagnosis of such problems as multiple personality disorder (Hacking 1995), eating disorders of various stripes, and attention deficit hyperactivity disorder (DeGrandpre 1999). All of these disorders seem to be tied in one way or another to the vulnerability of the self. Perhaps the most revealing of the proliferating diagnoses of the late 20th century is the co-dependency movement, documented in an excellent study by John Steadman Rice (1996) entitled *A Disease of One's Own*. Just as Lears connects the therapeutic ethos to the institutions that came into being to address the problems of the late-19th-century self, Rice points to the role of what he calls "liberation psychology" in both acting as the basis for the co-dependency movement and offering a cure for the problems of co-dependents.

Rice notes that although originally a co-dependent was a person who was somehow enmeshed in the behavior patterns of another person who suffered from an addiction, as the co-dependency movement gained traction in the late 1980s the concept expanded along with its popularity. Co-dependency was reconceived as a disease in its own right, no longer the result of association with an addict. Rather, co-dependency itself was the cause of all addictions (1996: 8). Furthermore, co-dependency was the result of oppressive practices of child rearing that stifled expression and development of the true self. This view expresses the most fundamental themes of liberation psychology, which had been developing in professional circles since the mid-20th century. The basic principle of liberation psychology is that emotional difficulties stem from the barriers that social institutions place in the way of expression of the true self. Rice (1996: 29) characterizes the core assumption of liberation psychology as follows: "Conventional culture and society make individuals sick by thwarting the development of the 'real self' in the interests of social conformity."

In liberation psychology, the inner self is understood to be so valuable that any external demands of family or other institutions are an insult that must be swept away, for the self is also so fragile that such demands will cripple it and render it unable to exercise free will. This position can be understood as an extreme manifestation of a contradiction that has haunted the notion of personality since its appearance over a century ago: we contemporary selves embark on a quest, a quest of self-discovery. We are convinced that our quest has an object: ourselves. But this quest depends on our being highly receptive to suggestions—conveyed in no small part by the culture of entertainment—about our possibilities. So, realizing ourselves turns out to be a process highly dependent on external social institutions that are capable of overwhelming us.

The problem is compounded by the fact that one's quest for inner uniqueness often comes to be organized in terms of a search for the kind of satisfaction and emotional stimulation that occur in experiences of becoming caught up. It is in such experiences that one glimpses—and feels—life as it should be. However, these ecstatic moments are not linked to one's actual struggles; they are not tied into one's personal history. That is, if the goal is realization of the self, one would expect that what is made real would be continuous with a person's experience, history, temperament, and so on. Thus those who seek self-realization in experiences of entertainment are likely to find that their goal remains elusive, and that what is hoped for remains just out of reach. Ironically, to the extent that we follow the path of self-realization through entertainment, many of our most sought-out experiences will foster our sense of the fragility of the self. In repeated experiences of becoming caught up, a flexible self grows, and the flexible self is by its nature vulnerable to being swept away by the power of stimulation. In cultivating our capacity for stimulation, we build a self that is ever receptive to the pleasures of entertainment experiences and therefore less likely to be able to resist their appeal.

The flexible self is a network of mental phenomena—beliefs, ideas, expectations, values, desires, emotions—that work together to encourage certain sorts of activity. This activity—a cycle of participating in and seeking out experiences of entertainment—is a component of the very foundation of our way of life. The consequences of this cycle ramify throughout contemporary life, and tracing these consequences would be an extensive project in its own right. In my concluding comments, I make a few suggestions about how to begin.

Conclusion

I BEGAN THIS BOOK by describing Skip, a man who becomes so caught up in playing a game that his body, and at least part of his mind, falls into the game. I hope I have subsequently portrayed enough varieties of becoming caught up so that most readers will recognize they too at times become caught up in the play of entertainment. But what does it matter? Skip is just having fun, as are the rest of us when we play games or immerse ourselves in fictions or lapse into fantasies about our desires for activities or relationships or consumer products.

The phrase "just having fun" is interesting. It suggests that when people are having fun, it's *just* that; this is the end of it, and there is no sense in inquiring further about why they are acting this way. Fun is such a powerful and transparent motive that anything undertaken because it is fun needs no further explanation.

As a long-term admirer of the deviousness of human beings, I am suspicious. When the conventional way of looking at some activity suggests the activity needs no explanation, I wonder whether the conventional view is hiding something. Throughout this book I have argued that an entire set of values and motives (associated with pleasure, release, and leisure) is sustained and satisfied through experiences of becoming caught up in entertainment activities. The fact that we would prefer to limit our exploration of these experiences by describing them as "just having fun" points to the conclusion that we would rather not think too carefully about the contradictions between the motives of the day and those of the night. It turns out no massive propaganda apparatus is required to sustain doublethink.

In the previous chapter, I argued that among the most important of these subterranean values and motives is one important part of our conception of the self. In closing, I want to touch on one more implication of this partially hidden, flexible self-concept, because doing so allows me to frame some questions about what all of this means.

As I have mentioned, how a group of people conceptualizes what a person is has implications for many aspects of their collective life and worldview. Here I want to call attention to one more important cultural realm that is closely tied to concept of self: community. Contemporary concepts of personhood have been not only shaped by religious and political ideas that developed over centuries but also a response to changing forms of community, particularly in the past 150 years or so. The changes in forms of self and community I outlined in the previous chapter can be understood as two sides of the same coin.

By the early 20th century, social and economic transformations demanded a form of social character that could be displayed and evaluated in ephemeral encounters, as short-term relationships became increasingly important. The emerging mass production economy provided a convenient means to accomplish this. Through purchase and use of commodities such as clothing, automobiles, cigarettes—the list could be extended forever—consumers assembled the props they needed for whatever sort of performance they had in mind. From one perspective, this configuration is a way of organizing persons; as Susman (1984) points out, it is what we call personality. But this social arrangement is also a means of organizing communities, of creating associations tied together by a peculiar set of symbolic resources.

The relationships between the flexible self I have described and forms of community is a topic worthy of another book, and there is no prospect for treating this matter in any detail here. However, a very general description of some of these relationships is an appropriate way to close this book in that such a description bears directly on the question of the implications of this analysis. The book *Bowling Alone,* by Robert Putnam (2000), calls attention to the fact that participation in the civic and religious groups vital to our social and political life has been declining over the last several decades. In fact, the years during which communal participation has declined correspond to the years in which, as I mentioned earlier, a number of previously unknown or rare cognitive and emotional disorders began to proliferate. Here is now Putnam (2000: 27) describes the situation:

> For the first two-thirds of the twentieth century a powerful tide bore Americans into ever deeper engagement in the life of their communities, but a few decades ago—silently, without warning—that tide reversed and we were overtaken by a treacherous rip current. Without at first noticing, we have been pulled apart from one another and from our communities over the last third of the century.

Putnam's is a very careful and circumspect book, and he is perfectly aware that America remains a society in which groups of various sorts—families, soccer teams, fraternities, churches, circles of friends—remain vital and active. It cannot be maintained that the culture of entertainment has significantly undermined American communities, not only because innumerable such communities carry on just fine but also because the culture of entertainment, or parts of it, generates its own forms of community. For example, Daniel Boorstin (1973) used the term "consumption communities" to refer to the increasing importance, in the period after the American civil war, of groups whose public symbols of membership were consumer products. Those who smoke a particular brand of cigarette or drive a certain car are bound together. Admittedly, consumption communities are ephemeral and the social bond on which they are based is not particularly deep. As Boorstin (1973: 147) writes, "These consumption communities, even while they became ever more significant in the daily life of the nation, were milder, less exclusive, and less serious than the communities that had held men together in an early New England Puritan village or in a westward-moving wagon train." But it does not follow from this that consumption communities are culturally insignificant. In our society, much gets transacted in fleeting encounters, and consumption communities are the expression, on a communal level, of this fact.

Nevertheless, it is also true, as Putnam demonstrates in voluminous detail, that any number of sorts of groups have seen declining participation in recent decades. (His examples include clubs of all kinds, public meetings, church attendance, union participation, and so forth.) He considers several possible causes for the precipitous decline in civic participation, and the factor to which he assigns the greatest importance is television viewing. Some of the connections here are fairly obvious; he who is watching television is likely in his house rather than out and about. Furthermore, each hour in front of the TV is one hour less to interact with fellow citizens. But Putnam also believes that TV may have psychological effects that discourage participation in groups.

I offer for consideration the possibility that the processes I have discussed in this book are relevant here. Specifically, those experiences that sustain the flexible self conduct something of an ongoing campaign against civic participation. The connection here is at a very basic level. The liberation psychologists are correct: to be maximally flexible, one must eschew the commitments and strictures of enduring groups in favor of the capacity to adopt the commitments of the moment. But—unlike liberation psychologists—I do not accept that these commitments are expressions of the unique inner self. Rather, these commitments are largely to symbols intentionally fashioned by commercial interests to excite and stimulate us. Thus we come to seek meaning and purpose in stimulation (and in its absence, we are prone to boredom, apathy, and disorientation). In sum, the values of the flexible self do not suggest to people that they will find pleasure or fulfillment in the firm commitments entailed by participation in social communities; in fact, those values suggest that social communities may interfere with one's pursuit of stimulation. At this point, one can begin to see that the ideals cultivated in entertainment may have wide-ranging implications, extending for example to such matters as our communal life and political order.

My fondest hope in writing this book is to provoke conversation about these implications and their relationship to entertainment, a topic that is at once terribly important and terribly mystifying to us. I close, then, with some questions.

For my fellow social scientists: Why is the analytic apparatus for studying entertainment weak, when entertainment itself is such a potent cultural force in the world today? How can we cultivate our capacity to stand outside of the assumptions of entertainment culture and contemplate it critically? What are the political implications of the rapid spread of entertainment values outside of the West? Is it true, as I suggest, that play is a more useful category for analysis of entertainment than ritual is? Is it true that entertainment activities are a form of meta-action that often work to valorize ideals denied or downplayed in official discourse? If so, does entertainment culture undermine or promote contradictions in cultural value systems? Is it true that contemporary culture is characterized by forms of meta-action that are woven into everyday life, as in the oscillation between boredom and becoming caught up?

In addition, I would add some questions for my readers who are not social scientists, while at the same time thanking them for hanging with me: Why do we find it plausible that a new product or a new relationship will utterly change our situation? Why are we are drawn, moth-to-flame-like, to any story of transformation: the "reality" drama, the celebrity, the romance, our own therapeutic narratives? Is it possible to resist the values of the culture of entertainment, either in personal or in public life? Is it desirable to do so? Why is there so much talk about (say) celebrities and so little insightful talk about why there is so much talk about celebrities? Why do those on the political left or the political right who value communities often support those economic forces that produce entertainment? At the end of the day, does entertainment enhance or detract from our liberty?

Because I have primarily sought to raise questions, I have few if any answers. I do know that we inhabitants of contemporary society receive the message, every day and in many ways, that fulfillment is the proper goal of life, and that the possibilities for fulfillment are all around us. But as is ever the case with romance, the dream proves more powerful than the reality, and many assert that true fulfillment continues to evade us. For those caught in these unhappy circumstances, surrounded by riches that fade away as they grasp them, experiences of becoming caught up are opportunities for satisfaction. When we become caught up, we step for a brief time into that other world in the guise of imaginary beings who dwell there. To the extent we possess the psychological skills necessary to enjoy the play of entertainment, we become those beings and experience the compelling meanings and feelings that are so elusive in the day-to-day world. But it is also possible that in doing so we undermine our own capacity for autonomy and the sense of authorship of our own action.

Am I making a claim about the quality of life in the 21st century? I do not intend to do so, except perhaps peripherally. Rather, I am trying to introduce a concept—becoming caught up—and its implications for sustaining a particular sort of socioeconomic order. I am suggesting that the processes I have described here may bear on a number of important issues in contemporary social science. These issues include theoretical questions about the nature of order and action, practical questions about issues such as politics and consumption, ethnographic questions about the nature of contemporary society, and psychological questions about the self in a high-consumption society. Some may want to tie these observations to social commentary, to criticize or defend a way of life. The current work aspires only to outline a way of looking at our situation. I hope that this perspective is helpful to those who are ready to assess and reflect on the culture of entertainment and its place in our society.

Notes

Notes to Chapter 1

1. These imaginary worlds are specified by the rules of the game and the stipulations of a player-referee (see Fine 1983). As I write this, role playing is more likely to occur on the Internet than in the back room of a fast food restaurant, and every time I turn around I see updated examples of people becoming caught up in the imaginary worlds of electronics. You will have to accept that any book on this topic will be at least partially out of date by the time it reaches you.

2. Fine (1983) lays the groundwork for a discussion of becoming caught up in role-playing games, although he does not use this term. He points out (1983: 185) that unlike games in which the goal is something like winning, role-playing games are not directly competitive and thus can be considered explicitly directed toward engrossment. Fine, however, does not consider role-playing games to entail physical movement (1983: 184) and thus considers this engrossment to be a purely "internal" phenomenon. This is where our accounts diverge somewhat, although I hasten to add that Fine may have observed a different sort of game from the ones I concentrate on in this book.

3. Many authors have looked at the phenomenon of getting lost in play or other fictional worlds. See Nell (1988) for an extensive discussion of absorption in reading that offers many parallels to this work. This book also has an excellent bibliography of other sources related to the topic.

4. I have offered only a sketchy definition of play here because the reader's understanding of the term is likely to be firmer than any formal definition I can devise. This definition is intended to be a boiled-down restatement of the classic definition of play offered by Huizinga (1950: 28): "Play is a voluntary activity or occupation executed within certain fixed limits of time and place, according to rules freely accepted but absolutely binding, having its aim in itself and accompanied by a feeling of tension, joy and the consciousness

that it is 'different' from 'ordinary life.'" As I note below (and following Bateson 1972), it is especially important to emphasize that play is set off by metacommunicative conventions (typically implicit) that distinguish it from action in the day-to-day world.

5. These are by no means the only authors who have described the importance of ecstatic states in play. Many who have written on play name the experience of being caught up in play as its very essence. Huizinga (1950: 2–3) writes, "In this intensity, this absorption, this power of maddening, lies the very essence, the primordial quality of play." Or consider Gadamer 1975: 92): "Play fulfills its purpose only if the player loses himself in his play." Koepping (1997) provides an admirable review of the scholarship on his topic, which extends back at least to the philosophers of the Romantic period. Many readers of anthropology will recognize the term deep play from Clifford Geertz's well-known study (1973) of the Balinese cockfight. Both he and Ackerman have taken the term from Jeremy Bentham, although Geertz seems to use the concept in a way that is closer to Bentham's original formulation.

6. As this book went to press, I discovered another group of scholars who have studied a phenomenon very similar to what I am designating as becoming caught up; these are psychologists who have turned their attention to the process of what they call "narrative transport." (See, for example, Green, Brock, and Kaufman, 2004; and Green, Strange, and Brock, 2002.) I encountered this interesting research too late to integrate it into the present argument but encourage readers who are interested in this topic to consult these works and their bibliographies.

7. Somewhat atypically for an anthropologist, I have confined this study to the cultural context in which I myself dwell, that of the early 21st century in the United States. This is in part because I am a somewhat atypical anthropologist, and my work focuses on contemporary European and North American society. The covert assumption that non-Western societies are the most appropriate target for anthropological scrutiny is at times a thinly disguised form of racism that serves to protect Western ideological systems from examination. However, this certainly does not imply that non-Western cultures are any less appropriate for study than Western ones; rather, all human cultures are equally worthy of study. In this light, I note that recently a literature on entertainment in non-Western societies has begun to emerge. See, for example, the detailed studies by Allison (2000) and Derne (1995). Several of the articles in Miller (1995) are relevant to this topic, especially the introduction and the articles by Das (1995) and Abu-Lughod (1995). Liebes and Katz (1990) is an oft-cited study in this vein; see Spitulnik (1993) for a general review up to that time.

8. As noted earlier, there is also the danger of adopting an overly expansive notion of play, in which the border between play and the activities of everyday life begins to erode. Some of the most insightful students of play, among them Huizinga, can be accused of extending the concept of play to the point that it loses its utility (see Koepping 1997: 7). The point to keep in mind here is simply that play is set apart from the everyday world (Bateson 1973). At the same time, I want to emphasize that this does not necessarily mean the actor classifies the activity in question as play.

9. Schutz (1967) uses the term everyday world, and I mean more or less what he does by my term.

10. Many authors have discussed the domination of entertainment values in recent presidential elections, for example. A good example is Gabler (1999).

11. See, for example, Gabler (1999) or De Zengotita (2005).

12. I do not mean to deny here that there are significant continuities between the popular amusements of earlier centuries—such phenomena as carnivals, public executions, spectacles such as rat baiting, freak shows—and what I am calling contemporary entertainment. But those continuities are peripheral to my purpose here, which is to characterize the distinctive characteristics of contemporary entertainment.

13. I say that my examples are likely to be entertainment because there are always exceptions. Watching narrative fictions on television is likely to be entertainment, but someone could be doing so in pursuit of study of narrative fictions in order to write a scholarly article, and so on.

14. I advocate caution when it comes to employing certain widely used terms, proposing my own alternatives. One problematic term is anthropology of mass media, or media anthropology. In the last decade or so, anthropologists have begun attending to the phenomenon of entertainment (especially its manifestations outside the West), and one of these terms is most often used to label this interest. Both may be too well-established to dislodge, but they have some significant disadvantages. The term media draws boundaries around the object of interest in a way that reproduces Western assumptions about the primacy of technology and ultimately disguises the cultural, political, and historical foundations of technological innovation.

15. Anthropologist John Caughey (1984) interviewed many Americans who developed intense imaginary relationships with celebrities, and he estimates that millions of Americans participate in such fantasy relationships. These relationships often start in adolescence, but they may persist well into adulthood. His interviews with fans reveal typical patterns of behavior that should not be completely unfamiliar: collecting information and memorabilia about celebrities; falling in love with them; fantasizing about knowing them, adopting their favorite foods, clothing, and speaking styles, and so forth. It is somewhat more unusual, but by no means rare, for fans to do such things as pray to celebrities or believe that touching celebrities may heal them of disease.

16. Humphrey and Laidlaw are in turn following Rappaport (1979) here. Throughout this book I assume a distinction between play and ritual that can legitimately be criticized as ethnocentric. Many authors have pointed out that play and ritual are often combined (see Turner 1982: 35 ff, for example), and an argument can be made that separating these categories is an artifact of Western history, especially since the Reformation. I work within the assumptions of a play-ritual distinction, acknowledging that such a distinction may not be viable in non-Western traditions.

17. To speak of symbolic valorization is to borrow a term from John B. Thompson: "'Symbolic valorization' is the process through which symbolic forms are ascribed 'symbolic value'" (1995: 27). Agreeing with Randall Collins (2004: 102) that "values . . . are cognitions infused with emotion," I would say that symbolic valorization is the process whereby this infusion occurs.

18. An enormous amount of research has been done on the question of how media imagery influences behavior, perhaps especially in the areas of advertising and depictions of violence. The skepticism of commentators such as Michael Schudson (1984), who asserts that advertising has little influence over behavior, is overstated. As I note in the following chapter, the conclusion should rather be that social science research methods are not adequate to either establish or dismiss such influence. The approach I advocate here is in part

an attempt to circumvent some of these difficulties by thinking about how media imagery might have significant social effects without directly causing specific behaviors.

19. The extent to which fictions may be accepted as real has been a topic of discussion for a long time. For example, Samuel Johnson, in an introduction to the plays of Shakespeare, written in 1765, writes, "The truth is, that the spectators are always in their senses, and know from the first act to the last that the stage is only a stage, and that the players are only players" (Vickers 1979: 70). (I was alerted to this reference by reading Lamarque 1981.) Unwise as it may be to contradict Samuel Johnson, my position in this book is that he oversimplifies the matter here. (This point is nicely made in Metz 1982: 72.) My position is that although sane people are typically able to distinguish fiction from reality, enjoying fictions often entails participants' not being entirely "in their senses." Of course, the relationship between reality and art has been discussed for millennia; see the articles in Spariosu (1984) for a general account.

20. D. W. Winnicott argues that the adult's ability to engage in and benefit from imaginative activities such as art and religion is an extension of the child's capacity for play (Winnicott 1964: 145).

21. Many readers will recognize that this account of the effect of becoming caught up in the play of entertainment directly parallels Durkheim's classic analysis of the effect of ritual. I have more to say about this parallel later in the book.

22. Thomas More's original joke about utopia (the word means "no place") remains relevant in this book.

23. As I discuss in the final chapter, it is not far off the mark to equate what we call "personality" with a person's entertainment value.

24. For an account that stresses the sociological aspects of contemporary entertainment and its development in the early 20th century, see Nasaw (1994). Gabler (1999) offers a readable account of the development of entertainment in late-19th-century American society.

25. Although it is no doubt obvious, I should say here that considering becoming caught up does not exhaust everything one might want to know about how people engage entertainment. The category of entertainment is vast and difficult to delimit, and a lot goes on under this umbrella. Entertainment can be informative, or it can simply furnish images of attractive persons for the viewer to stare at, or it can be genuinely artistic, provoking reflections on the subtleties of our existence. Becoming caught up is important to study, but there are also other important patterns in our engagement of entertainment.

Notes to Chapter 2

1. A brief formulation of the utopian function of entertainment, similar in some ways to mine, is contained in Dyer (1981).

2. In this book I use the phrase "the day-to-day world" to refer to the commonsense world of everyday reality. The theoretical fashions of the last several decades have made it more difficult than it should be to talk baldly about "real-world events," so I want to clarify this briefly. Of course, reality is socially constructed, and there are some genuinely interesting questions about the nature of our realities, but it does not follow that it is fruitful to problematize reality in all contexts. For some purposes, we may take reality to be a straightforward concept. Some people, failing to understand this, are not nearly as interesting as they think they are when they question any use of the word. In much of the day-to-day world,

we need and depend on a commonsense conception of reality (see Bowlin and Stromberg 1997), and anyone who claims not to do this is either posturing or mad.

3. An alternative theory explaining the magical qualities of the work of art is contained in the work of Alfred Gell (1992) and also mentioned by Umberto Eco (1986). This is, to reduce the point to a sentence, that we are so dazzled by the technical mastery obviously required to produce the artwork that we attribute a special charisma to it.

4. Careful readers of Durkheim's classic book *The Elementary Forms of Religious Life* (1995) will recognize parallels, on a number of levels, between what I am calling romantic realism and what he called an ideal. Of course, many authors have focused on aspects of human experience that partake of both the immediacy of the everyday and the perfection of the beyond; Campbell (1987: 83), for example, discusses the daydream in these terms.

5. On Disneyland, see Fjellman 1992.

6. Not all entertainment is based on romantic realism. Most spectator sports, for example, do not present fictions in any obvious sense. (Contemporary professional wrestling is an instructive exception to this generalization.)

7. Here are a few more places one can observe romantic realism in action: The "news," in which romantic realist images, polished to improve their entertainment value, are presented in the guise of what is happening in the day-to-day world (see Boorstin 1961, Gabler 1999, Esslin 1982a, chapter four). Or contemporary architecture (Huxtable 1992). The minor institution of the "makeover," available on television, in women's magazines and in the mall (the makeover will change you into a romantic realist version of yourself). A somewhat less obvious but intriguing possibility is the museum, in which some aspect of the past is typically romanticized and may become the object of nostalgic longing (Appadurai 1996, Stewart 1984). Any "reality-based" television show.

8. Murray Smith (1995) has argued that the idea of identification with fictional characters is ultimately crude and misleading; he offers a more nuanced interpretation of how readers engage fictional characters. I draw on his formulation in later chapters, but in the context of the argument I am making here, the commonsense conception of "identification" is sufficient.

9. *USA Today Sunday Magazine*, Dec 27, 1997.

10. One could certainly argue about my assertion here (that the celebrity is a 20th-century phenomenon). Simon Schama (1989: 123 ff.), for example, locates a very similar mechanism at work in late-18th-century (immediately prerevolutionary) France. Establishing the genealogy of celebrity in this way fits in with the argument of the next chapter, and thus I have no inclination to deny the validity of this perspective. My point is simply that the social phenomenon of the celebrity becomes much more significant and widespread in the 20th century than in earlier periods.

11. Richard Schickel (1973: 35) writes: "The screen gave actors, in the month or two of a film's release, exposure of a kind they could not achieve in a lifetime of touring. Moreover, it was an intimate and realistic (or at least realistic-seeming) medium. People actually thought they knew these people, these new stars, right down to their smallest habits and mannerisms, in a way they had never known any other public figures."

12. Here again I am drawing on Schickel (1973, 1985). See also Susman (1984: 282). Other recent works on celebrity include Braudy (1997), Gamson (1994), Dyer and McDonald (1998), and Marshall (1997).

13. This is why we are so interested in personal details about celebrities. These details prove that celebrities are like us and different from us, that they do indeed mediate between the day-to-day world and a world beyond (Stromberg 1990). The agonies that do occur even in the world of the celebrity—divorce, addiction, at times even suicide—are fascinating because they reveal these celestial creatures to be just like us.

14. In Boorstin's (1961: 57) well-known formulation, the celebrity is "known for his well-knownness."

15. *Newsweek*, June 9, 1997: 61.

16. The analysis I am offering here of television advertising could be, and has been, extended to advertising in other media. For an insightful look at the romantic realism created by mail-order catalogues, see Brubach 1993.

17. Schudson (1984, see especially pp. 217–218) makes a similar point about romantic realism, although he uses the term "capitalist realism"; see also Ewen (1988) on "style" and Gladwell (2000) on "stickiness." More broadly, many historians of advertising make arguments about the utopian images presented in advertising. For starters, see Marchand (1985), Ewen (1976), Snow (1983), Esslin (1982b), and Berger (1972).

18. Although it might be regarded as obvious, in fact this is a controversial claim. Social scientists and advertisers have conducted thousands of studies in the last half-century in an attempt to determine whether and how advertising works. The studies show, among other things, that viewers tend not to play close attention to television commercials; nor do they remember them very well (Schudson 1984; Draper 1986). So any sort of statement about the efficacy of advertising is open to immediate question. But suppose advertising sometimes works in ways that subjects cannot articulate. After all, it is a simple truth about human beings—and sufficiently obvious so that one would think even social science researchers would recognize it—that people cannot always articulate how events affect them. The problem here, in other words, may be with the research methods that are endorsed by the current social scientific establishment in the United States. Many advertisements may influence people in ways that cannot be observed using the research methods social scientists are usually trained to employ. In part, this book is an attempt to impart one way of thinking about how nonintentional processes may be implicated in our responses to advertising and entertainment. Other researchers have pursued other avenues for investigating the possibility that nonconscious cognitive processes may influence viewers' reactions to advertising (see Krishnan and Trappey 1999 for a short review).

19. It would seem, for example, that Zoroastrianism is a clear example of a millennial movement arising outside the Judaic tradition.

Notes to Chapter 3

1. This was also a central theme of the work of German critics of the Weimar era; see Arato and Gebhardt 1982. Walter Benjamin (1968) argued that the effect of art in premodern society was often to create an aura, an effect of absorption that at different periods in his work he identified negatively with passivity or positively with organic communities (Arato and Gebhardt 1982). Contemporary mass culture, he argued, all but eliminated the possibility of auratic works. The effect of modern cinema, for example, was to bombard the subject with ever higher levels of distracting sensations (see also Kracauer 1995), effectively diverting her from any possibility of absorption or empathy. Theodor Adorno (1982) devel-

ops a position that is in at least some ways more similar to my own, arguing that a form of inauthentic aura persists in contemporary art. I hasten to distance myself, however, from Adorno's pomposity, elitism, and the content of his critical judgments.

2. My claim that becoming caught up is a phenomenon associated with modernity in Western culture must not be taken as an assertion that very similar phenomena could not have occurred at other times and places. I will leave such judgments to scholars who are experts on such other times and places. One could, of course, write a very different history of becoming caught up than the one I present here. One possibility would be to consider the relationship between becoming caught up and other forms of ecstatic states. As E. R. Dodds (1951) shows in his classic study *The Greeks and the Irrational,* "slightly altered" mental states were a focus of considerable interest among the early Greeks, who considered these states as evidence of contact between human beings and the beyond. Especially relevant for this history would be the fact that such mental states were associated with, among other things, storytelling and the Dionysiac rituals out of which our theatrical tradition grew. Again, I have no interest in denying the possible relationship between getting caught up and trance states in other cultures. I do want to insist, however, that becoming caught up must be understood first in the context of its present historical and cultural circumstances. I hope that those who have the expertise to compare this tradition to those of other times and places will undertake the task.

3. Throughout the book, Fried stresses that this was the fundamental principle of Diderot's criticism throughout most of his career: works that acknowledge the viewer or audience are fatally flawed. In my own interpretation, this can be glossed as a demand for a basic level of realism. The work must allow the viewer to sustain the illusion of its reality.

4. Compare the very similar formulation for the mechanism of ideology in general set out by Althusser (1971).

5. Of course, there are many traditions that have developed such conventions.

6. Fried also links absorption to the development, in the 19th century, of Realism proper. See Fried (1990).

7. Dating the novel to this period is somewhat controversial (see McKeon 1987). However, this debate is not directly relevant here, for my goal is simply to sketch, in very broad strokes, some of the cultural developments of the early Romantic period. Surely no expert would deny the importance of this period for the development of the novel.

8. Of course, others who have studied the novel would attribute priority to other candidates. For a particularly broad view of the domain of the novel, see Bakhtin (1981).

9. Fried (1980) expresses this, for paintings, as the contemporary demand (articulated in particular by Diderot) that the scene comprise a tableau.

10. I am echoing Campbell's 1987 analysis of *Sense and Sensibility* here.

11. McKendrick, Brewer, and Plumb (1982) and Campbell (1987) date the origin of the fashion pattern to the mid-18th century. McCracken is doubtful of this (1988: 6ff), arguing that a form a fashion became established among the English aristocracy in Elizabethan times. Clearly, however, the consumption McCracken documents is a variation on age-old patterns of the use of display goods to establish and maintain status. That is, though the fashion system McCracken finds in Elizabethan times may well be a precursor of the full-blown fashion pattern that emerged over a century later, it is also a fundamentally premodern phenomenon. I should also note that in linking the fashion pattern to the 18th century

I am referring to the center of Western Europe; fashion came later to other areas. For an interesting treatment of the case of Russia, see Ruane (1995).

12. McCracken (1988) does not see this period as the first incursion on the dominance of the patina system; he regards the Elizabethan era as the earliest manifestation of a relatively widespread demand for novelty in consumer goods.

13. See also Taylor (1989): 249ff.

14. As many have observed, this is the problem with life these days.

15. For an extended discussion of the linkage between romance and consumption, see Illouz (1997).

16. If one were to undertake a comprehensive history of becoming caught up, one would certainly have to attend to the general fascination with trance states in European art, science, and popular culture during the late 18th and the 19th centuries. Such a study would have to consider, among other things, the extraordinary vogue of Mesmerism (see Darnton 1968), the conventions of artistic response in the romantic period (see, for example, Campbell 1987), and, emerging somewhat later the fascination with hysteria (see Beizer 1994) and Mesmerism in Britain (Winter 1998).

17. Of course, many authors find similarities between advertising and entertainment and religious systems in general. See for example, Twitchell (1992), Esslin (1982b), and Goethals (1990). Then there are treatments of the religious aspects of other areas of secular culture, such as shopping malls (Zepp 1997) and "Generation X" culture (Beaudoin 1998); Leigh Schmidt (1995) examines the intertwining of religious and consumerist themes in American holidays. Finally, for a discussion of the relationship between ritual and communication more generally, see Carey (1989).

18. Lears (1994: 57) writes: "By popularizing a pattern of self-transformation that would prove easily adaptable to advertisers' rhetorical strategies, evangelical revivalists like [Charles Grandison] Finney played a powerful if unwitting part in creating a congenial cultural climate for the rise of national advertising."

19. "My Afternoons among the Dry Goods," *Harper's Weekly* 1 (Oct. 31 1856, 689–690). Cited in Harris (1990: 178).

20. Raymond Williams (1993) points out that it was not only mass production that paved the way for the new advertising techniques of the 20th century. In addition, the growth of monopoly capitalism and the need to rationalize distribution were important factors here.

21. Ewen (1976); see also sources cited in Featherstone (1991: 14).

22. See Ewen (1976), Berger (1972).

23. For example, historian Jackson Lears (1983: 18) says of Claude Hopkins, an influential advertising man who worked in the early 1900s: "Hopkins refused to appeal to a buyer's reason by listing a product's qualities; on the contrary he addressed non-rational yearnings by suggesting the ways his client's product would transform the buyer's life."

24. Obviously public spectacles did not originate in the 19th century; nor did events such as carnivals and fairs. However, the elements of the exhibitionary complex were unique in several ways. Above all, they displayed symbolic resources such as art or consumer goods in organized ways so as to provoke awe for the organizer—ultimately, the society.

25. Schwartz (1998) would question the contrast between education and entertainment here. But I do not think she would disagree that exhibitions and the like were increasingly forms of entertainment during this period.

26. Again, I would follow Schwartz in arguing that "education" and "entertainment" are but two phases within an overall process of public exercise of power over viewing publics.

27. Improbably, even the history of marketing in the department store shows close links between these practices and Evangelical Protestantism. See, for example, Leach's (1993) discussion of the role of John Wanamaker.

28. It would be difficult to separate the growing power of advertising during this century from the history of the mass media of radio and television. In a sense, these two phenomena, advertising and mass media, have made one another. Radio and eventually television came to be the forces they are because of the enormous funds available to them through advertising. The form these media have taken in our society has been heavily influenced by their role as carriers of advertising. For a thorough discussion of this relationship, see Barnouw 1966.

29. For an informative account of the exhibitionary methods that led up to the motion picture, see Nasaw 1993, whose account I am following here.

30. There is an enormous literature covering various aspects of film history. Some books that I have found helpful are Williams (1992), May (1980), Sklar (1994), Nasaw (1993), and Cook (1996).

31. As Williams (1992: 215) points out, the relationship between motion pictures and absorption was immediately picked up by contemporary critics.

Notes to Chapter 4

1. Anyone who is interested in this problem should consult Fine (1983) for an alternative account that is empirically rich and theoretically sophisticated. Fine repeatedly touches on the problem of the relationship between the consciousness of the player and that of the character in fantasy role playing. For the most part, he approaches this matter through the work of Erving Goffman and other ethnomethodologists, which from my perspective leads to a theoretical position that never really properly locates the nature of the cognitive and emotional states of the player. In discussing the situation of player and character, for example, Fine tries to locate the player's consciousness of character in terms of a contrast between open and closed awareness. (Here he is following Glaser and Strauss, 1964.) In open awareness, the social actor is aware of the personae she creates; in closed awareness (for example, multiple personality), she is not. Really, the situation of the fantasy game-player is neither of these, a problem Fine recognizes when he writes (1983: 188), "Open awareness denies the engrossing character of fantasy."

2. Although I have discussed play at several points in this book, at no point do I systematically review the literature on this topic, because to do so would be a separate project from the one I am embarked on here. I recommend that the reader who wants to learn about contemporary work on play start with Harris (2000) and Sutton-Smith (2001).

3. I will have a good deal more to say about how all this happens, in the next chapter.

4. Some would in fact argue that role playing is a significant component of day-to-day behavior in our society, a manifestation of what Warren Susman (1984) called the culture of personality. After all, isn't our self-presentation on a first date or a job interview a fairly transparent variety of role playing? Taking the argument in this direction, however, will lead me away from the entertainment I want to focus on in this book, and for the time being I use the term *role play* to refer to activities that occur in play and drama. The question of the dividing line between fictional worlds and socially constructed worlds that are accepted as

nonfictional is something I touch on throughout the book, but to actually attempt to clarify this line is beyond the scope of my work here.

5. My thanks to Susan Smith, the documentary filmmaker who worked with me on this project.

6. "DM" stands for dungeonmaster.

7. Many have concluded, in part from such observations, that people pay little attention to, say, TV commercials. As I discussed in a note in the second chapter, I think it may be instead that attentiveness is harder to spot than has been assumed.

8. This point, of course, has been prominently elaborated by postmodernists such as Baudrillard (1981, 1983) and Michael Taussig (1993). Other recent and interesting treatments in this vein are those of Thomas De Zengotita (2005) and Neal Gabler (1999). Here is Gabler (1999: 58), giving a more recent version of the Frankfurt School's claim: "Life [is] . . . the biggest, most entertaining, most realistic movie of all."

9. See Harris (2000: 60 ff) for a discussion of this issue that is based on experimental evidence showing how even children engaged in pretend play remain clear about the boundaries between fantasy and reality.

10. Again, my findings for role players are paralleled by the results of studies of children's pretend play: "Role play is striking because children temporarily immerse themselves in the part that they create. They frequently start to act on the world and to talk about it as if they were experiencing it from the point of view of the invented person or creature. This perspectival shift is manifested in various ways. First, children use the terms of reference, including deictic terms that are appropriate to the role that they have adopted" (Harris 2000: 30).

11. There are other possible interpretations here. Perhaps player 5 is plotting a complex activity for which he needs to know both real time and game time; perhaps his concerns about game time provoke a largely conditioned glance at his watch; and so on. All of these interpretations, however, point (albeit in slightly different ways) to the same conclusion: the player's real-world concerns and game concerns are very closely intertwined here.

12. This situation is complicated by the observation that Skip is not in fact wearing a watch. Although again I cannot claim to know exactly what is going on here, the most likely interpretation is that he is in the habit of wearing a watch but is not currently doing so. In any case, this points to the fact that Skip is somewhat dissociated from what we might call the real situation here.

13. Player 4 is probably committing a gaffe here. One indication of this is that there was a relatively long pause after his comment. His error is in connecting that world too closely to this one by assuming an overweight man could not be playing the character of an attractive woman.

14. See Haviland (2000) for a discussion of gesture oriented to narrated space. This is a commonplace in many parts of the world; in fact, McNeill's introductory discussion (1992) of gesture is based on a speaker telling a story.

15. A recent and very useful study of how readers engage fictions, particularly in film, is Murray Smith's *Engaging Characters* (1995). Smith summarizes much of the work in philosophy and drama criticism; for my purposes one of the most important distinctions he draws is between central and acentral imagining. This distinction is drawn from the work of Richard Wollheim (1984). Very briefly, central imagining is the practice of putting oneself in a fictive situation and experiencing it. Acentral imagining is the practice of observing an

experience in one's mind. Both are important in engaging narratives. Becoming caught up is closely related to central imagining and as such is, as I have repeatedly stressed, but one component of a reader or spectator's response to a fiction.

16. Fine (1983) also reports such phenomena. He writes (1983: 217), "In playing a character for a long time, identification grows and the player begins to feel what his character 'feels.'"

17. Indeed a number of commentators have perpetuated this story in their own work, so that the Green Slime is by now a much-discussed villain indeed. Of course, with this work, the tradition continues.

18. I have not discussed film viewing as an example of becoming caught up in this book, except in passing. This is not because such activity is irrelevant; on the contrary, commercial cinema is probably the most widespread context in contemporary society in which people become caught up. As John Ellis (1982: 40) points out, "The audience is seated in rows, separated from each other to some degree, and the image is projected in near-darkness. This induces a particular kind of mental state in the commercial cinema viewer." This mental state often presumably entails some level of becoming caught up. Although I have done some research in this area (for example, I have filmed audiences viewing horror films), I lack sufficient material on the topic to offer an account here.

19. A number of other commentators have expressed similar reservations about this part of Walton's account. See, for example, Skulsky (1980).

20. Again, this is a commonplace development in more familiar games. I may be genuinely upset with my teammate who misses an easy shot that causes us to lose the basketball game, and for some players such emotions may not be left behind at the gym. Fictive realities spill over into the real world in various ways, and emotion is among the most compelling examples of this.

21. Much ink has been spilled by literary critics debating whether it is correct to say that readers identify with fictional characters. A useful and balanced summary of the issues can be found in Smith (1995); Currie and Ravenscroft (2002) is also useful. In this work, I sometimes use *identification* in a loose and commonsense sort of way, without attending much to the question of whether this is the most accurate term for the nature of a reader's engagement with a character. What is important in this work is that I hold that readers, and other sorts of players, sometimes adopt the perspectives of fictional agents, and in doing so they are likely building on fundamental aspects of human cognition.

22. Decety and Chaminade (2005: 121) trace the basis of simulation theory to work by N. Humphrey (see, for example, Humphrey 1982). See Tomasello (1999: 70ff) and Currie and Ravenscroft (2002: 91ff) for alternative genealogies.

Notes to Chapter 5

1. In support of this assertion, Tomasello cites Kummer and Goodall (1985).

2. As Goldman (2005: 92) goes on to note, the model "need not be an actual person."

3. One of the fullest and most sophisticated discussions of the implications of multiple voices in discourse remains Bakhtin (1982).

4. As I discuss shortly, shifts in perspective of this sort need not depend on a shift to a fictional perspective.

5. Of course, not all who study imitation agree on precisely the same definition of the behavior. To complicate the issue, it may well turn out to be the case that imitation is a

function not only of mental ability but also of the nature of a species' adaptation to a particular ecological niche. So arguments about whether humans are the only creatures who imitate will likely continue.

6. Readers who are interested in pursuing the anatomy of the mirror neuron system in monkeys and its probable relationship to human brain structure might want to begin by reading Brass and Heyes (2005), which also contains extensive references on these questions.

7. A number of subsequent authors (see, for example, Rizzolatti and Arbib 1998; McNeill 2005) have developed theories about how a mirror neuron system could be implicated in human language. These findings are both exciting and promising, but at this time what is established has to do with reaching and grasping behaviors in macaques, and evidence for a mirror neuron system in humans remains (as I understand it) strong but indirect.

8. Obviously, the neural activity associated with observation and execution of movements cannot be exactly the same, or we would always execute movements on observing them. Lotze et al. 1999 (cited in Decety and Chaminade 2005) describe experimental results suggesting cerebellar activity is responsible for inhibiting execution of movements when the subject intends to merely imagine a movement.

9. Of course, any situation is subject to differing descriptions, and people with diverse interests may disagree on which one is correct (Goffman 1986: 8).

10. See the discussion in Currie and Ravenscroft (2002: 97–98).

11. This term, which I use repeatedly in explaining Collins's theory, comes originally from Erving Goffman (see Collins 2004: xi). For reasons I have already covered, I personally prefer to avoid extending the term *ritual* in this way.

12. I have borrowed the terminology of "authorship" of action from Humphrey and Laidlaw's description of ritual action (1994).

13. Summing up the research on this issue, Hatfield et al. (1994: 62) write, "In a variety of studies then, we find that people tend to feel emotions consistent with the facial expression they adopt and, conversely, have trouble feeling emotions inconsistent with those poses."

14. Like several of the terms I use in this part of the book, "emotional contagion" has something of a bad odor in contemporary social science, perhaps because of its association with the "crowd psychologists" such as Le Bon, whose work was subsequently studied by those (such as Adolph Hitler) who sought to manipulate crowds. (See Lindholm 1990.) However, contemporary empirical work leaves little doubt that emotional contagion exists, and it is not really all that mysterious.

15. To be fully accurate here, this is Hatfield's definition of what she calls primitive emotional contagion, or what is "relatively automatic, unintentional, uncontrollable, and largely unconscious" (Hatfield et al. 1992: 153). This is what I refer to as emotional contagion.

16. Plantinga (1999) discusses this issue at length and reviews some of the experimental evidence supporting this point. For a more recent empirical study, see Wild et al. (2001).

17. Roy D'Andrade first suggested the importance of absorption for this argument (personal communication).

18. As is the case with entrainment, absorption is frequent in the day-to-day world, not just the world of play. One could become absorbed in a skilled task, for example, or a demanding situation. The psychologist Mihály Csikszentmihalyi (1990; Csikszentmihalyi and Csikszentmihalyi 1988) has carefully studied this sort of absorption, which he labels "flow." (Csikszentmihalyi makes no reference at all to absorption in his most widely cited works on

flow, and evidently regards these phenomena as unrelated). Some of the earliest and still most interesting work on absorption was done by Josephine Hilgard (1970), and she was careful to distinguish absorption in imaginative situations from absorption in skilled activities. For Hilgard, this distinction was rooted in the fact that absorption in imaginative activities is strongly correlated with hypnotizability, while absorption in skilled activities is not.

19. The mere mention of hypnosis and trance may produce in some readers the same sort of reaction that is sometimes produced by the terms "altered states of consciousness" or "emotional contagion." As Hacking (1995) says, phenomena that fit no broader vision of the world make many of us uneasy.

20. One could, for example, posit that the mind consists of, as Hilgard (1986: 217) puts it, "a hierarchy of possible thoughts and actions determined by the competitive strengths of the activated subsystems, whether habits or cognitive structures."

21. Hypnosis is notoriously difficult to define. For hypnosis to occur, one needs, in the first place, a person who can be hypnotized, because hypnotic susceptibility varies. Some small percentage of the population (Hilgard offers an educated guess of 1–5 percent; 1986: 158) is highly hypnotizable and able to enter trances characterized by extreme suggestibility, selective amnesias, and so on. A much larger part of the population displays some level of susceptibility to hypnosis, but here a profound complication emerges: there is no obvious way to delimit the lower boundaries of hypnosis. That is, it is possible to demonstrate response to suggestion among subjects who have experienced no hypnotic induction, and many subjects who might be classed as hypnotized because of their suggestibility report that after an attempted hypnotic induction they feel little different from their everyday state (Hilgard 1986: 157). In sum, no one is sure of the dividing line between a mild hypnotic state and everyday consciousness. None of this, however, suggests that hypnosis does not exist. It suggests instead that hypnosis, like many other mental processes, is not so much an either-or state as a matter of degree. One may be slightly hypnotized, very hypnotized, not hypnotized at all, and so on. It is also interesting to note in this context that typically hypnotic states can only be established with the genuine consent of the hypnotic subject (Hilgard 1986: 224). It may occasionally happen that someone is inadvertently hypnotized, but for the most part establishment of these states depends on what Hilgard calls an initial contract between subject and hypnotist. One could take this point to be parallel to Coleridge's famous observation that a "willing suspension of disbelief" must be established to enable enjoyment of literature or poetry.

22. Pointing out the relationship among becoming caught up, hypnosis, and other trance states paves the way for hypothesizing that becoming caught up may be a historically conditioned variant of certain pan-human mental processes, processes that have manifested themselves in other times and places as such things as spirit possession or ecstatic trance. This suggests that the frequency of becoming caught up in our society is not a sign of social perversity, but rather a predictable feature of human life and a sign of our kinship with people from other times and places.

23. I want to attend to the issue—a rather touchy one as it turns out—of this term "states of consciousness." In the passage above, Rossi uses the term "altered states" of consciousness. Although the term is common enough, it (like others I have commented on here) retains what John Nell (1988: 221) has called a "raffish air," because of its appearance in inquiries into the effects of drugs and certain religious practices, topics that some scientists suspect are pursued only by those who are themselves involved in unscientific

consciousness-altering practices. I am anxious to avoid the possibility of seeming raffish myself by association, so I will for the most part avoid the term. At the same time I wish to point out that, so far as I know, no expert denies the existence of different states of consciousness, that "psychological processes operate within one or another frame or state that by definition excludes for the time being other states" (Pribram 1977: 221). Taking a conservative approach, then, I simply assert that there are both continuities and variations in consciousness that account for widely observed mental states such as (partially following Pribram 1977) ordinary perceptual awareness, dreaming, reverie, hypnosis, and trance. None of this need be thought of as eerie; to take a single example, Kubey and Csikszentmihalyi (1990: 172) suggest that television viewers may experience altered states of consciousness. For some other studies of altered states of consciousness, see Ludwig 1966, Winkelman 1986, Wolman and Ullman 1986, and Zinberg 1977.

24. My thanks to Roy D'Andrade for alerting me to this study.

25. See Hollan 2000 for a persuasive discussion of the possibility that what some authors call "normal consciousness" is neither normative nor psychologically normal. Hollan argues for a "constructivist" theory of mind in which alert consciousness is but one aspect of everyday cognitive orientation, and splits or dissociations in consciousness are an expected and adaptive part of mental functioning (Hollan 2000: 539).

Notes to Chapter 6

1. Daniel Lende criticizes this view as outmoded, pointing out that the primary significance of play behaviors is more likely to have to do with integration of different brain systems of motor control. See his blog post "The Neurobiology of Play", posted February 17, 2008, at www.neuroanthropogy.net.

2. Of course, practice need not involve play. See Fagen (1976) for a more detailed discussion of why play should be especially effective for practicing routines.

3. I want to be careful here regarding claims about the uniqueness of human beings, because ethological research continues to expand our knowledge of the often marvelous cognitive capacities of nonhuman animals, which seem to be a lot smarter than we have traditionally assumed. However, I think I am safe in saying that the sort of abstraction I am talking about here is much more in evidence in human life than in the life of other animals.

4. As I have already acknowledged, this generalization about play and ritual may be more appropriate in contemporary Western culture than in other places.

5. Serious students of play should note the word *often* in this sentence. I am not saying here that play is inevitably or even typically associated with one type of values. Experts on play have been debating this matter for decades, and I can only note that the relationship between play and social values, or the relationship between play and valued skills, is a matter of controversy. One book that summarizes and makes some sense of this controversy is Sutton-Smith (2001).

6. The phrase comes from Marshall Sahlins (1976: 66), who points out this has been a truism in anthropology since the work of Boas. For a discussion of Boas relevant to this point, see Stocking (168: 133–233).

7. In this sense, looking at meta-action reveals a truth that Goffman (1986) uncovered through what he called frame analysis: our grasp of human action is typically based on it being interpreted relative to a goal, or in humans a frame. Of course, this is also close to the basic outlook of simulation theory.

Notes to Chapter 7

1. I learned of this reference through Grant (1976).

2. This argument has also been around for a while. As Illouz (1997) points out, this is the premise of Flaubert's *Madame Bovary*.

3. If other social scientists listened to their interview subjects as closely as Swidler did, I suspect other such paradoxes would be discovered. Although these mysteries are not confined to the realm of romantic relationships, they are especially likely to be found in areas of life subject to romantic imagery more broadly conceived. That is, this sort of contradiction is likely to turn up as people formulate their desires and aspirations: for their lives, for consumer goods, for what they should be, for what the world should be. The reason is that, as I note throughout this book, we fall prey to a particular sort of doublethink: often the sorts of values endorsed through our play contradict our articulate values and hence must be denied.

4. Radaway also distributed a questionnaire to her subjects, and she reports that a large majority of the respondents saw similarities between their own feelings and those of the heroine (1984: 98).

5. Certainly, gender roles can often be interpreted in this light.

6. See Campbell (1987: 211) and Bell (1976).

7. Sandra Harding (1986: 88) argues, persuasively I think, that the leisure-work contrast is based on a male perspective, in that many traditionally female occupations (childrearing, for example) do not comfortably fit into either side of the dichotomy. This, however, does not diminish the cultural salience of the contrast in contemporary society.

Notes to Chapter 8

1. There has been a good deal of interesting anthropological work on consumption. See, for example, Miller (1998).

2. Although it is possible that this point also has relevance for illegal drug consumption, in the present context my argument is meant to apply only to the use of legal drugs. Self-administration of legal drugs is, of course, likely to be more open and more closely tied to the routines of day-to-day life than is self-administration of illegal drugs. Therefore it would be imprudent to assume that the practices I discuss here are similar to those characterizing illegal drug use.

3. Obviously, there are limits to the range of subjective interpretations of a drug's effect; some drugs are stimulants, others depressants, and so on. However, the fact that in American culture smoking a cigarette is often undertaken to relax should alert us to applying even these global distinctions with care. As Daniel Lende (2005: 101) has written, "The overall impact of drugs is not limited to the pharmacology—social learning and context can powerfully shape the perceived effects of drugs." Or, to quote Vuchinich (2002: 99) again, "After several decades of research in behavioral pharmacology, researchers now know that little, if anything about the behavioral effects of drugs or the conditions under which they are self-administered is 'solely determined by the drug's pharmacology'" (Alessi et al., 2002: 82).

4. I encountered this conception in reading Holland et al. (1998), and my account here closely follows theirs.

5. Throughout this discussion, I am arguing not simply that tobacco use may take the form of play, but more generally that tobacco use may be embedded in (and a component

of) broader play activities involving conventions of self-presentation, conversational norms, mock and serious seductive behavior, and so on.

6. The final sentence again illustrates the importance of entrainment in smoking activity.

7. Mark Nichter points out (personal communication) that these expectations about the uses of tobacco are strongly embedded culturally and are perhaps especially likely to be reinforced through mass media such as films.

8. This point, as it applies to imaginative play in general, is thoroughly documented and discussed in Harris (2000).

9. There is not, so far as I know, any professional consensus on the precise relationship between the terms *drug dependency* and *addiction*. There does seem to be a tendency among those who study these phenomena to reject the term *addiction* (labeled by one prominent behavioral pharmacologist, Brady 2005, as "absolutely useless") because it has been used in so many ways. In this chapter, I prefer the term *dependency*; when I use "addiction" or quote others using the term I intend it as a looser, more general synonym for dependency. As will become clear, I hold that there is an ideology of addiction in our society based on interpretations of chemical dependency, but it should be understood as a metaphor for describing certain characteristics of the conception of self in contemporary society.

10. As Harold Shaffer (1997: 1574) of the Division on Addictions at Harvard Medical School writes, "Trying to identify the most important unresolved issue in the field of addictions is similar to trying to identify the most needy person among the impoverished masses of the world."

11. Here my view overlaps with that of Elster (1999: 138), who writes, "The seduction [of the drug] operates in part through the belief that the desire is overpowering, so that any resistance will be fruitless."

12. Although I cannot treat the complexities of the matter here, it is popularly (and for the most part professionally) accepted that one may become addicted to some forms of play, gambling being an obvious example. Whether or not one agrees with this extension of the concept of addiction, the very suggestion further supports the argument that play processes themselves can assume a character at least very similar to being addictive.

13. Much of the current thinking among those who treat addictions is based on the assumption that dependency is a strictly physiological process, a disease, and is based solely on the chemical effects of the addictive substance. Although I think this view is oversimplified (see Falk 1983, Gossop 1990, Akers 1991, Orford 1985, Thombs 1994), my argument here does not necessarily contradict this view. I am saying that the concept of addiction (not any physiological process) arises in part from the idea that the substance has the power to override the will.

14. Once again, my account here is a conscious parallel to Durkheim's account of ritual (1995: 222). The ritual participant feels "that he is lifted above himself and that he is participating in a life different from the one he lives ordinarily." The participant naturally seeks to "connect those experiences to some external object in a causal relation." In the rituals Durkheim discusses, the object is of course the physical symbol of the clan totem. In the case I am presenting, it is a drug.

15. This is not part of Sedgwick's explanation of the paradoxes of addiction. She raises this possibility only to dismiss it. In my view this is an error on her part.

16. Once again, my argument is intended as a close parallel to Durkheim's. My brand of neo-Durkheimianism has been strongly influenced by Randall Collins (2004), although I also deviate considerably from Collins's approach, and he therefore bears no responsibility for my actions.

17. This is a point that has been repeatedly made about ritual practice, and in particular ritual language. As I noted in Chapter Six, in ritual the sense of not being fully the author of one's own actions (Humphrey and Laidlaw, 1994) is harnessed to reinforce the conviction of a greater power. See Keane (1997) for a review of the many studies that have examined aspects of this process.

18. This point has taken shape over a number of personal communications with Mark Nichter.

19. Of course, I am not the only observer in recent times to suggest that this is necessary; see Rose (1996: 1–21) for a short and clear review.

Notes to Chapter 9

1. As readers of Durkheim will recall, he refers to these poles as the sacred and the profane.

2. See, for example, Klapp 1986. He argues (23ff), among other things, that the word *boredom* was used much more often in written sources in 1961 than it was in 1931.

3. Our idea of boredom has kin among the concepts of other times and places. Spacks cites as an example the medieval notion of acedia. But acedia, though similar to our conception of boredom, is also decisively different from it, in that boredom as we think of it (and we think of it a lot) seems unique to our time.

4. Also cited in Musharbash (2007: 311).

5. All of the examples here come from the speech of young people, and it is commonplace to observe that younger people are especially likely to complain about boredom. One can speculate about why this is so. Without firmly established social identities, young people may be especially vulnerable to boredom because they are typically less engaged with the potent symbolic realms of career and family.

6. "We" refers to Mark and Mimi Nichter and myself. This discussion of boredom closely follows ideas that were developed in close collaboration with my co-researchers.

7. Here I am describing the passive form of boredom. Most of us are also familiar with a more active form of boredom, exemplified by a repetitive task or an interlocutor who goes on too long about some less-than-compelling topic. This active form of boredom is certainly not unknown among first-year college students; one's anthropology professor, for example, may be boring. But this is not the phenomenon I wish to discuss here. There is a relationship between passive and active boredom, of course, but I will not explore it in this context. It is interesting to note, however, that the "just" verb phrase is a clear marker separating the two forms. If your interlocutor is boring you, this is the active form. If, however, you begin to characterize the situation as "he's just going on and on about cross cousins," you have passed into passive boredom. This formulation means you are no longer trying to engage the topic; you have retreated into negativity.

8. The relationship between boredom and lack of social interaction is often noted by other researchers; see, for example, Musharbash 2007 or Conrad 1997.

9. I am by no means the first anthropologist to study Star Trek and its fans. For an early

example, see Claus (1976). More recent examples of my predecessors are Jindra (1994) and Wagner and Lundeen (1998).

10. Thus note the proliferation of support groups for the loved ones of those deeply involved in Internet role playing, such as "Worlds of Warcraft Widows."

11. The strongest evidence here is that the time is specified as 800 years ago in the script of the original program. Thus when Chris tells me that this happened 800 years ago, he is assuming the frame of reference of the program. I know about the script not because I have seen the program but because I posted an inquiry on an Internet newsgroup devoted to the Star Trek world of the Bajorans. I quickly received a reply from a fan who wrote: "The episode says it was eight hundred years ago. That puts it in 1571 A.D., if you want to take that reference literally." Note, then, that my correspondent does precisely what Chris does: the time referent in his communication to me assumes the temporal framework not of the present but rather of the Star Trek world.

12. The information on Chris allows further interpretation; it is not only in the domain of entertainment that Chris feels overwhelmed. He mentions this theme in discussing his engagements in the day-to-day world as well (his hometown, the public-relations crowd in college). In my interviews with him, Chris testified (indirectly, through his stories) that any form of engagement can become constrictive and suffocating for him. This may represent something about Chris's psychological situation or about a broader group; I lack sufficient evidence to pursue the matter here.

13. A thoughtful and well-worked out version of such an argument can be found in Jensen 1990.

14. Jon Elster (1984) felicitously discusses this problem by referencing the story of the sirens in the *Odyssey*.

15. My understanding of the situation here is not the same as that proposed by Davidson, although there is no direct contradiction between our views.

16. Radicalism often takes the form of asserting the primacy of one side of a long-recognized duality, and in recent decades many anthropologists have styled themselves as radicals who reject the possibility of generalization and assert that local variation is the only thing worth documenting in the study of humanity. Happily, as time passes and a less fevered perspective becomes possible, the inanities of such radicalism typically come more clearly into view.

17. I am generalizing here in a way that can be easily and effectively criticized by the reader. The oscillation between boredom and entertainment is undoubtedly more prominent among young people than among older adults, but even in the former category there are entire communities in which this is not true. However, the generalization, taken in the proper spirit, is still worth making, because it says something about widespread and important tendencies in contemporary life.

Notes to Chapter 10

1. This is a specific instance of a broader point made by Thompson (1990), namely that the 19th-century theorists who laid the foundations of contemporary social science had little inkling of the role that institutions such as advertising and entertainment would come to play in the 20th century. Thompson suggests, sensibly, that the jaw-dropping neglect of these institutions in contemporary social science is in part simply a reflection of the fact that the theories social scientists have elaborated on assume a 19th-century social reality.

2. As Sut Jhally (2002: 327) has written, "The marketplace (and its major ideological tool, advertising) is the major structuring institution of contemporary consumer society."

3. Some may dispute this generalization. Certainly, social interaction with smaller groups of people remains a central aspect of social life, and as Randall Collins (2004) has shown, this form of social interaction is vital in the process of symbolic valorization. Those who attend rock concerts and sporting events may want to point out that large-scale public gatherings continue to exist. However, the cultural importance of such events pales beside that of electronic media. There is simply no comparison between the number of people attending the Super Bowl and those watching it on television. Social scientists therefore need to develop sophisticated theories of how valorization occurs through interaction with media.

4. Though there can be no doubt that the work of the Frankfurt School of sociology offers insights into what we could characterize as the institutions of advertising and entertainment, taken as a whole the "critical theory" approach is unusable today. This is in large part because the approach—especially in the hands of Adorno—remained committed to a firm value distinction between high art and popular culture. In a sense, the present work is an attempt to salvage one powerful strand of thought from the Frankfurt School, one that is articulated especially in the thought of Walter Benjamin.

5. In referring to a "flexible self," I am echoing the terminology of Emily Martin (1994). Her work is primarily about ideas on the immune system, but she also discusses the prevalence of the metaphor of flexibility throughout contemporary culture, including our understandings of the self. Occasionally I also use an even stronger term to designate some of our ideas about the self, that being *transformability*. At times we seem to believe not only that the self is and should be flexible but that it is and should be transformable, capable of total and essential change. The metaphor of transformation is also an important notion that unites diverse realms of our ideology. Gabler (1999:51) quotes Warren Susman's judgment (regarding the form of culture that took shape in the early 20th century) that "transformation seemed to be what the new culture was all about."

6. One could make a similar statement about the culture of entertainment, for as I noted in the first chapter we seem to have a lot of trouble grasping the nature of our engagement with entertainment. Even books on entertainment written by social scientists often vacillate between offering analysis and straightforward fascination with entertaining entities such as celebrities.

7. Collins is in turn following Goffman (1967) here.

8. Another understanding of the contemporary self is offered by Shore (1996: 150), who construes what I am calling the flexibility of the self as its capacity to be repeatedly reconfigured. Here Shore seems to be calling attention to the same characteristics in the contemporary self that I am trying to sketch, while at the same time linking them to his broader understanding of the importance of modularity in contemporary culture.

9. This statement about the nature of social character in contemporary society is explicitly offered as a generalization, a way of designating an enormously complex phenomenon so that it can be isolated and discussed. This is a necessary first step toward increased understanding, and eventually more refined terms. The claim here is not that all people who live in contemporary society have this sort of idea about the self, or even that this description applies perfectly to any person.

10. Relatively early statements of this position are Riesman, Glazer, and Denny (1961) and Rieff (1966). More recently, see Susman (1984), Lears (1983), Giddens (1991), Lasch (1978), Lifton (1993), Gergen (1991), Martin (1994). Strathern (1988) and Battaglia (1995) are examples of the extensive literature in anthropology that takes up the question of the unity and autonomy of the self in non-Western cultures.

11. For a classic discussion of the differences between self and society in rural and urban settings, see Simmel 1971 (original 1903). Simmel's analysis is framed in an outdated social evolutionary idiom, but the essay nevertheless has many interesting insights.

12. The distinction between character and the contemporary organization of subjectivity that I am outlining here is closely related to (although somewhat different from) the well-known distinction between "inner directed" and "other directed" personality types that was first formulated by David Riesman (Riesman, Glazer, and Denney 1961) and his colleagues.

13. Another excellent example of the interrelationship among consumption, interaction, and forms of person is Collins's study of practices of tobacco use (2004). Collins prefers to classify these practices as a form of ritual, and as I have argued I feel we may get more mileage by investigating them under the rubric of play. But otherwise, his account parallels my own in any number of ways. I should perhaps add that although I have learned a great deal from Collins on these issues, my own argument on tobacco use was developed in conjunction with Mark Nichter and Mimi Nichter prior to reading Collins's study. I prefer to see the convergence of these approaches, then, as evidence that we are all onto something.

14. In the early part of the 20th century, a minister involved with the crusade against nervous exhaustion "estimated that there were about 500,000 neurotics in a nation of eighty million people" (Hale 1971: 233). George Beard, a physician who more than anyone else was responsible for bringing the situation to the attention of the public, believed the number of sufferers to be much higher, perhaps a few million (Meyer 1980: 26).

15. The epidemic of nervous disease in the late 19th century was the context for the birth of the "mind cure" movement, which embraces a range of religious viewpoints (such as Christian Science) and led directly to 20th-century self-help ideologies (see Meyer 1980). It is worth noting, in this context, the affinity of all of these phenomena to what I have called romantic realism: they are moral systems based in the promise of an earthly utopia, to be attained in the form of a perfected life.

16. As Richard Sennett (1977: 151) has written, "As the gods are demystified, man mystifies his own condition; his own life is fraught with meaning, yet it remains to be played out."

17. As was briefly discussed earlier, there is an exception to this generalization, that being celebrities. Celebrities are thought to have the power to initiate trends *ex nihilo*.

18. The paradox that the individual who is utterly free to develop her own ideas often ends up being highly influenced by the opinions of those around her was noted long ago, by de Tocqueville (2000).

References

Abrams, M. H. 1971. *Natural Supernaturalism*. New York: Norton.

Abu-Lughod, L. 1995. The Objects of Soap Opera: Egyptian Television and the Cultural Politics of Modernity. In *Worlds Apart: Modernity Through the Prism of the Local*. Ed. Daniel Miller. 190–210. London: Routledge.

Ackerman, Diane. 1999. *Deep Play*. New York: Random House.

Adorno, Theodor W. 1982. On the Fetish Character in Music and the Regression of Listening. In *The Essential Frankfurt School Reader*. Eds. Andrew Arato and Eike Gebhardt. 270–299. New York: Continuum.

Akers, Ronald L. 1991. Addiction: The Troublesome Concept. *Journal of Drug Issues* 21: 777–793.

Alessi, S. M., J. M. Roll, M. P. Reilly, and C. E. Johanson. 2002. Establishment of a Diazepam Preference in Human Volunteers Following a Differential-Conditioning History of Placebo Versus Diazepam Choice. *Experimental and Clinical Psychopharmacology* 10: 77–83.

Allison, Anne. 2000. *Permitted and Prohibited Desires*. Berkeley: University of California Press.

Althusser, Louis. 1971. *Lenin and Philosophy and Other Essays*. New York: Monthly Review Press.

American Psychiatric Association. 1994. *Diagnostic and Statistical Handbook of Mental Disorders: DSM-IV*. Washington, D.C.: American Psychiatric Association.

Appadurai, Arjun. 1996. *Modernity at Large*. Minneapolis: University of Minnesota Press.

Arato, Andrew and Eike Gebhardt. 1982. Esthetic Theory and Cultural Criticism. In *The Essential Frankfurt School Reader*. Eds. Andrew Arato and Eike Gebhardt. 185–224. New York: Continuum.

Arlen, Michael. 1980. *Thirty Seconds*. New York: Farrar, Straus, and Giroux.

Austen, Jane. 1995. *Sense and Sensibility* (original 1811). New York: Penguin Books.

Bailey, Beth. 1988. *From Front Porch to Back Seat*. Baltimore: Johns Hopkins University Press.

Bakhtin, M. M. 1982. *The Dialogic Imagination*. Austin: University of Texas Press.

Barnouw, Erik. 1966. *A Tower in Babel: A History of Broadcasting in the United States, volume I*. New York: Oxford University Press.

Bateson, Gregory. 1956. The Message 'This Is Play.' In *Group Processes*. Ed. Bertram Schaffner. 145–242. New York: Josiah Macy, Jr., Foundation.

———. 1972. A Theory of Play and Fantasy. In *Steps to an Ecology of Mind*. 177–193. New York: Ballantine Books.

Battaglia, Debbora. 1995. *Rhetorics of Self-Making*. Berkeley: University of California Press.

Baudrillard, Jean. 1981. *For a Critique of the Political Economy of the Sign*. St. Louis: Telos Press.

———. 1983. *Simulations*. New York: Semiotext(e).

Beaudoin, Tom. 1998. *Virtual Faith: The Irreverent Spiritual Quest of Generation X*. San Francisco: Jossey-Bass.

Beizer, Janet. 1994. *Ventriloquized Bodies: Narratives of Hysteria in Nineteenth Century France*. Ithaca, NY: Cornell University Press.

Bell, Daniel. 1976. *The Cultural Contradictions of Capitalism*. New York: Basic Books.

Benedict, Ruth. 1934. *Patterns of Culture*. Boston: Houghton Mifflin.

Benjamin, Walter. 1968. *Illuminations*. New York: Harcourt, Brace, and World.

Bennett, Tony. 1994. The Exhibitionary Complex. In *Culture/Power/History*. Eds. Nicholas B. Dirks, Geoff Eley, and Sherry B. Ortner. 123–154. Princeton, NJ: Princeton University Press.

Berger, John. 1972. *Ways of Seeing*. Harmondsworth: Penguin.

Berger, Peter. 1967. *The Sacred Canopy*. Garden City, NY: Anchor Books.

Boorstin, Daniel. 1961. *The Image*. New York: Atheneum.

———. 1973. *The Americans: The Democratic Experience*. New York: Random House.

Borsari, Brian. 2004. Drinking Games in the College Environment: A Review. *Journal of Alcohol and Drug Education* 48 (2): 29–51.

Bowlin, John and Peter Stromberg. 1997. Representation and Reality in the Study of Culture. *American Anthropologist* 99: 123–134.

Brady, Joseph V. 2005. Conversation with Joseph V. Brady. *Addiction* 100: 1805–1812.

Brass, Marcel and Cecelia Heyes. 2005. Imitation: Is Cognitive Neuroscience Solving the Correspondence Problem? *Trends in Cognitive Sciences* 9: 489–495.

Braudy, Leo. 1997. *The Frenzy of Renown: Fame and Its History*. New York: Vintage.

Brubach, Holly. 1993. Mail Order America. *New York Times Magazine*. November 21, 1993.

Bruner, Jerome. 1976. Nature and Uses of Immaturity. In *Play—Its Role in Development and Evolution*. Eds. Jerome S. Bruner, Alison Jolly, and Kathy Sylva. 28–64. New York: Basic Books.

Burke, Kenneth. 1952. *A Rhetoric of Motives*. New York: Prentice-Hall.

Caillois, Roger. 1961. *Man, Play and Games*. New York: Free Press of Glencoe.

Campbell, Colin. 1987. *The Romantic Ethic and the Spirit of Modern Consumerism*. Oxford, UK: Basil Blackwell.

Carey, James W. 1989. *Communication as Culture*. Boston: Unwin, Hyman.

Caughey, John L. 1984. *Imaginary Social Worlds*. Lincoln: University of Nebraska Press.

Cawelti, John G. 1976. *Adventure, Mystery and Romance*. Chicago: University of Chicago Press.

Claus, Peter. 1976. A Structuralist Appreciation of "Star Trek." In *The American Dimension: Cultural Myths and Social Realities*. Eds. W. Arens and Susan Montague. 15–31. Sherman Oaks, CA: Alfred.

Cohn, Norman. 1961. *The Pursuit of the Millennium* (second edition). New York: Harper Torchbooks.

Collins, Randall. 2004. *Interaction Ritual Chains*. Princeton, NJ: Princeton University Press.

Condon, W. S. and L. W. Sander. 1974. Neonate Movement Is Synchronized with Adult Speech: Interactional Participation and Language Acquisition. *Science* 183: 99–101.

Conrad, Peter. 1997. It's Boring: Notes on the Meanings of Boredom in Everyday Life. *Qualitative Sociology* 20: 465–475.

Cook, David A. 1996. *A History of Narrative Film* (third edition). New York: Norton.

Crary, Jonathon. 1990. *Techniques of the Observer*. Cambridge, MA: MIT Press.

———. 1999. *Suspensions of Perception*. Cambridge, MA: MIT Press.

Crawford, Robert. 1984. A Cultural Account of "Health": Control, Release, and the "Social Body." In *Issues in the Political Economy of Health Care*. Ed. J. McKinley. 60–101. London: Tavistock.

Currie, Gregory and Ian Ravenscroft. 2002. *Recreative Minds*. Oxford, UK: Oxford University Press.

Crystal, David. 1987. *The Cambridge Encyclopedia of Language*. Cambridge, UK: Cambridge University Press.

Csikszentmihalyi, Mihaly. 1990. *Flow*. New York: HarperCollins.

Csikszentmihalyi, Mihaly and Isabella Selega Csikszentmihalyi, Eds. 1988. *Optimal Experiences: Studies of Flow in Consciousness*. Cambridge, UK: Cambridge University Press.

Darnton, Robert. 1968. *Mesmerism and the End of the Enlightenment in France*. Cambridge, MA: Harvard University Press.

———. 1985. Readers Respond to Rousseau: The Fabrication of Romantic Sensitivity. In *The Great Cat Massacre and Other Episodes in French Cultural History* (original 1984). 215–256. New York: Vintage Books.

Das, V. 1995. On Soap Opera: What Kind of Anthropological Object Is It? In *Worlds Apart: Modernity Through the Prism of the Local*. Ed. Daniel Miller 169–189. London: Routledge.

Davidson, Donald. 1980. *Essays on Actions and Events*. Oxford, UK: Clarendon Press.

Decety, Jean and Thierry Chaminade. 2005. The Neurophysiology of Imitation and Intersubjectivity. In *Perspectives on Imitation: From Neuroscience to Social Science, Volume 2: Imitation, Human Development and Culture*. Eds. Susan Hurley and Nick Chater. 119–140. Cambridge, MA: MIT Press.

DeGrandpre, Richard. 1999. *Ritalin Nation*. New York: Norton.

Derne, Steve. 1995 Popular Culture and Emotional Experiences. In *Social Perspectives on Emotion, volume 3*. Eds. Michael Flaherty and Carolyn Ellis. 171–197. Greenwich, CT: JAI Press.

De Zengotita, Thomas. 2005. *Mediated*. New York: Bloomsbury.

DiClemente, Carlo C. 2003. *Addiction and Change.* New York: Guilford Press.

Dodds, E. R. 1951. *The Greeks and the Irrational.* Berkeley: University of California Press.

Douglas, Mary. 1992. The Person in an Enterprise Culture. In *Understanding the Enterprise Culture.* Eds. Shaun Hargreaves Heap and Angus Ross. 41–62. Edinburgh: Edinburgh University Press.

Draper, Roger. 1986. The Faithless Shepherd. *New York Review of Books.* June 26, 1986: 14–18.

Duffy, Margaret. 1994. Body of Evidence: Studying Women and Advertising. In *Gender and Utopia in Advertising: A Critical Reader.* Eds. Luigi Marca and Alessandra Marca. 5–30. Lisle, IL: Procopian Press.

Durkheim, Emile. 1995. *The Elementary Forms of Religious Life* (original 1912). Trans. Karen E. Fields. New York: Free Press.

Dyer, Richard. 1981. Entertainment and Utopia. In *Genre: The Musical.* Ed. Rick Altman. 175–189. Boston: Routledge and Kegan Paul.

Dyer, Richard and Paul McDonald. 1998. *Stars* (second edition). London: British Film Institute.

Eco, Umberto. 1986. *Travels in Hyperreality.* New York: Harcourt Brace Jovanovich.

Ellis, John. 1982. *Visible Fictions.* London: Routledge and Kegan Paul.

Elster, Jon. 1984. *Ulysses and the Sirens.* Cambridge, UK: Cambridge University Press.

———. 1999. *Strong Feelings.* Cambridge, MA: MIT Press.

Erikson, Erik H. 1968. *Identity, Youth and Crisis.* New York: Norton.

Esslin, Martin. 1982a. *The Age of Television.* San Francisco: W. H. Freeman.

———. 1982b. Aristotle and the Advertisers: The Television Commercial Considered as a Form of Drama. In *Television: The Critical View.* Ed. Horace Newcomb. 260–275. Oxford, UK: Oxford University Press.

Ewen, Stuart. 1976. *Captains of Consciousness.* New York: McGraw-Hill.

———. 1988. *All Consuming Images.* New York: Basic Books.

Fagen, Robert. 1976. Modelling How and Why Play Works. In *Play—Its Role in Development and Evolution.* Eds. Jerome S. Bruner, Alison Jolly, and Kathy Sylva. 96–115. New York: Basic Books.

Falk, John L. 1983. Drug Dependence: Myth or Motive? *Pharmacology Biochemistry and Behavior* 19: 385–391.

Featherstone, Mike. 1991. *Consumer Culture and Postmodernism.* London: Sage.

Fields, Jeff and Henry Sappenfield. 1997. Fantasy Role-Play as a Form of Ritual. Unpublished paper, files of the author.

Fine, Gary Allen. 1983. *Shared Fantasy.* Chicago: University of Chicago Press.

Fjellman, Stephen M. 1992. *Vinyl Leaves.* Boulder: Westview Press.

Fried, Michael. 1980. *Absorption and Theatricality.* Berkeley: University of California Press.

———. 1990. *Courbet's Realism.* Berkeley: University of California Press.

Frijda, Nico H. 1986. *The Emotions.* Cambridge, UK: Cambridge University Press.

Gabler, Neal. 1999. *Life the Movie.* New York: Knopf.

Gadamer, Hans-Georg. 1975. *Truth and Method.* New York: Seabury Press.

Gallie, W. B. 1968. *Philosophy and the Historical Understanding.* New York: Schocken Books.

Gamson, Joshua. 1994. *Claims to Fame: Celebrity in Contemporary America*. Berkeley: University of California Press.

Gell, Alfred. 1992. The Technology of Enchantment and the Enchantment of Technology. In *Anthropology, Art and Aesthetics*. Eds. Jeremy Coote and Anthony Shelton. 40–63. Oxford, UK: Clarendon Press.

Geertz, Clifford. 1973. *The Interpretation of Cultures*. New York: Basic Books.

Gennep, Arnold van. 1960. *The Rites of Passage*. Chicago: University of Chicago Press.

Gergen, Kenneth J. 1991. *The Saturated Self*. New York: Basic Books.

Gerth, H. H. and C. Wright Mills. 1946. *From Max Weber*. New York: Oxford University Press.

Giddens, Anthony. 1991. *Modernity and Self-Identity: Self and Society in the Late Modern Age*. Stanford, CA: Stanford University Press.

Ginsburg, Faye. 2005. Media Anthropology: An Introduction. In *Media Anthropology*. Eds. Eric W. Rothenbuhler and Mihai Coman. 17–25. Thousand Oaks, CA: Sage.

Gladwell, Malcolm. 2000. *The Tipping Point*. Boston: Little, Brown.

Glaser, Barney and Anselm Strauss. 1964. Awareness Contexts and Social Interaction. *American Sociological Review* 29: 669–79.

Goethals, Gregor T. 1990. *The Electronic Golden Calf*. Cambridge, MA: Cowley.

Goffman, Erving. 1967. *Interaction Ritual*. Chicago: Aldine.

———. 1986. *Frame Analysis*. Boston: Northeastern University Press.

Goldberg, Lewis R. 1999. The Curious Experiences Survey, A Revised Version of the Dissociative Experiences Scale: Factor Structure, Reliability and Relations to Demographic and Personality Variables. *Psychological Assessment* 11 (2) 134–145.

Goldman, Alvin I. 2005. Imitation, Mind-Reading and Simulation. In *Perspectives on Imitation: From Neuroscience to Social Science, Volume 2: Imitation, Human Development and Culture*. Eds. Susan Hurley and Nick Chater. 79–94. Cambridge, MA: MIT Press.

Gossop, Michael. 1990. Compulsion, Craving and Conflict. In *Addiction Controversies*. Ed. David M. Warburton. 236–249. Philadelphia: Harwood Academic.

Grant, Vernon W. 1976. *Falling in Love. The Psychology of the Romantic Emotion*. New York: Springer.

Green, Melanie C., Timothy C. Brock, and Geoff F. Kaufman. 2004. Understanding Media Enjoyment: The Role of Transportation into Narrative Worlds. *Communication Theory* 14 (4): 311–327.

Green, Melanie C., J. J. Strange, and Timothy C. Brock, Eds. 2002. *Narrative Impact: Social and Cognitive Foundations*. Mahwah, NJ: Erlbaum.

Hacking, Ian. 1995. *Rewriting the Soul: Multiple Personality and the Sciences of Memory*. Princeton, NJ: Princeton University Press.

Hale, Nathan G. 1971. *Freud and the Americans*. New York: Oxford University Press.

Harding, Sandra. 1986. *The Science Question in Feminism*. Ithaca, NY: Cornell University Press.

Harris, Neil. 1990. *Cultural Excursions*. Chicago: University of Chicago Press.

Harris, Paul L. 2000. *The Work of the Imagination*. Oxford, UK: Blackwell.

Hatfield, Elaine, John T. Cacioppo, and Richard L. Rapson. 1992. Primitive Emotional Contagion. In *Review of Personality and Social Psychology, vol. 14*. Ed. Margaret S. Clark. 151–177. Thousand Oaks, CA: Sage.

————. 1994. *Emotional Contagion*. Cambridge, UK: Cambridge University Press.

Haviland, John. 2000. Pointing, Gesture Spaces, and Mental Maps. In *Language and Gesture*. Ed. David McNeill. 13–46. Cambridge, UK: Cambridge University Press.

Hilgard, Ernest. 1986. *Divided Consciousness: Multiple Controls in Human Thought and Action* (expanded edition). New York: Wiley.

Hilgard, Josephine R. 1970. *Personality and Hypnosis*. Chicago: University of Chicago Press.

Hollan, Douglas. 2000. Constructivist Models of Mind, Contemporary Psychoanalysis, and the Development of Culture Theory. *American Anthropologist* 102: 538–550.

Holland, Dorothy, William Lachicotte Jr., Debra Skinner, and Carole Cain. 1998. *Identity and Agency in Cultural Worlds*. Cambridge, MA: Harvard University Press.

Horkheimer, Max and Theodor W. Adorno. 2002. *Dialectic of Enlightenment: Philosophical Fragments*. Stanford, CA: Stanford University Press.

Huizinga, Johan. 1955. *Homo Ludens: A Study of the Play Element in Culture*. Boston: Beacon Press.

Hughes-Freeland, Felicia and Mary M. Crain. 1998. *Recasting Ritual: Performance, Media, Identity*. London: Routledge.

Humphrey, Caroline and James Laidlaw. 1994. *The Archetypal Actions of Ritual: A Theory of Ritual Illustrated by the Jain Rite of Worship*. Oxford, UK: Clarendon Press.

Humphrey, N. 1982. Consciousness: A Just-so Story. *New Scientist* 19 474–477.

Hurley, Susan and Nick Chater. 2005. Introduction: The Importance of Imitation. In *Perspectives on Imitation: From Neuroscience to Social Science, Volume 1: Mechanisms of Imitation and Imitation in Animals*. 1–52. Cambridge, MA: MIT Press.

Huxtable, Ada Louise. 1992. Inventing American Reality. *New York Review of Books*. Dec. 3, 1992: 24–29.

Illouz, Eva. 1997. *Consuming the Romantic Utopia*. Berkeley: University of California Press.

James, William. 1887. Review of "Romantic Love and Personal Beauty." *Nation* 45: 237–238.

Jenkins, Henry. 1992. *Textual Poachers*. New York: Routledge.

Jensen, Joli. 1990. *Redeeming Modernity*. Thousand Oaks, CA: Sage.

Jhally, Sut. 2002. Image-Based Culture: Advertising and Popular Culture. In *The Anthropology of Media*. Eds. Kelly Askew and Richard R. Wilk. 327–336. Oxford, UK: Blackwell.

Jindra, Michael. 1994. Star Trek Fandom as a Religious Phenomenon. *Sociology of Religion* 55(1): 27–51.

Keane, Webb. 1997. Religious Language. *Annual Review of Anthropology* 26: 47–71.

Kinsbourne, Marcel. 2005. Imitation as Entrainment: Brain Mechanisms and Social Consequences. In *Perspectives on Imitation: From Neuroscience to Social Science, Volume 2: Imitation, Human Development and Culture*. Eds. Susan Hurley and Nick Chater. 163–172. Cambridge, MA: MIT Press.

Klapp, Orrin E. 1986. *Overload and Boredom: Essays on the Quality of Life in the Information Society*. New York: Greenwood Press.

Knauft, Bruce. 1987. Managing Sex and Anger: Tobacco and Kava Use Among the Gebusi of Papua New Guinea. In *Drugs in Western Pacific Societies: Relations of Substance*. Ed. Lamont Lindstrom. 73–98. New York: University Press of America.

Koepping, Klaus-Peter. 1997. The Ludic as Creative Disorder: Framing, De-Framing and

Boundary Crossing. In *The Games of God and Man*. Ed. Klaus-Peter Koepping. 1–39. Hamburg: LIT Verlag.

Kokoszka, Andrezej. 2000. Altered States of Consciousness: A Comparison of Profoundly and Superficially Altered States. *Imagination, Cognition and Personality* 19 (2): 165–184.

Kracauer, Siegfried. 1995. *The Mass Ornament*. Cambridge, MA: Harvard University Press.

Krishnan, H. Shanker and Charles V. Trappey. 1999. Nonconscious Memory Processes in Marketing: A Historical Perspective and Future Directions. *Psychology and Marketing* 16: 451–457.

Kubey, Robert and Mihaly Csikszentmihalyi. 1990. *Television and the Quality of Life: How Viewing Shapes Everyday Experience*. Hillsdale, NJ: Erlbaum.

Kummer, H. and J. Goodall. 1985. Conditions of Innovative Behavior in Primates. *Philosophical Transactions of the Royal Society of London*. B308: 203–214.

Lamarque, Peter. 1981. How Can We Fear and Pity Fictions? *British Journal of Aesthetics* 21: 291–304.

Lasch, Christopher. 1978. *The Culture of Narcissism*. New York: Norton.

Leach, William. 1993. *Land of Desire*. New York: Pantheon Books.

Lears, T. J. Jackson. 1983. From Salvation to Self-Realization. In *The Culture of Consumption: Critical Essays in American History 1880–1980*. Eds. Richard W. Fox and T. J. Jackson Lears. 3–38. New York: Pantheon.

———. 1994. *Fables of Abundance*. New York: Basic Books.

Lende, Daniel. 2005. Wanting and Drug Use: A Biocultural Approach to the Analysis of Addiction. *Ethos* 33: 100–124.

Liebes, T. and E. Katz. 1990. *The Export of Meaning: Cross Cultural Readings of "Dallas."* New York: Oxford University Press.

Lifton, Robert Jay. 1993. *The Protean Self*. New York: Basic Books.

Lindholm, Charles. 1990. *Charisma*. Oxford, UK: Basil Blackwell.

Lotze, M., P. Montoya, M. Erb, E. Hulsmann, H. Flor, U. Klose, N. Birbaumer, and W. Grodd. 1999. Activation of Cortical and Cerebellar Motor Areas During Executed and Imagined Hand Movements: An fMRI Study. *Journal of Cognitive Neuroscience* 11: 491–501.

Ludwig, Arnold. 1966. Altered States of Consciousness. *Archives of General Psychiatry* 15 (3): 225–234.

Luhrman, Tanya. 1989. *Persuasions of the Witch's Craft*. Cambridge, MA: Harvard University Press.

Lukes, Steven. 1973. *Emile Durkheim, His Life and Work: A Historical and Critical Study*. New York: Penguin Books.

MacAndrew, Craig and Robert B. Edgerton. 1969. *Drunken Comportment*. Chicago: Aldine.

Marchand, Roland. 1985. *Advertising the American Dream*. Berkeley: University of California Press.

Marshall, P. David. 1997. *Celebrity and Power: Fame in Contemporary Culture*. Minneapolis: University of Minnesota Press.

Martin, Emily. 1994. *Flexible Bodies*. Boston: Beacon Press.

May, Lary. 1980. *Screening Out the Past*. New York: Oxford University Press.

McCracken, Grant. 1988. *Culture and Consumption*. Bloomington: Indiana University Press.

McKendrick, Neil, John Brewer, and J. H. Plumb. 1982. *The Birth of a Consumer Society.* Bloomington: Indiana University Press.

McKeon, Michael. 1987. *The Origins of the English Novel 1600–1740.* Baltimore: Johns Hopkins University Press.

McNeill, David. 1992. *Hand and Mind: What Gestures Reveal About Thought.* Chicago: University of Chicago Press.

———. 2005. *Gesture and Thought.* Chicago: University of Chicago Press.

Mead, George Herbert. 1934. *Mind, Self, and Society.* Chicago: University of Chicago Press.

Metz, Christopher. 1982. *The Imaginary Signifier.* Bloomington: Indiana University Press.

Meyer, Donald. 1980. *The Positive Thinkers.* New York: Pantheon Books.

Miller, Daniel. 1995. *Worlds Apart: Modernity Through the Prism of the Local.* London: Routledge.

———. 1998. *A Theory of Shopping.* Ithaca, NY: Cornell University Press.

Musharbash, Yasmine. 2007. Boredom, Time, and Modernity: An Example from Aboriginal Australia. *American Anthropologist* 109: 307–317.

Nadel, J. and G. Butterworth. 1999. *Imitation in Infancy: Cambridge Studies in Cognitive and Perceptual Development.* Cambridge, UK: Cambridge University Press.

Nasaw, David. 1993. *Going Out: The Rise and Fall of Public Amusement.* New York: Basic Books.

Nell, Victor. 1988. *Lost in a Book.* New Haven: Yale University Press.

Nichter, Mimi. 2000. *Fat Talk: What Girls and Their Parents Say About Dieting.* Cambridge, MA: Harvard University Press.

Orford, Jim. 1985. *Excessive Appetites: A Psychological View of Addictions.* New York: Wiley.

Person, Ethel S. 1989. *Dreams of Love and Fateful Encounters: The Power of Romantic Passion.* New York: Penguin Books.

Plantinga, Carl. 1999. The Scene of Empathy and the Human Face on Film. In *Passionate Views: Film, Cognition and Emotion.* Eds. Carl Plantinga and Greg M. Smith. 239–255. Baltimore: Johns Hopkins University Press.

Powdermaker, Hortense. 1950. *Hollywood, The Dream Factory.* New York: Little, Brown.

Pribram, Karl H. 1977. Some Observations on the Organization of Studies of Mind, Brain, and Behavior. In *Alternate States of Consciousness.* Ed. Norman E. Zinberg. 220–229. New York: Free Press.

Putnam, Robert. 2000. *Bowling Alone.* New York: Simon and Schuster.

Radaway, Janice. 1984. *Reading the Romance.* Chapel Hill: University of North Carolina Press.

Rappaport, Roy. 1979. *Ecology, Meaning and Religion.* Berkeley, CA: North Atlantic Books.

———. 1995. *Ritual and Religion in the Making of Humanity.* Cambridge, UK: Cambridge University Press.

Rice, John Steadman. 1996. *A Disease of One's Own.* New Brunswick, NJ: Transaction.

Rieff, Philip. 1966. *The Triumph of the Therapeutic.* New York: Harper and Row.

Riesman, David, Nathan Glazer and Reuel Denney. 1961. *The Lonely Crowd.* New Haven, CT: Yale University Press.

Rizzolatti, G. and M. Arbib. 1999. Language Within Our Grasp. *Trends in Neuroscience* 21: 188–194.

Rizzolatti, G. and L. Craighero. 2004. The Mirror Neuron System. *Annual Review of Neuroscience* 27: 169–192.

Rose, Nikolas. 1996. *Inventing Our Selves: Psychology, Power, and Personhood.* Cambridge, UK: Cambridge University Press.

Rossi, Ernest L. 1986. Altered States of Consciousness in Everyday Life: Ultradian Rhythms. In *Handbook of States of Consciousness.* Eds. Benjamin B. Wolman and Montague Ullman. 97–132. New York: Van Nostrand Reinhold.

Rothenbuhler, Eric W. and Mihai Coman, Eds. 2005. *Media Anthropology.* Thousand Oaks, CA: Sage.

Rougemont, Denis de. 1956. *Love in the Western World,* revised and augmented edition. New York: Pantheon Books.

Ruane, Christine. 1995. Clothes Shopping in Imperial Russia: The Development of a Consumer Culture. *Journal of Social History,* summer 1995: 765–782.

Rymer, Russ. 1996. Back to the Future: Disney Reinvents the Company Town. *Harper's* 293, 1757: 65–76.

Sahlins, Marshall. 1976. *Culture and Practical Reason.* Chicago: University of Chicago Press.

Schama, Simon. 1989. *Citizens.* New York: Knopf.

Schickel, Richard. 1973. *His Picture in the Papers.* New York: Charterhouse.

———. 1985. *Intimate Strangers: The Culture of Celebrity.* New York: Doubleday.

Schmidt, Leigh. 1995. *Consumer Rites.* Princeton: Princeton University Press.

Schudson, Michael. 1984. *Advertising, the Uneasy Persuasion.* New York: Basic Books.

Schutz, Alfred. 1967. *Collected Papers, vol. 1: The Problem of Social Reality.* Hague: Martinus Nijhoff.

Schwartz, Vanessa. 1998. *Spectacular Realities.* Berkeley: University of California Press.

Sedgwick, Eve. 1993. *Tendencies.* Durham, NC: Duke University Press.

Sennett, Richard. 1977. *The Fall of Public Man.* New York: Alfred A. Knopf.

Shaffer, Howard J. 1997. The Most Important Unresolved Issue in the Addictions: Conceptual Chaos. *Substance Use and Misuse* 32: 1573–1580.

Shore, Bradd. 1996. *Culture in Mind: Cognition, Culture, and the Problem of Meaning.* Oxford, UK: Oxford University Press.

Simmel, Georg. 1971. The Metropolis and Mental Life (original 1903). In *On Individuality and Social Forms.* Ed. Donald N. Levine. 324–339. Chicago: University of Chicago Press.

Sklar, Robert. 1994. *Movie-Made America* (second edition). New York: Vintage Books.

Skulsky, Harold. 1980. On Being Moved by Fiction. *Journal of Aesthetics and Art Criticism* 39: 5–14.

Smith, Murray. 1995. *Engaging Characters: Fiction, Emotion, and the Cinema.* Oxford: Clarendon Press.

Snow, Robert P. 1983. *Creating Media Culture.* London: Sage.

Spacks, Patricia. 1995. *Boredom: The Literary History of a State of Mind.* Chicago: University of Chicago Press.

Spariosu, Mihai, Ed. 1984. *Mimesis in Contemporary Theory: An Interdisciplinary Approach.* Philadelphia: John Benjamins.

Spiegel, David. 1990. Hypnosis, Dissociation, and Trauma: Hidden and Overt Observers. In *Repression and Dissociation.* Ed. Jerome L. Singer. 121–142. Chicago: University of Chicago Press.

Spitulnik, Debra. 1993. Anthropology and Mass Media. *Annual Review of Anthropology* 22: 293-315.

Stewart, Susan. 1984. *On Longing*. Baltimore: Johns Hopkins University Press.

Stocking, George. 1968. *Race, Culture and Evolution*. Chicago: University of Chicago Press.

Stone, Lawrence. 1988. Passionate Attachments in the West in Historical Perspective. In *Passionate Attachments: Thinking About Love*. Eds. Willard Gayline and Ethel Person. 15–26. New York: Free Press.

Strathern, Marilyn. 1988. *The Gender of the Gift: Problems with Women and Problems with Society in Melanesia*. Berkeley: University of California Press.

Stromberg, Peter. 1985. The Impression Point: Synthesis of Symbol and Self. *Ethos* 13: 56–74.

———. 1990. Elvis Alive? The Ideology of American Consumerism. *Journal of Popular Culture* 24 (3): 11–19.

———. 2000. The "I" of Enthrallment. *Ethos* 27: 490–504.

Stromberg, Peter, Mark Nichter, and Mimi Nichter. 2007. Taking Play Seriously: Low Level Smoking Among College Students. *Culture, Medicine and Psychiatry* 31: 1–24.

Susman, Warren. 1984. *Culture as History*. New York: Pantheon Books.

Sutton-Smith, Brian. 2001. *The Ambiguity of Play*. Cambridge, MA: Harvard University Press.

Swanson, Guy E. 1978. Travels Through Inner Space: Family Structure and Openness to Absorbing Experiences. *American Journal of Sociology* 83: 890–919.

Swidler, Ann. 2001. *Talk of Love*. Chicago: University of Chicago Press.

Taussig, Michael. 1993. *Mimesis and Alterity: A Particular History of the Senses*. New York: Routledge.

Taylor, Charles. 1975. *Hegel*. Cambridge, UK: Cambridge University Press.

———. 1985. The Person. In *The Category of the Person*. Eds. Michael Carrithers, Steven Collins, and Steven Lukes. 257–281. Cambridge, UK: Cambridge University Press.

———. 1989. *Sources of the Self*. Cambridge, MA: Harvard University Press.

Tellegen, Auke and Gilbert Atkinson. 1974. Openness to Absorbing and Self-Altering Experiences ("Absorption"), A Trait Related to Hypnotic Susceptibility. *Journal of Abnormal Psychology* 83: 268–277.

Thombs, Dennis. 1994. *Introduction to Addictive Behaviors*. New York: Guilford Press.

Thompson, John. 1990. *Ideology and Modern Culture*. Stanford, CA: Stanford University Press.

———. 1995. *The Media and Modernity*. Stanford, CA: Stanford University Press.

Tomasello, Michael. 1999. *The Cultural Origins of Human Cognition*. Cambridge, MA: Harvard University Press.

——— and Malinda Carpenter. 2005. Intention Reading and Imitative Learning. In *Perspectives on Imitation: From Neuroscience to Social Science, Volume 2: Imitation, Human Development, and Culture*. Eds. Susan Hurley and Nick Chater. 133–148. Cambridge, MA: MIT Press.

Tocqueville, Alexis De. 2000. *Democracy in America*. Trans., Ed., and with an Introduction by Harvey C. Mansfield and Delba Winthrop. Chicago: University of Chicago Press.

Turner, Victor. 1967. *The Forest of Symbols: Aspects of Ndembu Ritual*. Ithaca, NY: Cornell University Press.

————. 1969. *The Ritual Process.* New York: Aldine.

————. 1982. *From Ritual to Theatre.* New York: Performing Arts Journal.

Twitchell, J. B. 1992. *Carnival Culture: The Trashing of Taste in America.* New York: Columbia University Press.

Urban, Greg. 1989. The "I" of Discourse. In *Semiotics, Self, and Society.* Eds. Benjamin Lee and Greg Urban. 27–51. New York: Mouton de Gruyter.

Vickers, Brian, ed. 1979. *Shakespeare, The Critical Heritage,* vol. 5. London: Routledge and Kegan Paul.

Voelkl, Bernhard and Ludwig Huber. 2000. True Imitation in Marmosets. *Animal Behavior* 60: 195–202.

Vuchinich, Rudy E. 2002. Still Necessary to State the Obvious: Comment on Alessi, Roll, Reilly, and Johanson (2002). *Experimental and Clinical Psychopharmacology* 10: 99–100.

Vygotsky, L. S. 1978. *Mind in Society.* Cambridge, MA: Harvard University Press.

Wagner, Jon and Jan Lundeen. 1998. *Deep Space and Sacred Time: Star Trek in the American Mythos.* Westport, CT: Praeger.

Wallace, Anthony F. C. 1956. Revitalization Movements. *American Anthropologist* 63: 264–181.

Walton, Kendall L. 1990. *Mimesis as Make-Believe.* Cambridge, MA: Harvard University Press.

Watt, Ian. 1957. *The Rise of the Novel.* Berkeley: University of California Press.

Weber, Max. 1958. *The Protestant Ethic and the Spirit of Capitalism* (original 1904–05). New York: Scribner.

Wild, Barbara, Michael Erb, and Mathias Bartels. 2001. Are Emotions Contagious? Evoked Emotions While Viewing Emotionally Expressive Faces: Quality, Quantity, Time Course and Gender Differences. *Psychiatry Research* 102: 109–124.

Williams, Alan. 1992. *Republic of Images.* Cambridge, MA: Harvard University Press.

Williams, Raymond. 1993. Advertising: The Magic System. In *The Cultural Studies Reader.* Ed. Simon During. 320–336. London: Routledge.

Williams, Rosalind H. 1982. *Dream Worlds: Mass Consumption in Late Nineteenth-Century France.* Berkeley: University of California Press.

Winkelman, Michael. 1986. Trance States: A Theoretical Model and Cross-Cultural Analysis. *Ethos* 14: 174–203.

Winnicott, Donald W. 1964. *The Child, the Family, and the Outside World.* Baltimore: Penguin.

Winter, Alison. 1998. *Mesmerized.* Chicago: University of Chicago Press.

Wollheim, Richard. 1984. *The Thread of Life.* Cambridge, MA: Harvard University Press.

Wolman, Benjamin B. and Montague Ullman, Eds. 1986. *Handbook of States of Consciousness.* New York: Van Nostrand Reinhold.

Zeldin, Theodore. 1995. *An Intimate History of Humanity.* New York: HarperCollins.

Zepp, Ira. 1997. *The New Religious Image of Urban America,* second edition. Niwot: University Press of Colorado.

Zinberg, Norman E., Ed. 1977. *Alternate States of Consciousness.* New York: Free Press.

Index